THE FRONTIER ABLAZE

The North-West Frontier Rising
1897-98

This edition first published in Great Britain 1996 by
Windrow & Greene Ltd
5 Gerrard Street
London W1V 7LJ

© Michael Barthorp
Colour plates © Windrow & Greene Ltd

Design by Frank Ainscough

Printed and bound in Hong Kong through
Bookbuilders Ltd.

A CIP catalogue record for this book
is available from the British Library

Standard edition
ISBN 1 85915 023 3

De luxe edition
ISBN 1 85915 033 0

THE FRONTIER ABLAZE

The North-West Frontier Rising
1897-98

Michael Barthorp

Colour plates by

Douglas N. Anderson

WINDROW & GREENE

LONDON

Dedication

To the memory of
Thomas Atkins, Jack Sepoy, Johnny Gurkha and their Officers,
who did the work and paid the price.

"The flying bullet down the Pass,
That whistles clear; 'All flesh is grass.'"
(RUDYARD KIPLING, *Arithmetic on the Frontier*)

Acknowledgements

The author gratefully acknowledges the assistance of many individuals and institutions who have helped in various ways during the preparation of this book. In alphabetical order they are: Major W.G.P.Aggett; RHQ The Argyll and Sutherland Highlanders (Lieutenant-Colonel A.W. Scott-Elliot); Mrs Stuart Battye; Mr George Caldwell; Mr George Dibley; Lieutenant-Colonel M.J.Evetts MC; The Gurkha Museum (Brigadier C.J.D.Bullock OBE, MC and Lieutenant-Colonel M.H.Broadway); Major Alan Harfield; Mr Peter Harrington; Mr R.G.Harris; Mrs D.Hill; Major T.C.S. Knox; The London Library; Mr R.J.Marrion; Lieutenant-Colonel David Murray; The National Army Museum; The Northamptonshire Regiment Museum (Colonel J.P. Wetherall and Mr George Durant); The Queen's Royal Surrey Regiment Museum (Colonel P.A.W.G.Durrant OBE); Mr Rulzion Rattray; The Royal Green Jackets Archive (Major T.L.Craze); RHQ The Royal Highland Fusiliers (Major W.Shaw MBE); Mrs Dawn Waring; Wellington College Archive (Mr R.C. Sopwith); Colonel D.R.Wood.
Special debts of gratitude are owed to: Mr Douglas Anderson, for his masterly colour plates which are so evocative of their period, as well as for much other help, advice and support; Lieutenant-Colonel P.J.Mercer MBE, for unearthing a fund of useful material and for reading and commenting upon the text's first draft; Miss Sara Woodcock, for her patient and efficient conversion of the author's typescript into a form acceptable to the publisher; and to Mr Martin Windrow, for initiating the work and persevering with it until publication.

CONTENTS

FOREWORD

"Lor', sir, them's our mudlarks!" shouted a gunner to his officer, who was about to open fire during one of the first expeditions ever to be mounted against hostile tribesmen on British India's North-West Frontier. The men whom the sharp-eyed gunner recognised just in time were not tribesmen, but belonged to what later became one of the most illustrious regiments of the old Indian Army - the Corps of Guides, then newly raised as part of the Punjab Irregular (later Frontier) Force to police the various Pathan tribes who inhabited this mountainous and lawless borderland which had recently become a British responsibility following the conquest and annexation of the Sikh kingdom of the Punjab in 1849. The "mudlarks" alluded to the Guides' new and singular uniform, of dust-colour or "khaki" to match the ground. They were the first troops ever to wear such clothing at a time when other soldiers in India, and elsewhere, still fought in their traditional uniforms of red, blue, green or white.

Nearly 50 years and some 40 expeditions later all troops engaged on the Frontier - British, Indian or Gurkha - were clothed in khaki. Instead of the muzzle-loading smoothbore muskets of 1849 they carried breech-loading rifles of far greater range and accuracy. Their artillery was more powerful, and they had machine-guns to supplement their rifle-fire. Years of campaigning on the Frontier had taught them the lessons of mountain warfare which, in 1849, they had had to learn by often bitter experience. Yet the tribesmen they fought remained as they had always been: proudly independent and, in the words of Winston Churchill, who encountered them as a young officer, "every man a warrior, a politician and a theologian."

The North-West Frontier of India always loomed large in the lives, minds and recollections of generations of British soldiers - even those who had also served in two World Wars. For many British Regular soldiers between 1849 and 1947, and even more so for their Indian Army comrades, it was on the Frontier that for the first time, as Kipling wrote, "an' now the hugly bullets come peckin' through the dust/ an' no one wants to face 'em, but every beggar must". The Frontier provided the only active operations against a live enemy that many would see throughout their service. It was on these harsh hills that the years of training would be put into practice; here the strengths and weaknesses of units, and the true mettle of individual officers and men, would become far more apparent than they had ever been in peacetime garrisons.

It was not only soldiers whose thoughts were fired by the Frontier. Politicians, proconsuls and pundits were constantly preoccupied with its security. Writers of fiction - for all ages - set their heroes' adventures against the backdrop of this perennially dangerous border country. Artists and illustrators re-created true and imaginary tales of derring-do against "the wily Pathan". Later their example would be followed by film-makers, with such epics as *Gunga Din, Lives of a Bengal Lancer, The Drum, King of the Khyber Rifles*, and others, some of which can still be seen today. Even after Partition in 1947, when the Frontier became the responsibility of the new Moslem republic of Pakistan, its days under British rule continued to be the subject of historical works, adventure stories and - curiously for the late 1960s - a fictional British television series called *Frontier*. (In arguing that the old names still conjured up an instantly recognisable image in the public mind we may perhaps be forgiven for mentioning one of the most entertaining of the *Carry On...* films, inevitably located *...Up the Khyber*.)

Everyone, from the Viceroy of India to the scribbler of boys' magazine yarns, once knew that there was never peace on the Frontier: this fact was taken for granted by five generations of our countrymen. Least of all was there peace just a century ago. In 1897-98, notwithstanding the losses and punishments which Pathan tribes had suffered in past years, there blazed up, over the space of eight months, such widespread uprisings that it would finally take the deployment of 64 British and Indian infantry battalions (23 more than the entire infantry strength of today's British Regular Army), plus cavalry, artillery and engineers in proportion, to restore the Queen's peace. This became known at the time as the Pathan Revolt or the Great Frontier War.

Books about some of its episodes appeared immediately afterwards; it has featured in subsequent works about the British on the Frontier as merely one of the many events in that hundred-year period; but the whole course of the war has not been covered before in one volume. Such is the aim of this book, thereby resurrecting an important Imperial campaign, and affording a closer look at the men who fought it.

MJB *Jersey CI*

Glossary

Abattis	*Defensive barricade of felled trees.*	**Mullah**	*Moslem preacher.*
Bhisti	*Water carrier.*	**Naik**	*Indian infantry corporal.*
Daffadar	*Indian cavalry sergeant.*	**Nullah**	*Dry watercourse or ravine.*
Dhoolie	*Litter, covered stretcher, slung on pole.*	**Poshteen**	*Sheepskin-lined coat.*
Ghazi	*Moslem fanatic pledged to kill unbelievers.*	**Ressaldar**	*Indian cavalry lieutenant.*
Havildar	*Indian infantry sergeant.*	**Rupee**	*Unit of Indian currency, 15 to £1.*
Jemadar	*Indian cavalry or infantry 2nd lieutenant.*	**Sangar**	*Field breastwork of piled stones.*
Jezail	*Flintlock musket.*	**Sepoy**	*Indian infantry private.*
Jehad	*Moslem holy war.*	**Serai**	*Enclosure.*
Jirga	*Council or deputation of tribal elders.*	**Sowar**	*Indian cavalry trooper.*
Khan	*Lord or chief; suffix to a name.*	**Subedar**	*Indian infantry lieutenant.*
Kotal	*Summit of a pass or col.*	**Tulwar**	*Curved native sword.*
Malik	*Headman of village or tribe.*		

CHAPTER ONE

The Frontier and its People

"A tilted wilderness of rock and scrub; hard, barren and jagged; split here and there by stony watercourses in which little water flowed; in summer, a blinding glare from the ochreous ridges; in winter, a cold breath shaking snow off the holly-oak on the mountain-sides; intense heat, intense cold, vivid storms, violent people - everything excessive". Thus did the soldier and author John Masters describe the Frontier as he found it in 1937 [1]. So it had been forty years before, and so it had been for centuries before that: a harsh, forbidding landscape offering few of life's necessities to the people who inhabited it, and whose characters were moulded by the extremes of their habitat.

In the far north-east of Afghanistan is a strip of land, the Wakhan, where the Pamir and Karakorum mountain ranges meet, which divided what was once the most northern territory of British India from the Russia of the Tsars. From this strip the mountains known as the Hindu Kush - "the killer of Hindus" - stretch slightly south of west across northern Afghanistan. More mountains reach south-westwards, through the regions of Chitral, Dir and Swat, until they are pierced by the Kabul River valley running east from Kabul, the capital of Afghanistan; some ten miles to the south of that river lies the famous Khyber Pass, leading to Peshawar, once the largest military base in the north-west of British India.

Between the Kabul River and the Kurram River valley to the south rises another east-west range, the Safed Koh, reaching out towards the western end of the Hindu Kush. South of it, but before the Kurram River, lies a long, wide valley called the Tirah Maidan, bounded on its south by the Samana Range. To the east lies the Kohat Pass. After the Kurram valley the general trend of the mountains continues south-westerly through Waziristan, eventually merging into the Sulaiman Range, which falls away southwards to the desert and hills of Baluchistan bordering the Arabian Sea.

From the Wakhan to the south of Waziristan is some 400 miles as the crow flies - roughly the distance between Edinburgh and Southampton - but very considerably more as a man walks. From Kabul to Peshawar via the Khyber is 200 miles, although the road through the pass from the Afghan border to Peshawar is only 35 miles. Besides the Khyber there are in the far north three passes, one of which, the Dorah, leads into Chitral, from where the Malakand Pass runs southwards towards the Punjab. South of the Khyber and Kohat the passes from the west are, first, the Kurram valley; then the Tochi and Gomal through north and south Waziristan respectively; and finally the Bolan, guarded by Quetta, which was another important British military garrison.

To the west of these mountains lay the independent kingdom of Afghanistan forming a buffer between British India, Russia to the north and Persia (now Iran) to the south. Should any invader, his covetous eyes fixed upon India, come out of the west - as had in the past Darius the Persian, Alexander of Macedon, the great Tamerlane, and the first Mughal emperor Babur - he would first be faced by the great natural obstacle of these mountains. Should he succeed in penetrating their passes he would then encounter a second natural obstacle, the mighty River Indus, flowing roughly parallel to the mountains and between 50 to 150 miles to their east, into which ran, from the west, the rivers through the passes. Besides the natural obstacles an invader would also encounter the inhabitants of these mountains: the Pathans.

Opinions as to their origins have varied: Iranian, Arab, Afghan aboriginals with an admixture of strains from the various invaders over the centuries - even a lost tribe of Israel. All are Moslems by religion, and all speak the Pushtu language, though with variations of pronunciation. All grouped themselves into family communities or sections, several of which would form a clan or *khel*, which itself would be part of a larger grouping, the tribe.

The tribes of the region are numerous but some, like the Chitralis of the far north, are not true Pathans and do not feature in this story, any more than do those bordering the Arabian Sea. Of those who will be met again in these pages the northernmost were the Yusufzai, from around Dir, part of whom were the Bunerwals to the south-east, and their allies the Swatis and Mamunds, all inhabiting the region northwards from the Malakand Pass towards Chitral, around the Swat Valley. West of the Malakand and north of the Kabul River valley were the tough and avaricious Mohmands, the nearest of the northern tribes to Peshawar.

South of the Kabul River, and also close to Peshawar and the Khyber, were the Afridis, a martial, mistrustful and lawless people of many clans who inhabited the Tirah Maidan and the region north-west of Kohat. Beyond them,

"A tilted wilderness of rock and scrub, hard, barren and jagged": North-West Frontier terrain in 1980, unchanged over the years. (Author's photograph)

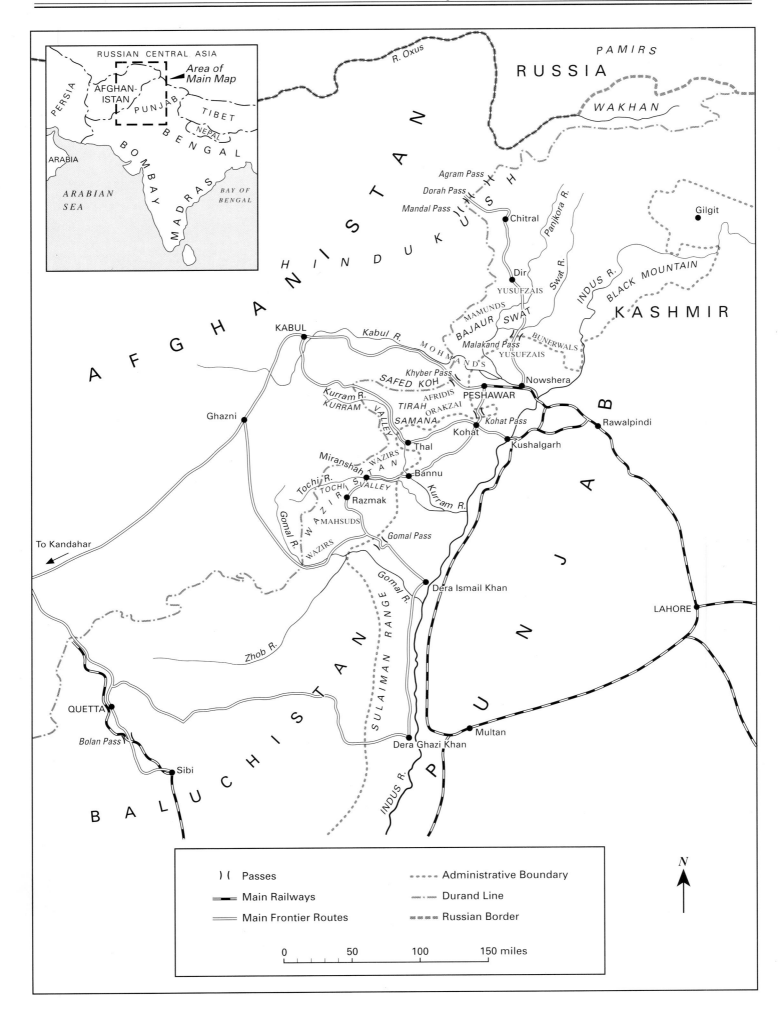

RUSSIAN CENTRAL ASIA

Area of
Main Map

PERSIA

AFGHAN-
ISTAN

PUNJAB

TIBET

NEPAL

BENGAL

ARABIA

BOMBAY

MADRAS

ARABIAN
SEA

BAY OF
BENGAL

PAMIRS

RUSSIA

R. Oxus

WAKHAN

A F G H A N I S T A N

H I N D U K U S H

Agram Pass

Dorah Pass

Mandal Pass

Chitral

Panjkora R.

Gilgit

Dir

YUSUFZAIS

Swat R.

INDUS R.

BLACK MOUNTAIN

KASHMIR

MAMUNDS

BAJAUR

SWAT

KABUL

Kabul R.

MOHMANDS

Malakand Pass

BUNERWALS

YUSUFZAIS

Khyber Pass

SAFED KOH

Nowshera

Kurram R.

AFRIDIS

PESHAWAR

Ghazni

KURRAM

VALLEY

TIRAH

ORAKZAI

SAMANA

Kohat Pass

Rawalpindi

Thal

Kohat

Miranshah

WAZIRISTAN

Kushalgarh

Tochi R.

TOCHI VALLEY

Bannu

Razmak

MAHSUDS

Kurram R.

Gomal R.

WAZIRS

Gomal Pass

To Kandahar

P U N J A B

Gomal R.

Dera Ismail Khan

LAHORE

SULAIMAN RANGE

Zhob R.

QUETTA

B A L U C H I S T A N

Multan

Bolan Pass

Dera Ghazi Khan

Sibi

INDUS R.

P

) (Passes

Administrative Boundary

Main Railways

Durand Line

Main Frontier Routes

Russian Border

0   50   100   150 miles

N

10

before the Kurram Valley was reached, lay their less warlike kinsmen the Orakzais. Together they could muster the largest number of fighting men on the whole Frontier – some 51,400 in all.

South of the Kurram, down to the Gomal Pass, were the Waziri clans, chiefly the Darwash Khel and – a law unto themselves – the Mahsuds. Sir Olaf Caroe, the last British Governor of the North-West Frontier Province, a man with vast experience of and admiration for the Pathans, likened "the Mahsud to a wolf, the Wazir to a panther. Both are splendid creatures; the panther is slier, sleeker and has more grace, the wolf-pack is more purposeful, more united and more dangerous"[2]. Fortunately for the British in 1897, the wolf-pack stayed at home, licking the wounds it had received two years before, but still dangerous – as it would prove again when the century turned.

Although there were characteristic variations between the tribes, and differences in their attitudes towards each other (and even between their clans), they all had certain traits in common. All lived according to a code of behaviour – *pukhtunwali* – infringements of which incurred drastic penalties. Two elements of this code required a generosity of spirit: any fugitive seeking sanctuary – even an enemy – had to be offered protection; and hospitality towards strangers – again, even enemies –

Pathan warriors, in this case Mahsuds, who were likened by an experienced British officer to a wolf-pack: purposeful, united and dangerous. (G.Russell)

was a binding obligation when requested. The third element was responsible for much of the Pathans' touchy pride, long memories, familiarity with weapons, and lack of respect for life: any sort of insult to, or theft from, an individual, a family or clan had to be avenged in blood, no matter how long it took.

Feuds between families and clans could be long-lasting, the Afridis being particularly prone to internal feuds; but the greatest insult offered to a tribe would obviously be an

Mohmand tribesmen from north of the Kabul River; some are armed with Snider and Enfield rifles, others with the long Frontier jezail. (Victorian Military Society Journal)

infringement of its lands and code by outsiders. Then internal feuds would be temporarily set aside while all united against the common foe.

With so much at stake it is not surprising that every village, every house was constructed as a defensive work, and that arms were always carried or readily to hand. These were, typically, a curved sword or *tulwar*; a straight, two-foot-long knife with a heavy back and a single razor-sharp edge; and, in earlier days, a long-barrelled matchlock or flintlock musket – the *jezail*, which had a range of about half a mile.

As time passed the tribes began to acquire muzzle-loading Enfield percussion rifles followed, in the early 1890s, by breech-loading Sniders and Martini-Henrys – the last, incidentally, giving them parity with Indian soldiers. These they obtained through gunrunners, by theft, and by manufacturing copies (with astonishing skill, given their technical resources) in their own arsenals, particularly those of the Adam Khel Afridis, the armourers of the Frontier.

All males were skilled in the use of these weapons, as indeed were some females, at least with edged weapons – "the women come out to cut up what remains", as Kipling warned any soldier who had the misfortune to be wounded and left behind [3]. Any non-Moslem taken alive was, according to John Masters, liable to be castrated and beheaded, usually by the women.

Alongside the Pathans' passionate desire to preserve their independence and way of life was their fanatical belief in and devotion to their Islamic faith, in the name of which they would perform great deeds, both noble and ignoble. They might ignore their *maliks* or headmen, they might argue – endlessly – in their council meetings, no Pathan ever calling any man his master; but when the call came from the *mullahs*, especially a call to arms against the infidel, no prior commitment, no clan feud, no lack of enthusiasm for danger or discomfort would deter a tribesman from his duty to his faith. In its name he would zealously inflict death, torture and mutilation; if his own life was forfeit, then his place in Paradise was assured.

Alongside this often heroic, frequently cruel zeal for blood, there could co-exist – as at least some British on the Frontier perceived – a curious sense of respect, mingled with a sometimes macabre humour, towards their opponents. This could make a Frontier campaign somewhat akin to a sporting contest in which, while it lasted, no holds were barred in the effort to win, but when it ended animosity would be forgotten – until, of course, the next time. "Did we fight well?" the Zakka Khel once asked a British official. "I wouldn't have shaken hands with you if you hadn't", he replied [4].

When Pathans enlisted, as many did, in Indian regiments like the Corps of Guides, they would fight as loyally for their regiment against their own kinsmen as they would later, after discharge back to their tribe, against their former comrades. At Ambela in 1863 the tribesmen, seeing that the Pathan and Gurkha sepoys opposing them were as skilled at hill-fighting as themselves, used to shout at them to send up the brave but less agile Sikhs and British, who made "better *shikar*" (sport) [5].

Some British in the 19th century (usually those unfamiliar with them) took a less generous view of the Pathans, emphasising their lawlessness, treachery and cruelty while overlooking their courage and honour, and the environment and history which had inevitably shaped them as they were.

A Political Officer (centre right, bareheaded) with a group of Khyber Afridis - martial, mistrustful and lawless, the Khyber clans alone could put some 27,000 fighting men into the field. In three days of late August 1897 they would take all the Khyber Pass forts. (Author's collection)

But few ever underestimated them as fighting men and mountain guerrillas. Not many soldiers, British or Indian, could match them man for man in their own terrain - neither their powers of endurance on a bare minimum of food, water and rest, nor their inbred tactical sense and cunning. A senior British officer believed the Pathans were "probably the finest individual fighters in the East, really formidable enemies, to despise whom means sure trouble" [6].

The years immediately before the campaigns described in this book had witnessed a change in the Pathans' fighting methods against forces sent to oppose them. In earlier days, although they would fire their jezails at anything within range (often longer than most of the shorter-barrelled smoothbore weapons returning their fire), and would sometimes concentrate their marksmen to produce a fusillade, their favoured method of attack was a sudden rush in mass with sword and knife from a concealed position, often at close range to the enemy, and whenever possible downhill. The speed at which they moved, the surprise they aimed to achieve, allied to the slow rate of fire of the muzzle-loading weapons facing them, would get them among the troops with minimum loss. Then it would be lightly-equipped, strong and wiry swordsmen against more heavily-burdened, less athletic men with discharged firearms and only bayonets with which to defend themselves.

The advent of breech-loaders, of greater range and accuracy and a higher rate of fire, and subsequently of bolt-action, magazine-loaded rifles, altered both sides of the equation. The sudden rush became far more vulnerable, initially to the Martini-Henry's stopping power and easier re-loading, and later to the sheer volume of fire produced by magazine rifles. Furthermore, as Pathans obtained breech-loaders themselves they quickly appreciated how much damage, delay and disruption they could cause by long-range firing from their own heights into the often ponderous, concentrated columns of their enemies far below (and particularly the unarmed, unwieldy baggage trains), as well as by sniping into camps at night, depriving tired troops of their rest. High above, with their lines of escape well worked out, they could continue to fire while the troops clambered up the steep slopes to dislodge them, slipping off at the last minute to their next position.

No Pathan worth his salt believed in wasting his life, his precious rifle and ammunition in fighting to the last ditch and the last round. Better by far, he thought, to run away to fight another day - or in the next hour, when the breathless troops, having attacked a by-now empty hilltop, began their always vulnerable descent (often hampered by the wounded who could never be left behind) to rejoin their column below. Then it would be back to the hilltop, or to some other piece of commanding ground, to re-open fire into the backs of the retreating troops as they tried to keep their footing on the treacherous scree of the downhill slope. Their stumbling descent would be in marked contrast to the tribesmen's who, if they chose to pursue, would "come down hillsides like falling boulders, not running but bounding" [7].

If the tribesmen assessed the body of troops opposing them as inexperienced, unwary, lacking covering fire to mask their movement, or simply too few, then it would be time for a swift unseen move to some vantage point from where they could launch one of their old rushes with sword and knife - but with marksmen held back ready to deal with the unexpected. Sharp-eyed, sure-footed and speedy, the Pathan was a master of his ground and of his arms, always alert to seize a sudden opportunity.

* * *

The British had been in India for nearly 250 years before they came into contact with the Pathans. In 1600 Queen Elizabeth I granted a charter to the East India Company for the purpose of trading in the East Indies and in India, then part of the great Mughal Empire. For the next 150 years England's Indian trade prospered through settlements established by the Company around the coasts from Bombay in the west, via Madras in the south, to Calcutta in the east, gradually ousting first its Portuguese, and then its

A Pathan watchtower, key to the defences of the typical defended Frontier village; these substantial stone towers were vulnerable to artillery or sappers' charges, but not much else.(G.Russell)

Dutch rival companies.

From the early days the East India Company had organised a few bodies of armed Europeans to protect its warehouses and factories. To supplement these it began to add, in the early 18th century, some small units of locally-raised *sipahis* (the original spelling) or *sepoys*; but their role was purely defensive and there had been no conflict with either the local rulers or the rival trading companies.

This notion of raising armed guards from the indigenous population and training them as soldiers had come first to France's trading company in India, partly as a means of demonstrating its prestige to the native rulers - who, though owing nominal allegiance to the Mughal Emperor in Delhi, were often virtually independent and at odds with one another. The French company had raised more such troops than the East India Company, and from the mid-18th century began to progress from mere trading to empire-building. By exploiting the differences between native rulers it planned to further French ambitions, at both their expense and that of the East India Company.

To maintain its position the EIC had no recourse but to follow suit. There ensued fifteen years of struggle for supremacy; but by 1763, thanks to leaders like Robert Clive, Eyre Coote and Stringer Lawrence, the French and their allies were defeated. Britain, through the EIC, now controlled Bengal and most of Madras, and the Company's army had grown in size and efficiency.

This was more than ever necessary to protect what had been won because, although Britain was now the dominant European power in India, there were still powerful Indian rulers prepared to dispute any further expansion. Four wars had to be fought against the Sultans of Mysore before their threat to the Company was finally defeated in 1799. Next came the confederation of Mahratta princes whose domains covered much of central and western India. Another four wars, between 1803 and 1819, were required before Mahratta power was broken; it was in the first of these that Sir Arthur Wellesley, later the Duke of Wellington, first made his name as a general in the field. Before the overthrow of the Mahrattas was accomplished three attempts to subdue the Gurkha hillmen of Nepal were undertaken, ending with a treaty of friendship; Nepal was not annexed, and Gurkha volunteers were accepted into the Company armies.

In the wake of conquest came administration and settlement by the officials of the Company, which had long since ceased to be a purely commercial concern. Since 1784 it had become answerable to the British Parliament and was effectively the agency through which Britain governed its Indian possessions. Its activities were supervised by a Board of Control in London, whose President had a seat in the Cabinet, and which was advised by the Company's Court of Directors. The latter appointed the Governors of the three "Presidencies", of Bengal, Madras and Bombay, those of the two latter being subordinate to Bengal's, who was styled Governor-General.

By the early decades of the 19th century British territory had increased vastly since the days of Clive. The Company armies, aided by troops from the Royal army at home, had carried all before them. Behind them the people of the conquered regions usually found a fairer and more just - though different - rule than they had known under their own often avaricious and despotic rulers. By 1830 British

India's border marched with the Punjab lands of the wise and powerful ruler of the Sikhs, Ranjit Singh. London felt it was time to call a halt and consolidate what had been won.

However, beyond the Punjab lay Afghanistan - no friend to Ranjit Singh, with whom the Company had contracted an alliance. Beyond Afghanistan lay Russia, expanding gradually southwards into Persia and with, it was feared, her eyes fixed on further expansion eastwards. With Persia bending to Russia's will, and with reports of Russian overtures made to the Afghan Amir, it seemed to the Governor-General, Lord Auckland, and to Ranjit Singh, that a different ruler in Kabul - one who had earlier held the Afghan throne but, having been deposed, had found sanctuary in India - would be more congenial to them both.

The result of this ill-conceived plan to install a more malleable Amir was the First Afghan War of 1839-42. It ended, without Sikh participation, in failure, disaster and humiliation for the Company's armies, although a fresh "avenging army" was able to restore British prestige somewhat in the final year of hostilities. There was no change of Amir, and he whom Auckland had distrusted was to prove a friend in testing times to come.

More trouble quickly followed. After the death of Ranjit Singh in 1839 the Sikh court became rent by feuds and the Sikh army, organised and trained on European lines, became aggressive. Contemptuous of the British showing in Afghanistan, and alarmed at the British occupation of Sind to the south in 1843, it feared the Punjab would be next. In 1845 it struck first, invading British India in the first of the two Sikh Wars, the hardest fighting that the Company's armies had yet experienced. Eventually, in 1849, the Company was victorious and the Punjab was annexed; and so the British came up to their final frontier, with its Pathan inhabitants, for the first time.

* * *

Before the Company's conquest of the Punjab its Sikh rulers had never been able effectively to prevent the Frontier tribes from raiding towards the Indus to plunder, from richer and more fertile lands, the better things of life which their own barren, unproductive, feud-riven mountains could not yield. There had been no demarcated boundary between tribal lands and Sikh territory, nor was there one on the Afghan side.

When the Company's troops came up to the Frontier after defeating the Sikhs, the tribesmen saw again the redcoats they had watched passing through their lands to the First Afghan War less than a decade before. They knew what had befallen the army retreating from Kabul in 1842 - from which, notoriously, only one man survived. They would also have heard what a hard struggle the Company armies had faced in the two Sikh Wars. When they found these armies on their borders in 1849, therefore, they saw no reason to change their ways; and given their liking for "trial by combat", they may even have welcomed the chance to pit their wits against these new potential adversaries. They acknowledged no mastery, whether exercised by the Amir in Kabul or the Company in the Punjab. They wanted no more and no less than to continue their traditional, feral way of life free of interference.

The Company established its administration up to the foothills of the tribal lands. Should the tribes commit misdemeanours within the Company's administrative border then, in the interests of good order and justice, they would be punished by military means, but not before

conciliatory measures had been tried first. What they did amongst themselves in their own hills was not the Company's concern. This remained the policy - commonly known as "butcher and bolt" - until the Company's next, greatest and final crisis: the Great Sepoy Mutiny of 1857.

The insurrection of the Company's Bengal Army and its allies posed the greatest threat to British rule for a hundred years; but it will not be considered further here. As far as the Frontier was concerned, the Company's position thereon was saved by a combination of decisive action by admirable men on the spot, and the faithfulness to his given word of the Afghan Amir. By 1859 it was over; and so was the Honourable East India Company.

"John Company's" rule now passed to the Crown. The President of the Board of Control became Secretary of State for India with his own department, the India Office, and advised by a Council of India replacing the Court of Directors. Responsible to the Secretary of State in India itself was the Governor-General, henceforth commonly known as the Viceroy, who was also advised by a Council and who presided over the Government of India, divided into different departments - Home, Foreign, Finance, Military, Legal - and staffed by the Indian Civil Service.

Responsibility for the Frontier region was vested in the Lieutenant-Governor of the Punjab, who answered to the Foreign Department of the Government of India. The policy of "butcher and bolt" continued; but there was soon a greater preoccupation than the tribes, one that exercised the minds of great men in offices in London and Calcutta [8], more than those in cantonments of the Punjab Frontier Force or the headquarters of British battalions stationed in Peshawar.

Beyond the Frontier and Afghanistan still lay Imperial Russia, expanding since the 1860s into Central Asia. To many thoughtful minds in the 1860s and 1870s it seemed only a matter of time (particularly after a less reliable Amir succeeded in 1868) before Afghanistan went the way of Turkestan, and the Tsar's armies were poised at the western gates of the vital passes into India.

This preoccupation, and the consequent need to ensure that British, not Russian, influence prevailed in Kabul, had

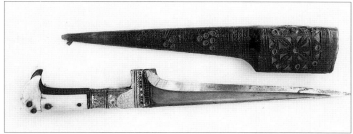

The "Khyber knife", notorious among generations of British soldiers; this example is 12ins. long, but some were made considerably larger. The hooked pommel gave a lightning-fast draw from the wooden scabbard; the heavy-backed T-section blade tapered to a needle point, with a single razor-sharp edge. One horror story told by "old sweats" to terrify recruits was that a Pathan would stab home, then, with a single upward tug, both disembowel the soldier and cut clean through his belt, the easier to snatch away his equipment and ammunition pouches. (Private collection)

The start of things to come: the last stand of the 44th Foot during the retreat from Kabul in 1842, in the famous painting by W.B.Wollen. Compare with the illustration on page 110 of an episode 55 years later. (The Royal Anglian Regiment)

led to the First Afghan War. Its failure, proving the unwisdom of antagonising the Afghans and the Frontier tribes, resulted in the "close-border policy": hold firm on the Indus, and let any invader come to grief in the passes – whose inhabitants would resist intruders whether from east or west. But that policy had been formulated and maintained before the major Russian advances into Central Asia. Those advances lent weight to a different view, the "forward policy": hold the western approaches to the passes, some said as far forward as the Hindu Kush, which would necessitate some form of control over Afghanistan . Such a policy would, however, leave the far-flung defenders' lines of communication through the passes vulnerable to tribal interference. Not until 1874, when Disraeli's new Conservative Government appointed Lord Lytton as Governor-General, was the forward policy adopted. The Second Afghan War of 1878-80 followed, sparked off by the Afghans' acceptance of a Russian mission and denial of a British one.

The hostilities involved operations not only against regular and irregular Afghan forces, but also, as the close-border theorists had predicted, against hostile tribal activity on the lines of communication. The war ended with the return of Gladstone's Liberals to power; with neither British forces nor British influence in Afghanistan; with the Russian threat undiminished – but with a strong new Amir in Kabul, Abdurrahman, who was to maintain good relations with British India despite his determination to exclude all foreign influences from his country.

Lytton's forward policy died with the change of administration in London and his resignation, but there were some changes to the old close-border system. It in fact became more "forward" than before, with areas around Quetta and the Kurram Valley coming under British control, as did the Afridi end of the Khyber Pass. Strategically important though these areas might have been for the defence of India, their occupation inevitably increased the risk of tribal confrontation. So it proved: in the 16 years after the war there were more counter-tribal expeditions than in the same period before it.

These troubles, plus uncertainties about the respective responsibilities for the tribes of the Indian and Afghan Governments, together with the institution, from 1885, of a more effective infrastructure for Indian defence - the construction of strategic roads and railways, and of firm bases to counter threats to the passes - all caused tensions along the Frontier and between Kabul and Calcutta. Eventually, in 1893, the two Governments agreed upon a formal demarcation of the Indian-Afghan border in the region. This, the Durand Line (named after the Indian Government's Foreign Secretary), began to be physically marked out with pillars - not without opposition - from 1894. With the Amir's agreement the lands of Chitral, Bajaur, Swat, Buner, Dir, the Khyber, Kurram and Waziristan all formally became British territory.

Although this agreement placed the border further forward than ever before, the new territory was not administered in the same way as was the rest of India up to the old administrative border. It was regarded as tribal territory whose inhabitants became "British protected persons", not governed but supervised by Political Agents. These agents - some from the Indian Civil Service, some from the Indian Army - were to acquaint themselves with the tribes of their agency and, having established some rapport with them, were to try to wean them from violence and depredation by a mixture of inducements of various kinds on the one hand, and the threat of punishment on the other.

The model for these agencies was that established for the Khyber after the Second Afghan War by Colonel Robert Warburton, the son of a British officer and an Afghan mother. He was not only very able but had a perfect command of Pushtu, an obvious asset for political agents (though one not acquired by some, who had to rely upon interpreters with consequent risk of misunderstandings or even misrepresentation). Warburton's concern was control of the Pass, not of the Afridis, but such was the mutual regard between him and these notoriously difficult people that there was no trouble on the Khyber for fifteen years. Elsewhere it was different. Work had not long begun on the Durand Line in the Waziristan agency when the working

party and its escort were attacked by Mahsuds who inflicted heavy casualties. An all-arms force of three brigades had to be sent against the whole Mahsud country over the very cold winter of 1894–95. The "wolf-pack" was harried, its hostile villages destroyed and reparation eventually extracted.

Almost at the same time, but far to the north, an uprising in Chitral left the Political Agent with his small escort besieged in a fort for nearly two months while two relief columns, from east and south, fought their way over difficult country to the rescue. After the successful conclusion of this campaign a permanent garrison was established on and around the Malakand Pass, which had

Sir Robert Warburton's domain: the Khyber Pass seen from Fort Ali Masjid at the Peshawar end. (Author's collection)

Guardians of the Frontier: types of the Punjab Irregular Force in the 1850s, in a watercolour by W.Carpenter. (Private Scottish collection)

had to be forced against strong opposition by the southern column; and a new political agency, embracing Dir, Swat and Chitral, was established with its headquarters at Malakand. Within a short space of time the country had settled down, the tribesmen appearing content enough with the prosperity which the new agency was bringing.

By the end of 1895 the Durand Line had been demarcated, order had been restored at its either end, the Afridis in the centre were quiet under Warburton's knowing eye, and the Khyber was secured by the forts manned by the Khyber Rifles - the Afridi-recruited levies which he had established. In 1896, with not a single expedition mounted that year, there seemed reasonable grounds for hope that the Pathans' age-old "content with discord, with alarms, and with blood" [9] might just be responding to the good intentions and wishes of their political masters for a more civilised, prosperous and harmonious tribal territory. Warburton, nearing the end of his distinguished career, was even planning to take leave in the spring of 1897.

But of course, as the more pessimistic might have forecast, it was all too good to be true. Warburton got away on leave as planned; but within days of his going the Frontier was ablaze from south to north, even unto his own centre. The political agents had done their best to be fair, understanding and conciliatory. Now it was to be soldiers' work - and not just a brigade here and there, but the greatest number of troops ever deployed on the Frontier. Alongside the Frontier Force regiments would be many other elements of an Indian Army reorganised and revitalised since the Great Mutiny 40 years before, together with British troops whose own army had also undergone many reforms over the same period.

CHAPTER TWO

The Soldiers

The Indian Army

The Indian troops who retreated from Kabul in 1842 were from the largest of the East India Company's three armies - that of Bengal. They were predominantly high-caste Hindus from Oudh, whose greater height and fairer skins gave them, it was thought, a more martial appearance on parade than the smaller, darker men of the less caste-conscious Madras and Bombay Armies. Those who did not die from exposure were slaughtered in the passes, easy prey for their Moslem adversaries. The same sort of men formed the majority of the troops that fought the Sikhs between 1845 and 1849. The Sikhs were unimpressed by them, and felt much antipathy towards them when they paraded as victors after the war; but learned to respect both the British troops who had borne the brunt of the fighting, and the subsequent administrators of the Punjab, for their justice and incorruptibility. A few years later, in 1857, it would be the same men of the same Bengal Army who were foremost in the Great Mutiny.

The causes and course of the Mutiny need not be recapitulated here; but it spelled the end of the old Bengal Army, only three of its 88 Regular units not having mutinied, been disarmed or disbanded. In contrast, only parts of two units of the Bombay Army mutinied; the Madras Army remained loyal, as did the Punjab Frontier Force.

The latter played an important part in the suppression of the Mutiny. Recruited on the principle that the reformed poacher makes the best gamekeeper, its men had been drawn initially from the Frontier area, then from among Punjabis, Sikhs and Gurkhas - the latter another class who had proved loyal in 1857. Because this force alone was not sufficient to reinforce the greatly-outnumbered European troops, a number of new regiments of horse and foot were raised in the Punjab where men, after some initial hesitation, proved willing to pit themselves against the Bengal sepoys on behalf of their former conquerors.

The invaluable service rendered by these "northerners" against the hitherto-preferred "easterners" led to a British theory that the former were the true "martial classes" who would best serve the post-Mutiny native army, and consequently they were increasingly recruited. By 1892 the Indian infantry contained 34 battalions from the Punjab (including Pathans, Sikhs, Jats, Dogras and Punjabi Moslems), 15 of Gurkhas, 15 from Hindustan (mostly Rajputs or Hindustani Moslems), 26 from Bombay and 31 from Madras; ten years later even 14 of the Madras-designated battalions were recruited from the Punjab.

The type of men recruited - all volunteers - were predominantly of yeoman or peasant stock, from small, closely-knit village communities, physically tough, of limited intellect, unquestioning and amenable to discipline (providing it was fair). They were enlisted initially for three years, with the option thereafter of claiming their discharge or re-engaging to complete 21 years. They joined because soldiering was an honourable career, for the pay and other rewards, for the opportunity of advancement and distinction, and often to follow a family tradition.

Since recruiting was done on a regimental rather than an army basis they would join, not the Indian Army, but a regiment - say the 2nd Punjab Cavalry or the 36th Sikhs - and would expect to remain in that regiment all their service. Providing it was well-officered and they were well-treated they would give it loyal and devoted service; if not, they could become difficult and resentful, as had occurred in the old Bengal Army.

After the Mutiny the principle of having three separate armies was retained, and initially those of Madras and Bombay remained much as before. In the new, reorganised Bengal Army the regiments, both cavalry and infantry, were

Types of the "martial classes" found in the Guides Infantry of the Punjab Frontier Force. (R.G.Harris)

Representatives of some PFF, Gurkha, Sikh and Punjabi regiments, c.1890. Watercolour by Maj.A.C.Lovett. (Maj.A.G.Harfield)

of two types: single-class, i.e. all Gurkhas or all Sikhs; or class–company/troop regiments. In the latter type, for example the 11th Bengal Lancers, there was one troop of Punjabi Moslems, one of Pathans, three of Sikhs, and one of Dogras; the 31st Bengal Infantry (Punjab) had two companies of Punjabi Moslems, four of Sikhs, and two of Dogras.

This system ensured that the men of a company or troop were homogenous by religion, their home circumstances, speech, eating habits and so on, thereby forming a close-knit group whose concern for its honour and prestige would promote a spirit of friendly rivalry with other companies, which in turn would contribute to the efficiency of the regiment as a whole. Furthermore it aided recruiting and administration in a way which would not have been so practicable had all the classes been mixed throughout the regiment. On the other hand it could cause difficulties that did not exist in a single-class regiment if the need arose for inter-company transfers to facilitate promotions or to make good casualties. The supposed need for diversity within a regiment had been bred of mistrust inspired by the Mutiny; since total diversity was impractical, the class-company system was adopted. Despite its advantages, however, it was obviously not as flexible as the single-class unit, which had become more usual by the end of the century.

Stereotypes are always a gross oversimplification; but some general variations in the character of the "martial classes" were observable. For instance, the Sikhs and their kin the Jats were natural fighting men, hardy, brave and reliable; but they needed to be well-led and worked hard all the time to get the best out of them. Gurkhas, besides their well-known capacity for courage and endurance, were cheerful and faithful, and since such matters as caste and religion sat relatively lightly upon them they identified more easily with British troops than with other native regiments. Punjabi Moslems made good, steady, dependable soldiers, but without the more positive qualities of the Sikhs, or the fiery dash and natural skill-at-arms of the more independently-minded Pathans. The latter, fighting as soldiers on the Frontier, could often be faced by a conflict of loyalties.

For some time after the post-Mutiny reorganisation the three armies remained localised, but as the internal security problem diminished and the strategic emphasis shifted to the North-West changes were made in the higher organisation. First, the Madras and Bombay Armies were reduced. In 1886 the Punjab Frontier Force (PFF), hitherto a separate element under the Lieutenant-Governor of the Punjab, was brought into the Bengal Army, but still retaining its own identity. Finally, in 1895, the three armies were abolished in favour of four commands: Punjab (including the Frontier Force), Bengal, Madras (including Burma), and Bombay (including Sind and Baluchistan), each under a lieutenant-general responsible to the Commander-in-Chief, India. The units were no longer localised, but retained their old Presidency names in their designations. Thus, serving on the Frontier in 1897 will be found, besides many PFF and Bengal regiments, the 3rd Bombay Light Infantry and the 21st Madras Infantry.

By the 1890s there were 39 cavalry regiments, of which 19 were Bengal, numbered consecutively with six designated as lancers, and five were PFF, including the Guides Cavalry; the remainder were Madras (3), Bombay

(6), the Central India Horse (2), the Poona Horse, and Hyderabad (3). Every regiment had four, two-troop squadrons each of 164 all ranks, the NCOs and *sowars* being armed with sword, carbine and, where appropriate, lance.

After the Mutiny the only Indian artillery units were mountain batteries. These, by the 1890s, totalled eight, each of six guns with 138 pack-mules. The gun was the 2.5-in. Rifled Muzzle-Loading "screw-gun", so called because the muzzle and breech were in separate parts which were screwed together for action. It fired a 7lb. projectile - either shrapnel, shell, canister (case) or star-shell (for illumination) - and had a maximum range of 4,000 yards. Two guns, each carried on five mules, formed a section, whose other 36 mules carried ammunition, tools and spares, or were reserve animals. A battery had five officers and 106 NCOs and gunners, plus the mule-drivers.

Engineer tasks were undertaken by the independent companies, each some 150 strong, of the Bengal, Madras and Bombay Sappers and Miners. Those of Madras, whose men were no longer considered good enough for the infantry under the "martial class" principle, were nevertheless rated highly as sappers on account of their higher intelligence. Their British officers, like those of the mountain batteries, were seconded from the British Army, not commissioned into the Indian Army. Sappers were used for the more complex engineering requirements, such as bridge-building. The more straightforward tasks, such as road improvement or construction of simple defences, could be undertaken by certain infantry battalions designated and trained as Pioneers; of these, three each were Bengal (23rd, 32nd, and 34th) and Madras (1st, 4th and 21st), and one Bombay (28th).

The 121 Regular infantry battalions in 1892 were all from single-battalion regiments, except for the five senior Gurkha regiments which each had two battalions. Apart from those five regiments and the ten of the PFF, all were designated Bengal, Madras or Bombay Infantry and numbered consecutively within each group. Many had subsidiary titles denoting their class composition or territorial affiliation, as in 10th (Jat) Bengal Infantry, 26th (Baluchistan) Bombay Infantry, etc.; or marking the grant of a Royal title, as in 4th (Prince Albert Victor's) Bengal Infantry; or even both, as in 20th (Duke of Cambridge's Own) (Punjab) Bengal Infantry. In general usage such titles would usually be abbreviated to 10th Jats, 20th Punjabis, and so forth.

The Frontier Force regiments were numbered separately, as 1st to 4th Sikh Infantry, 1st to 6th Punjab Infantry (less the 3rd, disbanded in 1882), and the 5th Gurkha (Rifle) Regiment, with the Guides Infantry un-numbered; all had (PFF) after their titles. The four senior Gurkha regiments, all Rifles, were numbered 1st to 4th; the five junior regiments were numbered within the Bengal Line (9th, 42nd, 43rd and 44th) and as the 10th Madras Infantry (1st Burma Gurkha Rifles) [1].

Indian Army battalions, of some 700 all ranks excluding officers, had formerly consisted (like British battalions) of eight companies, divided into two wings each under a British officer, additional to those in battalion headquarters, each company being commanded by an Indian officer *(subedar)*. This had proved unsatisfactory in the Second Afghan War due to British officer casualties and the limited command abilities of their Indian counterparts. By the 1890s, therefore, the battalion was organised into four double-companies, each

Recruits for the Gurkha Rifles; the kukri knife will be retained as part of their military equipment. (Author's collection)

with two British officers, and further subdivided into four half-companies, all under Indian officers, each of two 20-strong sections under sergeants *(havildars)*.

Although by 1897 the Mutiny was 40 years in the past, and the new Indian Army was a very different force from that which had once turned its weapons on its officers, the policy adopted in the aftermath of that shocking episode - of always ensuring that Indian troops had inferior weapons to those of British regiments in India - still held good. In the Afghan War the British infantry had been armed with the Martini-Henry rifle, the Indian with the Snider. From 1892, when the bolt-action, magazine-loaded Lee-Metford began to reach the British garrison, the Martinis were handed over to the Indian infantry and remained their weapon for the rest of the century.

The Martini fired a .45in. round, was sighted to 1,450 yards and, for Indian troops, had an 18in. sword bayonet. It was a good weapon, with great stopping power; but being single-loading, with a fierce recoil and a 33in. barrel, both of which could impair accuracy (particularly when the long bayonet was fixed), it had neither the rate of fire, accuracy nor range of the shorter and handier Lee-Metford. Furthermore, as stated earlier, it gave the Indian sepoys no fire advantage over their tribal adversaries, many of whom had the same weapon.

* * *

Success in all military operations, and the performance of the troops committed to them, depend greatly on the

Bugler, jemadar (second lieutenant), NCOs and riflemen of the 2nd Goorkha Rifles in the 1890s. With the 3rd Gurkha Scouts, Col. Travers' 1st Bn. 2nd Goorkha Rifles would lead the second assault at Dargai on 20 October 1897; see also Plate F. (Maj. A. G. Harfield)

quality of the officers, both high- and low-ranking. In mountain warfare on the Frontier the nature of the operations and of the terrain often saw relatively small bodies of troops functioning on their own, divorced from their main body, whether as advance or rear-guards, defending a remote post, picquetting the heights to protect an advance or withdrawal, reconnoitring, or providing escorts. As Lord Wolseley wrote of such operations: "the real fighting unit will be the company" [2].

Without any of the modern means of instant communication between widely-spread bodies of troops, tactical decisions depended greatly on the officer - often quite young - who was immediately confronted by them. Even the then-usual means of communication, by Semaphore and Morse flags (see commentary to Plate H2) or heliograph - assuming he had them with his party - might be rendered inoperable by terrain or weather, and the meaning of field calls by bugle could well be familiar to tribesmen who had served in the Army.

Such warfare made great demands on the regimental officers, from the battalion commander down to the half-company subaltern. Their men, however brave, well-disciplined, well-trained and skilled in their arms, would rely upon their officers' quick thinking, tactical sense, alertness, initiative and, above all, their example and leadership. This applied with any troops, but particularly when they were "men of an alien legion" [3].

In Indian units the cavalry troop and infantry half-company commanders were Indian officers, *ressaldars* and *subedars* and the more junior *jemadars*. All were men of much experience in their regiments, but of a certain age,

having been promoted on seniority after considerable service in the ranks. They knew their men and they knew their work, they were loyal and trusted subordinates, and they had the strengths, but also the educational weaknesses, of the "martial classes". In the 18th century Indians had commanded companies, and they were to do so again from 1863; but the above-mentioned experiences in the Afghan War having led to an increase in the number of British officers, their status and perceived abilities as commanders had declined, so that they were, essentially, commissioned NCOs who would need the direction of a properly-trained (i.e. British) officer. This, it should be stressed, was how they were judged at that time - as fine men, but with limited command potential; but there had been instances when individuals had proved otherwise. One example had been during the Guides' epic defence of the British Residency at Kabul when, with all the British officers dead, an Indian took command and fought on to the end. There would be other episodes which would give the lie to the conventional wisdom of the day, as will be seen hereafter.

By the 1890s all British officers with Indian regiments were the products of the Royal Military College, Sandhurst or, if with mountain batteries and sappers, of the Royal Military Academy, Woolwich. Except for the latter they were commissioned not into individual regiments but into the Indian Staff Corps, which had been combined in 1891 from the Bengal, Madras and Bombay Staff Corps. These had been established after the Mutiny to provide a pool of British officers which would be used to fill not only staff appointments in the various headquarters and departments but also the command and staff functions in regiments. In the latter it had been intended that the British officers, apart from the commanding officer and his headquarters staff, should act more as advisers and supervisors to the Indian officers commanding companies. However, as has been seen, this had not worked; hence the double-company system with more British officers in executive roles and the now more advisory Indian officers acting as the link between them and the sepoys.

Unless officers went on the staff they could in theory be moved from one regiment to another, but in practice they generally tended to remain with one. The sepoy was a long-service volunteer, and each class had its own idiosyncrasies; furthermore, following the Mutiny, much would depend on trust, mutual respect and mutual

Daffadar and sowar of the Central India Horse. (Maj. A. G. Harfield)

understanding between leaders and led. Long service with a particular regiment, though contrary to the original concept of the Staff Corps, helped to cement the loyalty of all ranks both to the regiment and, within it, to one another. The British officer owed his allegiance, first, to the Queen-Empress; then – for the sake of his regiment's good name, coupled with his admiration for them – to his responsibility to his men. The sepoy's allegiance, once it had been earned, was given first to his officer and, through him, to his regiment, but not much higher.

Some two-thirds of British Indian Army officers were the sons of officers, a third of whom had themselves been Indian Army. The remainder stemmed either from the lesser gentry or professional families - medical, clergy and the Indian Civil Service. All counted themselves gentlemen, which as officers they were bound to be, but their family circumstances were seldom affluent [4].

They were the products of the public schools, of the generation immortalised by Rudyard Kipling in *Stalky & Co.*, which was based on his own schooldays between 1878 and 1882 at the United Services College. This was a spartan establishment at Westward Ho! on the North Devon coast, founded by retired Army officers to provide a public school education at lower rates than other schools; it was expressly designed to get boys into Sandhurst or Woolwich, without the expense of going on to "crammers" as many boys from other schools had to do. Kipling recorded that 75 per cent of the boys in his time were born outside England and were destined for the Army [5].

However, not all future Army officers went to the United Services College; as one of its old boys remarked, when discussing Stalky's later adventures with a Sikh regiment: "India's full of Stalkies - Cheltenham and Haileybury and Marlborough chaps" [6]. To these he might

Jemadar and gunners of No.5 (Bombay) Mountain Battery assembling one of the unit's six 2.5in.RML "screw-guns", by far the most common artillery piece on the Frontier.

This particular battery will be encountered later in this book, supporting the old "52nd" Light Infantry with the Mohmand Field Force against the Kuda Khel on 27 September 1897, and covering the fighting withdrawal of the Tirah Field Force's 2nd Division in December. (Maj.A.G.Harfield)

have added two other particularly Army-oriented schools: Clifton, which was to field 35 officers in the Pathan Rising, and Wellington, 50 per cent of whose output between 1879 and 1898 went to the Army. At least 40 Wellingtonians served during the Rising; six died, in action or from disease, and another five were wounded [7].

In the last two decades of the 19th century there were at least 64 seats of learning for boys that counted themselves public schools [8], though some, like the five just mentioned, enjoyed much higher prestige than others like the USC. Indian Army officers tended to be products of the less expensive schools, although Wellington offered special terms for the sons, and particularly the orphans, of Army officers.

Whatever the school, the majority were turning out, in the late Victorian era, many boys whose characters and physique had been formed to prepare them as reinforcements for those administering the British Empire and those commanding the troops that held it. No fortunes would be made in such careers, and many lives would be forfeit –"Two thousand pounds of education drops to a ten-rupee jezail"[9]. But these were roles that most public-schoolboys accepted as laid upon them by their upbringing and education; and they would do their best to uphold the honour of their country, their service or their regiment. In the Stalky story *The Flag of their Country* Kipling suggests that this knowledge of their duty was

Indian officers of the 36th Sikhs in full dress. This regiment, led by Lt.Col.John Haughton, particularly distinguished itself in a number of engagements during the Great Rising, including the defence of Forts Lockhart and Gulistan in September 1897, and the operations of the Tirah Field Force that winter. See also Plate H. (R.G.Harris)

inbred, and that the vulgarly explicit exhortations to patriotism of "the Jelly-Bellied Flag-Flapper" - a Member of Parliament - disgusted them. Yet for any who were in doubt - or perhaps for the reassurance of some parents - Sir Henry Newbolt spelled out the code: "To set the cause above renown,/ To love the game beyond the prize,/ To honour , while you strike him down,/ The foe that comes with fearless eyes"; and, above all, to "Play up! Play up! And play the game!"[10]. However naive such a code may sound to younger readers in the late 1990s, the simple fact remains that most young gentlemen of the 1890s held it to be unquestionable. It is not for nothing that the famous line from L. P. Hartley's *The Go-Between* has become much quoted: "The past is a foreign country; they do things differently there". (Even today there are some who might say "and better, too".)

It was believed that playing the game for the honour of the house or school prepared a boy for upholding the honour of his regiment in a deadlier game. The corporate school spirit, allied to the prefect system, introduced him to the mutual dependency necessary within and between regiments in the field, and to the command of those who would look to him for leadership. The boy who had been a successful head of house, or who had led the First XV to victory, should have no trouble - given time and the advice of his Indian officers - in getting the best out of his Sikhs, Punjabis or Gurkhas, or in earning their loyalty whilst so doing.

The British Army in India

The officers of the British Army were out of the same stable, though with some differences. They joined not the Army, still less a Staff Corps, but a regiment, often one in which their forebears had served. Despite the abolition from 1870 of the old system whereby first commissions and subsequent promotions up to the rank of lieutenant-colonel were purchased (a system never applicable to the Indian service), their social backgrounds remained much as before. Just under half were from Army families, the remainder from broadly similar backgrounds to Indian Army officers but at a generally more affluent level. The rural landed gentry predominated, with additions from the higher-paid legal and clerical professions, from commerce and banking, and from titled families - whose scions seldom entered the Indian Army. As might be expected the schools they attended were often, though not always, of the more prestigious type. However, Etonian and Harrovian sons of peers and baronets probably opted for the Household Cavalry or Foot Guards, which did not serve in India, though quite possibly for the Line Cavalry - which did. The young Winston Churchill, son of Lord Randolph Churchill and educated at Harrow, entered the 4th Hussars and went with them in 1896 to India, where we shall meet him again.

So the young officer of a British regiment, when first encountering his contemporaries in an Indian regiment, would find men not very different from himself, and possibly some old school-fellows; but would nevertheless, like all his brother-officers, feel himself superior to them. Partly this was because he knew he was privileged to command British soldiers and not, in the pejorative term sometimes used, "black infantry"; partly, because he knew many of them were in the Indian Army simply because they could not afford to serve in the British Army, where even in Line regiments officers needed some private means to live like gentlemen; and partly for historical reasons - the Mutiny, the antiquity of his own regiment, the long-standing prejudices of the Queen's Army against the old Company Armies, and so on. Possibly, too, he was compensating for his hidden concern that, when the time came for a Frontier expedition, he and his men would not be as experienced or adept at the work as, say, the Frontier Force battalion to which he was currently condescending.

Every right-thinking officer naturally believed, or was taught to believe, that his regiment was the best in the Army, so all would share some prejudice towards other regiments, British or Indian. At best this would manifest itself in a spirit of friendly rivalry, thereby contributing to

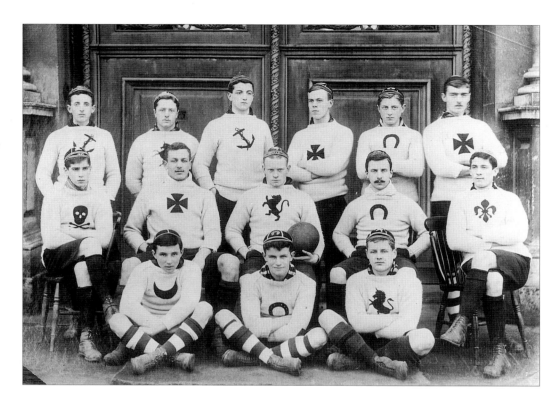

Officer material: the Wellington College rugby football First XV, 1893. Standing at right rear wearing the jersey of Blucher dormitory is L.L.Wheatley, later to serve on the Frontier with the 45th Sikhs (see the description of the defence of Fort Chakdara, pages 48-51). (Wellington College)

the overall effectiveness of the whole – the same principle which underlaid the Indian class-company system. Above all he would be expected to act, as Edward Spiers has written, "in accordance with the norms of gentlemanly behaviour, including an emphasis on honour, integrity and courage, a capacity for generosity and unselfishness, and a conformity with the etiquette, dress and deportment of persons in polite society" [11] – a type epitomised by "2nd Lieutenant Bobby Wick" in Kipling's story *Only a Subaltern* [12].

This was the end-product of the expensive education at a public school, of Sandhurst (also fee-paying in those days), and of the early years in a regiment, particularly in the fellowship of the Officers' Mess, conducted on the lines of a gentleman's club. Keener on field sports and team games than intellectual pursuits, the British officer of the 1890s was less of a "professional" than his modern counterparts; but, unlike many of them, he was more dedicated to his regiment than to furtherance of his own career. He was usually able to pass his promotion exam to the next higher rank when it became due by seniority, but few middle-ranking regimental officers chose to broaden their careers and military knowledge by entering for the Staff College, then less of a passport to the higher ranks than it is now. Ian Hamilton of the Gordons wrote of the 1880s that "no officer of the regiment had ever entered for the Staff College. This was one of their numerous, die-hard boasts"[13]. This attitude was still not uncommon ten years later, though more prevalent in the cavalry and infantry than amongst gunners and sappers; it was, however, growing less so.

Whatever their intellectual limitations, most British officers could be relied upon to lead from the front when the bugle called to arms, and "to play the game", not only by their brother-officers, but by their men, in a paternal care for their welfare.

* * *

At the close of the 19th century the NCOs and men of the British Army, though all voluntarily enlisted, were no longer the long-service men – mainly from rural areas and particularly from Ireland – who had filled the ranks in the Crimea and the Mutiny. Since the 1850s rural areas had suffered depopulation due to agricultural recession, with a consequent drift in search of work to increase the urban, especially slum populations, and mass emigration from Ireland after the famines of the 1840s. There had also been an increased demand for recruits, caused *inter alia* by the need for a larger British garrison in India after the Mutiny. All this had led to increasing reliance being placed on the large cities rather than the countryside as recruiting areas, with a consequent lowering of physical and moral standards.

Before 1850 the proportions of Scotsmen and Irishmen in the Army, at 14 and 40 per cent respectively, were greater than their proportions of the population as a whole; by 1897 these figures had fallen to 7.8 per cent and 12.4 per cent, although Ireland's contribution still slightly exceeded her proportion of the British population [14].

Despite measures, since 1870, to improve both the quantity and the quality of recruits, the two often conflicting, the men who enlisted still came from the less skilled section of the working class, many of them unemployed. Assuming that many of the men whose battalions will be met in these pages enlisted in the late 1880s and early 1890s, their former civil occupations would have been 64 per cent labourers, 15 per cent artisans, 11 per cent mechanics, the balance being chiefly shopmen, clerks and boys under seventeen years [15]. The minimum height and weight standards varied according to the recruiting response, but between 1889 and 1897 they were 5ft.4ins. and 115lbs.; the age bracket for recruits was 18 to 25 years.

Bearing in mind that soldiering was traditionally held in low regard by the public at large – much lower than among those sections of the Indian public which sent their sons into the Indian Army – the British recruits' motives for enlisting were primarily lack of work with consequent poverty and hunger, followed by such reasons as escaping domestic problems, joining relatives or friends, or indulging a fancy for travel, excitement and a smart uniform.

However unpromising the raw material, a glance at the faces and physiques of soldiers in photographs taken in the 1890s, particularly in India when they would have had some years' service, may recall a less well-known remark of the Duke of Wellington, who qualified his oft-quoted description of earlier British soldiers as "the scum of the earth" by saying: "It really is wonderful that we [the Army] should have made them the fine fellows they are"[16]. And so they appear: clean, well set-up, with evident pride in themselves, their uniforms and their regiments, many of them certainly having found a better life than that which they had left behind.

A soldier could not serve in India until he was either aged 20 or had completed one year's service. Even so, Kipling has a colonel complaining about a new draft as "pasty-faced, shifty-eyed, mealy-mouthed young slouchers from the depot"[17], comparing them unsatisfactorily with his older men and particularly those who had opted for long service (like the famous *Soldiers Three*, Mulvaney, Learoyd and Ortheris). For a picture of the ordinary soldier, his attitudes and his life in India in the latter part of the 19th century, Kipling's soldier stories and his *Barrack Room Ballads* – though presented in fictional form – are a most rewarding source, based as they are on his keen personal observations of such men between 1882 and 1889; and are only rivalled by the recollections of Private Frank Richards in his *Old Soldier*

The finished article. From top left: A.C.Bunny, Wellington and 1st Sikhs (killed 10 June 1897 - see Chapter Three); Hon.H.Cavendish, Harrow and 3rd Rifle Brigade (died Tochi, July 1897); R.D.Jennings-Bramly, Cheltenham and 1st Gordon Highlanders (killed 18 October 1897 - see Chapter Eight); and Richmond Battye, Clifton and 6th Bengal Cavalry (killed 1 December 1897 - see Chapter Nine). (R.G.Harris & author's collection)

Sahib, though Richards' service was post-1900.

Kipling's *The Young British Soldier* is full of what awaited "the 'arf-made recruity" who, on first arriving in the East, "acts like a babe an' drinks like a beast"; and gives an old soldier's advice on how best to make himself "fit for to serve as a soldier", by avoiding drink like "fixed Bay'nets that rots out your guts"; how to cope with cholera and the sun; down to the day when he comes under fire for the first time: "Be thankful you're livin' and trust to your luck and march to your front like a soldier". Curiously, one officer with much Indian experience believed that soldiers actually became more like Kipling's characters in the years immediately following these works' publication (1888-92) than they had been before[18]. If true, such were the men on the Frontier in 1897-98.

The chance of a Frontier campaign always seems to have lifted the spirits of British troops in India; Kipling makes this plain more than once[19]. When the men of the 2nd Highland Light Infantry were ordered to join the Malakand Field Force in 1897, one recorded: "Immediately a wild yell broke out and some men so far forgot themselves as to dance outside their barrack rooms". One party of sick discharged themselves from hospital so as not to be left behind[20].

Although they knew that hard, demanding work, discomfort and danger, possibly even death or mutilation awaited them, they welcomed it as a break from what Kipling called "the boundless monotony of cantonment life" in a peaceful Indian garrison, particularly in the hot weather. "They drilled morning and evening on the same dusty parade-ground. They wandered up and down the same stretch of dusty white road, attended the same church and the same grog-shop and slept in the same lime-washed barn of a barrack for two long years"[21].

In 1896 a colonel in the Indian Staff Corps wrote a cheerily optimistic article about the advantages for the British soldier of life in India compared with being stationed at home, extolling the "magnificent barracks", the food, the sports fields, game-shooting, the regimental clubs, institutes and canteens "with beer and spirits of unexceptionable quality", and the number of servants to perform menial tasks done in England by soldiers themselves. Yet even he had to weigh in the balance the climate, the life-threatening diseases, and the lack of amusements and entertainments outside barracks for young British working-class men. He refrained from mentioning explicitly the dearth of young British working-class women, and the prudish attitude of some Europeans towards regimental brothels. If these were closed, soldiers were left with little outlet save local brothels and what Frank Richards called "sand-rats", with the consequent severe risk of venereal disease, not so easily treated in those days. The optimistic colonel was honest enough to admit that "life could become colourless"[22].

The soldier of a hundred years ago did not usually consort with Indians, and his attitude towards the indigenous population would horrify today's liberal conscience. For a start, in India even "the humblest trooper was a white sahib"[23]. They had all picked up the horror-stories of the Mutiny, and firmly believed, like Frank Richards, that "what was won by the sword, must be kept by the sword". Lord Curzon, when Viceroy, was much disliked by British soldiers for his insistence on their better treatment of Indians, not to mention his American wife's widely-reported assertion that

the two ugliest things in India were the water-buffalo and the British private soldier; when the 9th Lancers were ordered to give "eyes right" to Curzon, their rank and file all turned their heads and eyes to the left [24].

Even with Indian soldiers of the martial classes the British rank and file's relations were correct rather than cordial. Only Gurkhas were welcomed in British camps and lines as comrades-in-arms. Echoes of the Mutiny reverberated in the consciousness of all British classes long after the old Bengal Army had passed into history.

Serving so far from his own familiar surroundings, the British soldier was thrown back on the comradeship of his fellows in the barrack room and, less closely, the paternal care of his officers. There was a wide social gulf between late Victorian officers and their men; but although the latter were quick to spot a martinet or one who was not up to his work, they did not generally resent this difference - indeed, they expected it. The rare officer promoted from the ranks could often be the cause of uneasiness.

Though remote in manners and mores, the best officers were not remote in spirit, the bond being closer in distant stations or on active service than in large cantonments or at home. Kipling believed that a subaltern who could lead a chorus round a camp-fire or "who plays cricket cleverly" would find that "Thomas Atkins will stand by him in time of need" more readily than he would another officer who might be better-qualified militarily. This notion Kipling further expanded in *The Shut-Eye Sentry*, in which he has NCOs and men covering for a young officer the worse for drink, ending "most depends on makin' friends with Privit Thomas A!" [25]. How an officer could win the trust, indeed the affection and admiration of his men when they were in need, as in a cholera epidemic, is movingly told in the above-mentioned story *Only a Subaltern*. Frank Richards summed up the relationship between his comrades and their officers of the Royal Welch Fusiliers as "mutual trust in military matters and sport, but no social contact. They took

Officers of the 1st Bn., Queen's Royal West Surrey Regiment, destined to see action with both the Malakand and Tirah Field Forces in 1897. (Author's collection)

The second-in-command and two subalterns of the 1st Northamptons in January 1898, hardened by a punishing winter campaign with the Tirah Field Force and one particularly ugly action against the Zakka Khel Afridis. (Maj. T.C.S. Knox)

"Clean, well set-up, with pride in themselves and their regiment":
British infantrymen - here apparently a tug-of-war team - pose with
their officer and NCOs. (Maj. T.C.S. Knox)

a keen interest in the men, were strict disciplinarians but [were] far from treating us with contempt" [26].

Between the officers and the men stood the NCOs, from the lance-corporals and corporals, to the sergeants and colour-sergeants - the latter then the senior NCO in a company - to the quartermaster-sergeants, and finally to the majestic figure of the sergeant-major: "the backbone of the Army", as Kipling called them. With his usual perceptive eye he tells us that when the ambitious young soldier first reaches the rank of "lance" he is "'arf o' nothin', an' all a private yet", ragged by the men from whom he has so recently been marked out, but learning "to sweat 'is temper an' 'is man". With time, luck and application he may ultimately attain the rank of colour-sergeant, "quick an' 'andy, uncommon set an' smart", experienced in handling men and in what to watch out for; until finally in action, with his captain dead, he "lifts 'em through the charge that wins the day" [27].

Since NCOs lived closer to the men, and since they enforced the discipline and orders laid down by officers as well as supervising much of the daily routine and administration, they were more likely to be the targets of any ill-feeling. To compensate for, and to assist in their heavy duties and responsibilities, they enjoyed privileges: higher pay, obviously; easier access to officers; more congenial living and feeding arrangements in the sergeants' messes, modelled on those for the officers; and for the corporals, who lived and ate with the men, the privacy of their clubs where they could talk and drink away from the raucous soldiery in the canteen.

Officers in good battalions, conscious of how much depended on the NCOs both in peace and war, would do their utmost to reinforce the latter's prestige and authority. It was always they who would be the first to spot signs of indiscipline, frustration, boredom or fear, all potentially disruptive to the regiment's good order, and more likely to arise in an Indian cantonment where there were fewer outlets than at home.

two-battalion regiment (as were the 1st - 25th Foot) or two single-battalion regiments (26th - 109th Foot) would be based, together with two Militia battalions and a varied number of Volunteer units, plus a brigade depot manned by the Regular battalions for training recruits. One Regular battalion or regiment was to be at home, not necessarily in the district, receiving recruits from the depot and feeding the other battalion abroad, the two rotating periodically. It was hoped that by strengthening ties between the area and the units based therein (most of which had a largely nominal territorial designation in addition to their numbers), the ensuing kinship would attract a better type of recruit and more of them, as well as inducing Militiamen to transfer to their Regular counterparts.

The imperfections of this scheme led to its further development in 1881. The brigade districts were converted to regimental districts, in which the Regular, Militia and Volunteer units of each became numbered battalions of one un-numbered, territorially-designated regiment served by a regimental depot. The old numbered single-battalion regiments became the two Regular battalions of the new regiment, though in some cases the former pairs were re-arranged with new partners. For instance, of those battalions which will be encountered later in these pages: the old 39th (Dorsetshire) - which had been linked somewhat incongruously with the 75th (Stirlingshire) - now became 1st Battalion, Dorsetshire Regiment; and received as its 2nd Battalion the former 54th (West Norfolk) - previously linked with the 95th (Derbyshire). The 75th, with the 92nd, became the 1st and 2nd Battalions, Gordon Highlanders; while the 95th joined the 45th (Nottinghamshire) to form 1st and 2nd Battalions, Derbyshire Regiment (Sherwood Foresters).

For the old senior regiments with two battalions the new system involved far less change of loyalties, uniform and badges; the 3rd (East Kent, The Buffs), for example, merely lost its numeral. For the others, while the 1872 Localisation had been unpopular enough, this further reform meant the loss of their time-honoured numbers, always far more significant than their subsidiary titles; the alteration of their ancient individual uniform facing colours to "national" colours, e.g. white for all non-Royal English

* * *

One advantage for British soldiers of the 1890s was that their spell of Indian service was never likely to be as long as that of their forebears. Among the reforms of 1870, besides improvements in food and living conditions (as well as the abolition of flogging in 1868), had been the change from long-service to short-service engagements. Primarily designed to build up a Regular Reserve of trained soldiers such as existed in Continental armies raised by near-universal conscription, the short-service system enlisted an infantryman for six years with the Colours and six on the Reserve (eight and four respectively for cavalrymen), with the option to extend to 12, and thereafter to 21 years' Colour service. Most men on the minimum Colour service did not extend, but among the others it was remarked that the longer they were in, the more likely they were to remain for 21 years.

Although short-service enlistment did build up a Reserve, it was less successful as a recruiting incentive. Another measure affecting the infantry was the Localisation Act of 1872. This divided the country into territorial "brigade" districts, on each of which one numbered

The .303in. Lee-Metford rifle; this in fact shows a Mk II, which differed in unimportant details from the Mk I with which all the British infantry battalions were armed in 1897-98. (Photos Ian Knight, Ian Castle collection)

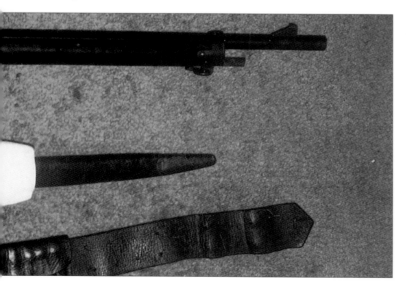

No.3 (Royal Artillery) Mountain Battery, with British gunners and Indian drivers, ready to advance. Each gun was carried in sections on five mules; each two-gun section required another 36 mules for ammunition, tools, spares, or reserve. (Navy & Army Illustrated)

regiments; and a grudging marriage to a partner with whom they had no previous bond. Some continued for many years to refer to themselves by their old numbers; of those on the Frontier in 1897, the 2nd Oxfordshire Light Infantry were always known as "the 52nd", the 1st Northamptonshire the 48th, the 2nd Highland Light Infantry the 74th, and the 2nd Argyll and Sutherland Highlanders the 93rd.

Not only was this loss of treasured identities resented, but some regiments had difficulty identifying with their counties - and vice versa; while others, now drawing predominantly upon thinly populated rural areas for recruits, found difficulty in filling the ranks, thus negating the purpose for which localisation had been introduced. Elsewhere, however, the desired effect began to take hold.

The principle of the home battalions feeding those overseas continued. But when recruiting fell short, and since the necessary parity of battalions between home and abroad was never fully achieved, it was only by lowering recruiting standards, accepting volunteers from other regiments, and reducing the strength of the home battalions that the overseas battalions could be kept up to strength.

* * *

An infantry battalion in India had an establishment of 29 officers, 2 warrant officers, 45 sergeants and 956 rank and file. It was organised into eight lettered companies, three commanded by majors, the remainder by captains, each having two half-companies under subalterns, with sergeants in charge of the two sections, which could be further sub-divided into sub-sections.

The weapons of all officers and warrant officers were sword and revolver, all other ranks being armed with rifle and bayonet except for the drummers (buglers in Light Infantry and Rifles), and pipers in Scottish battalions, who all had special edged weapons, some of the latter having

revolvers in addition.

By 1897 most British battalions in India had received the .303-inch Lee-Metford magazine rifle, sighted to 2,800 yards, with a 12in. sword bayonet. Although the magazine held ten rounds, fed into the breech by working the bolt action before each shot, it was at that time regarded as a reserve for rarely-used rapid fire, when one round could be fired every $2\frac{1}{2}$ seconds. To conserve ammunition - an important consideration during fighting in difficult country where ammunition re-supply could be a problem - a cut-out device was fitted; when closed this cut off the magazine from the chamber, the rifle then being reloaded with a single round after each shot, giving it the same rate of fire as the Martini-Henry of 12 rounds per minute.

Single round loading, as with the Martini, was the norm, but with the magazine kept fully charged ready for an emergency - such as, on the Frontier, a sudden Pathan rush from cover at short range. Firing, always controlled by the NCOs in accordance with the target, range and type of fire given by their officers, was either by company, half-company, section or sub-section volleys; independent fire, usually at shorter, more decisive ranges; or magazine fire, as already described.

Tactical manoeuvres were based on a three-line principle: a skirmishing or firing line, supports and reserves. The number of troops allotted to each would depend on the ground, the enemy and the aim of the operation; at company level, the reserve element would normally be found by another company. The purpose of the three lines was to give depth to the manoeuvre in hand, but against elusive opponents like Pathans, who had no artillery, the need for troops to outflank and cut off the enemy was of greater importance than depth.

The volume of infantry rifle-fire could be supplemented by a battalion's single Maxim gun, sighted to 2,500 yards and fed by belts of 250 rounds. The gun itself had a crew of three but its detachment included another eight men for local protection, ammunition re-supply and other duties around the gun. On operations the Maxims were normally under brigade, even divisional, but not battalion control; and their potential was not fully appreciated at this date. In Frontier warfare it was thought that worthwhile targets seldom presented themselves during offensive operations, but that Maxims could be useful when holding a static position such as a fort, particularly if the enemy attacked in mass. During the Relief of Chitral in 1895 the Maxim of the 1st Devons had a most successful shoot against such an attack by night, illuminated by star-shell. The same campaign adduced evidence of the morale effect of the Maxim's noise and rate of fire upon the tribesmen, who called it "the rattle gun"[28]. On the other hand, some indication of the low esteem accorded to the Maxim - partly due to its propensity to jam - was suggested by the fact that the death of the Devons' machine-gun officer left the force - a strong division - without a single officer experienced on the weapon.

Maxim detachments were also on the establishment of British cavalry regiments in India and one, of the 16th Lancers, was to feature in the 1897 operations. However, as it was the only representative of such regiments that arm will not be considered further here.

Of greater significance than the Maxim in hill warfare was the mountain gun, whose Indian batteries have already been mentioned. Besides the latter, with their seconded Royal Artillery officers, there were in India eight RA mountain batteries armed and organised like their Indian counterparts. All the officers, NCOs and gunners were British, men of some height and strength, only the mule-drivers being Indian. Again, Kipling tells us they were "the pick of the Army", who believed themselves superior to other gunners - "D'you say that you sweat with the field guns? By God, you must lather with us"; and whose advice to the tribesmen was: "You may hide in the caves, they'll be only your graves, but you can't get away from the guns!"[29]

Although the six guns of a battery might be worked together, or even massed with other batteries to produce a concentrated bombardment, this was the exception. More usually when supporting infantry, with whom they could keep up over most ground due to their mules' agility, the battery would work by two-gun sections. One would move with the infantry, covered by the other two, leapfrogging through each other so that at least one section could produce an immediate fire response when needed, and so that enemy positions could be engaged from different directions.

Owing to the terrain and the mountain battery's mobility, the 2.5in. screw-gun was the most commonly used artillery on the Frontier, although in the 1897 operations a total of five horse-drawn field batteries would also be deployed. In India each had a strength of 5 officers, 157 NCOs and men, again with six guns formed in three sections. The field gun they used was the 12-pounder RBL (Rifled Breech-Loading), firing shrapnel, shell and case-shot out to ranges up to 5,000 yards, and served by a crew of ten. Being drawn, with its limber, by a team of six horses, and accompanied by its ammunition wagon also with a limber and six horses, the field gun's opportunities for employment in mountainous terrain were obviously limited. If it could be got into action, its shell could have a more destructive effect upon stone buildings and defences than the screw-gun's 7lb. shell, though not always destructive enough. All artillery fire was likely to have considerable morale effect upon tribesmen; but to open fire too soon could cause them to vacate a position before they could be cut off by an outflanking force.

* * *

Before the Mutiny the proportion of British troops (Queen's and Company Europeans) to Indian had been about one to nine. From 1863 it was roughly one to two. In 1857 there had been 16 Queen's Line infantry battalions based in India; by 1896 there were 52 (out of a total in the Army of 141,[30]) of which 13 were in the Punjab Command, 18 in Bengal, 11 in Bombay and ten in Madras. In addition there were nine cavalry regiments and 88 RA batteries/companies allocated between commands in proportion - except in the case of mountain batteries, of which five out of eight were in the Punjab.

In peacetime garrisons neither British nor Indian units were allotted permanently to brigades and divisions, but

The means of communication in the field: regimental signallers of the 1st Northamptons in 1897 with Semaphore flags, heliographs and signalling lamps. This battalion would see hard marching and hard fighting with the Tirah Field Force, particularly at Saran Sar on 9 November. See also Plate G. (Maj. T. C. S. Knox)

were spread all over the sub-continent in districts, this being considered the best system for internal security. When a field force was required for Frontier operations the designated units were brigaded, but this afforded little time for the units, staffs and commanders to train together and to get to know each other's strengths and limitations. Furthermore, since units were drawn from all over India and not just from the Punjab Command, some might find themselves on operations without any prior knowledge of the Frontier region or the type of tactics they would be required to employ. Battalions like the 1st Dorsets and 1st Northamptonshire, ordered up to the Frontier in 1897 from Madras with no experience of mountain warfare, would have to learn the tricks of the trade as they went along – with results that will be seen in later chapters.

Infantry brigades were of either three or four battalions

and were usually mixed: either half British and half Indian, or with Indians predominating, the latter probably having more experience in Frontier tactics. Elements of the other arms – cavalry, gunners and sappers – might be included in the brigades, but more usually served unbrigaded as divisional troops so that they could be employed where most needed. Comparative numbers of battalions over the whole Pathan revolt were 21 British and 43 Indian.

Ten Indian or Gurkha battalions and only one British (2nd Border) had taken part in the Mahsud operations of 1894-95. The campaign to relieve Chitral, which began soon afterwards, was a larger undertaking and involved more British troops – seven battalions and three batteries, against the Indian contribution of six battalions, two cavalry regiments, one battery and three sapper companies. Whereas 14 of the Indian units that had been on these two

A British infantry battalion, 1897: 2nd Derbyshire Regiment, ready to take the field at Fort Jamrud, Peshawar. (Lt. Col. P. J. Mercer)

expeditions were to be present again in 1897-98, only three of the British battalions (1st Buffs, 2nd King's Own Scottish Borderers and 1st Gordon Highlanders) and two of the batteries would again take the field.

Not only would there be a higher proportion of Indian Army troops with recent campaign experience, but for the great majority of the men in the other 18 British battalions that were to see service it would be a case of "when first under fire an' you're wishful to duck"[31]. Some of their battalions had seen service in the mid-1880s in the Sudan or Burma, when a few of their more senior men might have been present, but others had not been in action since the Mutiny or the Crimea. Only two had been on a Frontier expedition during their current tour of duty in India (2nd Royal Irish and 2nd Royal Sussex, to Hazara or the Black Mountain in 1888), and both were to be involved only on

the periphery of the forthcoming operations.

When trouble broke out in Waziristan on 10 June 1897, the first sign of the great uprising to come, the 3rd Battalion Rifle Brigade was stationed at Rawalpindi in the Punjab[32]. It had been in India since 1889 and had seen no action of any kind for 34 years (when it had experienced a brief skirmish of one day's duration with the Mohmands during its previous Indian tour). Seven days after the outbreak the battalion was ordered to join the Tochi Field Force. "All were in the best of spirits and rejoiced that the long spell of bad luck was at last to be broken"[33]. For these Riflemen, however, it was to be a costly experience, and with little glory.

CHAPTER THREE

Treachery in Tochi

One could never be too careful on the Frontier; but when Pathans, even the panther-like Waziris, offered food and hospitality in the spirit of *pukhtunwali* to their guests, there seemed to experienced Frontier Force soldiers to be no cause for alarm. Another day, another place, it could well be war to the knife; but surely the laws of hospitality would be upheld? So it must have appeared to Colonel Bunny of the 1st Sikhs (PFF) at around midday on 10 June 1897, at the village of Maizar in the Tochi Valley.

Bunny was in command of 200 men of his own regiment, 100 of the 1st Punjab Infantry (PFF), two guns of No.6 (Bombay) Mountain Battery, and 12 sowars of the 1st Punjab Cavalry (PFF). This force was escort to the Political Officer for Tochi, Mr H.A.Gee, who was visiting Maizar to settle a dispute with its Madda Khel Waziri inhabitants over non-payment of their share of a fine imposed for the murder of a Hindu clerk the previous year. The party had marched westwards from the most advanced civil and military post in the Tochi Valley at Datta Khel and, passing through another Madda Khel village at Sheranni, had covered the twelve miles to Maizar by 9.30a.m.

All seemed quiet and peaceful. Women and children could be seen around the houses as the maliks came forward to suggest a shady halting place for the troops under some trees, close to a garden wall with water nearby. They proposed that a meal, then being prepared, might be acceptable to the Moslem sepoys of the escort. Reassured by this reception, Mr Gee with Captain Browne, Royal Artillery, and Lieutenant Higginson, 1st Sikhs, rode off with some of the maliks to visit another village, escorted by the sowars. Colonel Bunny ordered the two guns to be off-loaded from the mules and placed near the wall, ready for action. Once sentries had been posted the sepoys were told they could rest, but keeping their rifles with them. They had marched with only 22 rounds each in their pouches, presumably to spare them weight in the intense heat, but a reserve of 6,000 rounds in boxes had been carried on mules; none of this, however, was issued to the men. It seemed that, once Mr Gee had returned and the meal had been eaten, the party could return without further delay to Datta Khel.

The Political Officer rejoined at noon, having apparently reached an amicable settlement with the maliks. The Moslem sepoys settled down to the meal provided by the villagers while the Sikh troops ate their own rations. Mr Gee and the six British officers relaxed under the trees. Noticing that some of the villagers had come forward to watch this peaceful scene, Bunny ordered the pipers (which many Frontier Force battalions had, in emulation of Scottish regiments), to entertain them with a tune.

This was well received, so the pipers began again. Suddenly, a man appeared on a nearby tower waving a sword. All the villagers made off. Two shots were fired, one hitting Lieutenant Seton-Browne, 1st Punjabis, in the thigh.

Lt.Col.Bunny of the 1st Sikhs, Punjab Frontier Force (bareheaded, sitting on wall centre left) with officers and men of his battalion. Note the pipers (top left); the colonel had ordered his pipers to entertain the villagers of Maizar during the fatal halt of 10 June 1897. (R.G.Harris)

Bombay mountain gunners with the mule-loaded carriage of a 2.5in.RML gun; two guns of No.6 Mountain Battery accompanied Lt.Col.Bunny's column to Maizar. See also Plate B. (Maj.A.G.Harfield)

Immediately a fusillade followed, from riflemen concealed in buildings to the north, east and south, the fire being directed at first almost entirely at the group of officers. Colonel Bunny was the next to fall, shot in the stomach. Supported by two sepoys, he at once ordered fire to be returned.

Captain Browne and his subaltern, Lieutenant Cruickshank, reached their screw-guns in time to open with case-shot at tribesmen who were now charging forward from a hundred yards away. In their exposed position both were soon hit, Cruickshank twice, Browne in the upper arm by a shot that severed an artery. Despite their wounds both continued to direct their guns' fire, well served by their Sikh and Punjabi gunners; but as only 16 rounds per gun had been brought out, these were soon expended. Colonel Bunny, still just capable of exercising command, ordered the guns' withdrawal eastwards to a ridge, to be covered by the infantry.

The gun-fire had held the tribal rush at bay, but the enemy rifle-fire had increased in intensity as more tribesmen came up. This now rose to a crescendo as they saw the guns being dismantled prior to loading. With Captain Browne fainting from loss of blood and Cruickshank hit a third time, which killed him, Havildar-Major Muhammed Ismail took command. A mule carrying gun-wheels was shot; Havildar Amardin ran back under fire, picked up both wheels - 72lbs. each - and tried to catch up with his comrades until he was killed. Another man carried a 200lb. gun barrel to a mule, but the animal fell before he could load it; he got it onto another, then ran back to bring in Lieutenant Cruickshank's body. The battery farrier attempted to staunch Browne's wound regardless of the bullets striking around him, and managed

to get him onto Mr Gee's pony, but to no avail; when they reached the ridge the artillery officer was found to be dead.

While the infantry had been covering the gunners' withdrawal, Lieutenant Higginson had been badly wounded and Surgeon-Captain Cassidy shot in the knee. All the British officers except Mr Gee were now casualties, but the Indian officers more than rose to the occasion. Jemadar Sharzad, 1st Sikhs, carried Higginson to a safer place, then returned, picked up a rifle, and covered three sepoys as they carried Cassidy off. That done, he joined his Subedar, Narain Singh who, as the senior surviving officer, was conducting the retirement assisted by the 1st Punjabis' Subedar Sundar Singh.

Early in the fight Narain Singh, seeing the ammunition mules stampeding and conscious of how few rounds the sepoys had immediately available, organised a party to retrieve as many boxes as possible and distribute the ammunition packets to the men. Though under heavy fire, seven sepoys succeeded in bringing back 3,600 rounds; Sepoy Shiv Singh was hit three times while carrying the boxes, and Bugler Bala Singh constantly exposed himself to danger while distributing ammunition packets.

With the screw-guns out of action the tribesmen grew bolder. They pressed forward from all directions, covered by their marksmen; but the Sikh and Moslem sepoys stood their ground most gallantly until ordered to fall back. As soon as the guns and wounded were clear of Maizar the infantry began its withdrawal, one group covering the other. Seeing the move the tribesmen charged forward again. Instead of falling back in turn Subedar Sundar Singh and ten men of the 1st Punjabis faced them with a volley, fought hand-to-hand, and died to a man, buying their comrades time to put some distance between themselves and the seething village.

Even so the Waziris followed up, and the force had to make a fighting withdrawal interrupted by several stands rather than an unimpeded march back. All the wounded British officers were helped along by their men, Sepoy Allayar Khan carrying Lieutenant Seton-Browne much of the way. At 5.30p.m., having passed Sheranni and covered three hard-fought miles since leaving Maizar, they took up a good defensive position nine miles from the safety of Datta Khel. Here Colonel Bunny finally died from his wound. Despite great pain, he had done his best to extricate his men from the trap into which they had fallen. But, as another officer with Frontier experience later wrote: "Bunny of the 1st Sikhs was a frontier soldier, and had learnt so much of the game that he seemingly had forgotten it nearly all."[1].

Since the first shots were fired three and a half hours before the escort had lost three British officers and 24 of the Indian ranks dead. Although they were now in a better position, some thousand tribesmen were poised to move in for the kill; the sepoys were low on ammunition and encumbered with 28 wounded. Between watching his front for evidence of an enemy advance, Subedar Narain Singh must have occasionally glanced anxiously rearwards towards Datta Khel in the hope of some support.

When the first stand had been made at the ridge beyond Maizar some of the sowars had been despatched to Datta Khel to report the attack. In command at that post was Captain Cooper, 1st Sikhs; when a sowar rode in around 5p.m. he immediately ordered out two companies of his regiment, with the only two available British officers – Lieutenants De Brett, Royal Artillery, and Stockley, Royal Engineers – plus a supply of artillery ammunition. They had nine miles to go over bad roads, but they covered the distance in less than an hour and a half, reaching the escort – now down to less than five rounds per man – at 6.15p.m.

With this more than welcome addition to their firepower the sepoys re-opened fire at the surrounding hills and the guns shelled the village of Sheranni, setting part of it on fire and blowing up a mosque on whose roof a mullah could be seen waving a green flag. He must have been one of the last of the hundred-odd tribesmen killed that day; these losses, together with many wounded, seem to have persuaded them to break off the fight. The force was then able to withdraw without further harassment, but the weary men did not reach Datta Khel until after midnight.

Lieutenant Higginson, despite his two wounds, survived the return march and was recommended for the Distinguished Service Order; he was never to wear it, however, as two months later he died of enteric fever. In recognition of the loyalty and courage displayed by the Indian ranks in "a deed of arms second to none in the annals of the British Army"[2], when all their British officers were casualties, 25 decorations were awarded: six to the mountain gunners, 14 to the 1st Sikhs, and five to the 1st Punjabis; another 11 men would have been decorated had they survived.

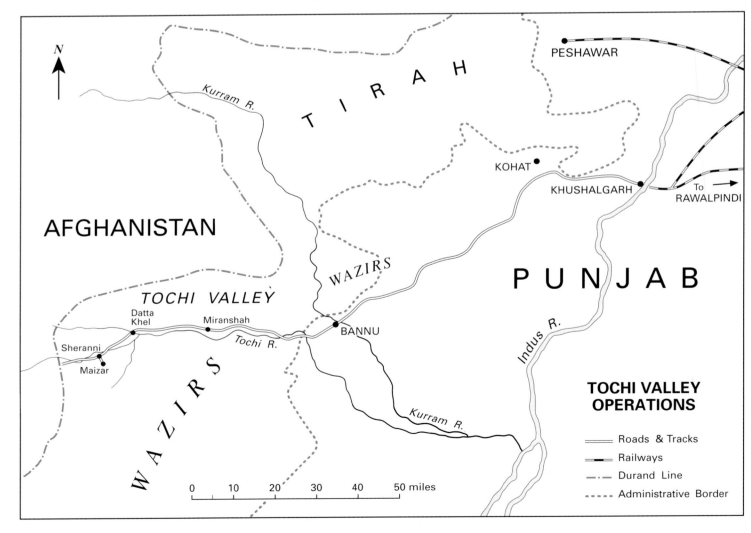

TOCHI VALLEY OPERATIONS

===== Roads & Tracks
==■= Railways
—·—· Durand Line
········ Administrative Border

Victims of Maizar: Lt.Higginson, 1st Sikhs; and (as a schoolboy at Wellington) Lt.Cruikshank, R.A. (Author's collection & Wellington College)

When the bodies of the slain sepoys were recovered later it was found that not only had the Sikh corpses been mutilated by the tribesmen (as was customary), but so had those of the Moslem sepoys. Abuse of the code of hospitality was a curious, though not unheard-of breach of Pathan ethics - and many of the abused were, after all, infidels - but the desecration of co-religionists' remains was another matter altogether. When calls for a holy war - *jehad* - were raised in the Frontier hills, as soon they would be, the loyalties of many Moslem sepoys were put to the test; but those who knew what had been done to their comrades at Maizar would face a less difficult choice.

* * *

In the immediate aftermath of Maizar there seemed no reason to suspect that it was anything more than an isolated attack by the Madda Khel, a rogue sub-section of the Darwesh Khel Waziris who hitherto had given no trouble. Later events would give cause to question this. What was indisputable was the treacherous nature of the attack, which deserved exemplary punishment without delay. Orders were issued for the assembly of a field force of two brigades under command of Major-General Corrie Bird at Bannu, and thence to Datta Khel.

Obviously the sooner the punishment was inflicted the more salutary it would be. However, it was now mid-summer, with temperatures of nearly 100 degrees Fahrenheit by night and well over that by day, which would be taxing enough for Indian troops, let alone British. Furthermore the railhead for troops from the Punjab was at Khushulgarh on the Indus, from which they would face a march of some 110 miles to Bannu via Kohat, a route ill-supplied with water. The marching would therefore have to be done at night, with special arrangements made for the provision of water and shade by day. Bearing in mind that all military activity during the hot weather was, under peacetime conditions, reduced to a minimum, the approach march alone to the forthcoming operations was likely to be a severe test of stamina and endurance.

Earmarked for the Tochi Field Force, in addition to the units which had suffered at Maizar, were two squadrons of the 1st Punjab Cavalry (PFF); another mountain battery, No.3 (Peshawar); four more Indian battalions[3] making six in all; and two British, the 2nd Argyll and Sutherland Highlanders from Nowshera and 3rd Rifle Brigade from Rawalpindi. Four field hospitals would accompany the force.

Cheered by their send-off from the Rawalpindi garrison, the Rifle Brigade entrained for Khushulgarh, arriving there very early next morning, 30 June, to occupy the camp vacated two days before by the 2nd Argylls, who had begun their march to Bannu. Having left a 200-strong rear party to provide reinforcements later if necessary, and with some of the officers away, the Rifles were somewhat under-strength and mustered only 21 officers (of whom two were attached from other regiments) and 801 men. Only E Company had its full complement of officers, A and D Companies having only one each. Temperatures in the tents of 115 degrees F gave an unpleasant foretaste of what was in store.

The march began that evening at 8p.m. It would be eight days before Bannu was reached, marching only at night and resting, or trying to do so, by day "in stifling heat, with horrible water, flies in plenty and, as often as not, a rainless dust storm in the afternoon"[4]. The heat by night of 98 degrees F was only slightly more endurable; the dust more choking; and the conditions, with the unaccustomed weight of 100 rounds of ammunition carried by each man, all aggravated by lack of proper rest by day, combined to make the night marches - averaging 14 miles each - an exhausting experience.

An officer wrote: "It is not a pleasant, but common enough sight to see most of one's men, as soon as a halt was ordered, drop at once on their hands and knees in the middle of the road, from sheer inability to stand up until the word was given to fall out". He remembered the march as "a perfect nightmare", but the Riflemen "behaved splendidly, singing and whistling to lighten the burden of the weary road, and they marched with a pluck beyond praise"[5]. Despite many cases of heat apoplexy the Rifles suffered no fatalities, unlike the Argylls ahead of them, who lost three men dead from that cause, and two more after leaving Bannu.

Sepoys of the 6th Jats, 2nd Brigade, Tochi Field Force; note the piled Martini-Henry rifles, as carried by all Indian troops in 1897. (Maj.A.G.Harfield)

After a much-needed rest of three days at Bannu the march was resumed westwards, the Argylls again two days ahead. Some seven miles out of Bannu the battalions crossed the administrative border into tribal territory at the mouth of the Tochi Valley. Though still marching at night each battalion was now preceded by its advance guard company, itself headed by a "point" to give early warning of hostile activity, and its main body and baggage train were closed by a rearguard. During the daytime rest the usual Frontier camp was pitched in a square within a perimeter wall, the men's tents close to its inner side so that they could instantly man the breastworks in the event of an alarm, with the officers' tents, hospital and baggage in the centre.

The countryside through which they passed, beside the

Tochi River, was "inhospitable and barren, rugged and bare hills on either side, nothing but stones everywhere, except along the bed of the river, where a certain amount of cultivation and a sprinkling of mud villages could be seen"[6]. But the ground was rising gradually, lessening the heat somewhat; and by the time Miranshah was reached, some 3,000 feet above sea level, the worst of the heat was behind them – though there was still the choking dust, only alleviated by sudden downpours of rain. Here the Rifles first encountered the 14th Sikhs, "a splendid set of men"[7], with whom they were to serve in the 2nd Brigade under Brigadier-General Symons.

As the Rifles were resting at Miranshah, the Argylls were marching into Datta Khel to join the rest of the 1st Brigade under Brigadier-General Egerton. With the arrival of the 2nd Brigade over the next few days the Tochi Field Force was complete and ready for operations at Datta Khel, 39 days after the Maizar attack. The Rifles marched in on

18 July, having covered the 170 miles from Khushulgarh in 19 days, including seven days' halts. When the concentration of the Field Force had first been ordered many experienced Frontier Force officers had warned that British troops were not up to such a march in such heat, particularly over the first and longest stage to Bannu. The Argylls and Rifle Brigade had proved them wrong. However, although not a single shot had been fired, the Argylls had lost five men dead, and of the 801 Riflemen who had begun the march only 726 had been able to complete it, the rest being left in various stages of sickness back along the route.

* * *

The first task at Datta Khel was to encircle the camps with defensive stone walls. The work was accelerated by reports that 7,000 Mahsuds were approaching from the south and would attack the Field Force at about 3.30a.m. on 19 July. By that hour every man was at his post, eager to forget, in the first brush with the enemy, the wretched approach march.

By sunrise not a single tribesman had appeared. Later and more accurate intelligence revealed that the great force of Mahsuds were no more than 70 or so malcontents lurking near the road in the hope of loot. Although it was believed that a well-known agitator, the Mullah Powindah - who had brought out the Mahsuds in 1894 - was again active in their country, his influence was not as compelling as it had once been and, as mentioned earlier, the formidable Mahsuds had decided to lie low in 1897.

The Tochi Field Force, somewhat disappointed at being deprived of this chance to show its mettle, was at least able to enjoy its breakfast in peace. But the anti-climax of the night of 18/19 July was to prove symptomatic of the whole Tochi expedition. A different foe would prove more lethal than the Mahsuds.

On the following day the 1st Brigade advanced unopposed to Sheranni. Over the ensuing week all the houses there and around Maizar of the Madda Khel, who had long since fled, were systematically destroyed as a part punishment for the treacherous attack of 10 June. Reconnaissances were made into the surrounding hills, but not a sign of the inhabitants was found. Only at night was there some sporadic firing into the camps, but by daybreak the snipers had disappeared and the baking hillsides were still and empty.

Back at Datta Khel life was no more exciting for the Rifle Brigade. The days were spent improving the defences, guarding supply convoys and securing the tents against the daily downpour of rain, always preceded by a gale blowing up a dust storm. No night sniper fire fell into their camp, only an incessant plague of flies attacking in thousands every meal time, while the air, even 5,000 feet up, was constantly pervaded by "an endless assortment of evil smells"[8]. Men soon began to go down with diarrhoea. On the 21st a Rifleman died of dysentery, the battalion's first fatality. Since no tribesmen appeared to entertain the men, a battalion sports day was held.

On 27 July the Rifles marched to Sheranni to join the 1st Brigade in time to take part in the final work of destruction. In the days that followed some companies went out as escorts for Survey or Intelligence officers and convoys, or as road-builders or forage-gatherers. But still not a tribesman was seen, the 100 rounds each man had carried up remained intact, and each night they returned to camp - where the busiest men were the medical staff.

Dysentery and fever were rife. The numbers of men reporting sick daily were soon in three figures. More men died. In late August and early September four Rifles officers had to be invalided back to India, and the battalion's popular second-in-command, Major Raikes, died. Fewer and fewer men were available for duty each day, and the hospital tents were overflowing.

The way in which the Riflemen kept up their spirits in the face of this insidious sickness won them many admirers, but in early August their morale suffered another knock. News was received of the other uprisings to the north in Malakand, and of other British regiments going into action. Yet here they sat - no mere Line regiment like the Argylls or the Royal West Kents, but the Rifle Brigade who, when action had first beckoned, had been "first in" like their

The camp at Datta Khel, 18-26 July. Any major movement of troops on the infertile and sparsely-inhabited Frontier required the transport of huge quantities of stores and forage. (Rifle Brigade Chronicle)

The 2nd Argyll & Sutherland Highlanders halted on the march in the Tochi Valley; the seated soldier with four gold reversed chevrons above his right cuff is the Drum Major. See also Plate B. (Argyll & Sutherland Highlanders)

famous Peninsular forebears[9]. Two months later they had seen no enemy, fired not a shot, and their comrades were dead, dying or debilitated around them. So much for their first chance of action in 34 years.

In fact the Argylls were also suffering from the same sickness - as were, from late September, even the better-acclimatised Indian battalions, though not as grievously as the Rifles. With more men fit for duty the Argylls could get away from the noxious flies and bad water, being sent out "on column" for up to three weeks at a time to the north, to the west as far as the Afghan border, and to the south to try to locate the elusive Madda Khel - or indeed anyone prepared to offer a fight. But all to no avail; the only hostile activity remained the occasional shooting into camps at night.

Reports reaching General Bird, commanding the force, suggested that the Madda Khel had sought sanctuary in Afghanistan. Letters were therefore sent on 5 August to the tribal leaders, urging them to come in under safe conduct to hear what was required of them. Not until 11 days later, with some persuasion from neighbouring tribes, did three Madda Khel maliks appear. General Bird demanded the restoration of government property lost at Maizar, the surrender of 18 headmen, payment of the still-outstanding fine for the murder of the Hindu clerk, and a further fine of 10,000 rupees (then about £650) for the attack on Mr Gee and his escort; ten days would be allowed for their reply.

The deadline came and went without reply. Not until 14 September was any communication received, and then it was to state that the terms were unacceptable. It was deadlock: without yielding the Madda Khel could not return to their lands for the winter, but without the Madda Khel no

retribution for the Maizar attack could be exacted. Despite the unhealthy situation of his base, Bird felt he had no alternative but to remain where he was to test the Madda Khel's patience.

Meanwhile, in the hope that a change would benefit the sickening Rifles' health, 460 of their fittest men, with the 1st Punjab Infantry, were sent to a place five miles away to guard a Sapper company improving a road and to escort forage convoys from the Maizar valley. Here they experienced rather more evidence of the enemy they had come so far and so fruitlessly to fight in the shape of more vigorous sniping than hitherto. There was no major improvement in the men's health, and on 8 September they marched back via Sheranni to Datta Khel.

Ten days later they went further back, to Miranshah; and in early October it was decided by the force headquarters that the battalion must be returned to India to recover its health. When it left Bannu on 30 October it had 425 men in the ranks, some of whom were hardly fit to march, and 205 sick in bullock carts; 100 were left behind, too ill to be moved, and 71 were buried in Waziristan. Of the original 21 officers who had marched up in June, only six remained with the battalion. So ended, for 3rd Battalion The Rifle Brigade, the Tochi expedition, "in the most unhealthy time of the year, in the always unhealthy valley" - an episode in the history of one of the most distinguished regiments in the British Army described by its chronicler as "an experience which none of us would willingly repeat"[10].

Back at Datta Khel and Sheranni the columns had continued to scour the countryside with no visible result. At least their patrolling enabled much useful surveying and mapping of the Tochi region to be undertaken without interference. However, the onset of the cold weather in October resulted in both an improvement in the soldiers' health and, given General Bird's persistent domination of the Madda Khel homelands, a weakening of the tribesmen's resolve.

Pencil sketches by L/Sgt. Stonor of the dress worn by NCOs and men of the 2nd Argylls in Tochi. Note the issue sunglasses. (Argyll & Sutherland Highlanders)

At the end of the month some headmen came in to surrender, followed by Sadda Khan, chief of the Madda Khel. On 14 November the whole tribe surrendered unconditionally. Once the question of the fines had been agreed and security for their payment was obtained the Madda Khel were permitted to return to their own territory. Sadda Khan was granted his life as an act of clemency, and in gratitude presented General Bird with a fine specimen of a mountain goat; this the general handed over to the Argylls, who adopted it as their regimental mascot, named after the chief.

As a precaution the Field Force remained in the area for another two months before dispersing. The Argylls, in six months' active service, had sustained only one casualty from enemy action - a corporal wounded by a sniper - but left behind them 41 men dead from disease. At his farewell to the battalion on 3 January 1898 their brigade commander commiserated with the men on their lack of action and the hardships and losses they had endured, but told them they "had done their duty like soldiers and like men"[11].

* * *

So ended the operations of the Tochi Field Force. It had ultimately achieved its aim of punishing the Madda Khel for Maizar with, it could be said, the minimum of bloodshed, but with little distinction for anyone and with much loss. If the Argylls and Rifles had derived satisfaction from being the first British battalions to be picked for active service back in June, this had been eroded by their misfortunes and the lack of any opportunity to add to their laurels. Furthermore, their morale could not have been improved by reports of the actions fought by battalions more recently ordered to the Frontier against the uprisings to the north, which had been continuing while they dragged out the summer in the fever-camps of Tochi.

News of the risings from late July onwards by other tribes between Malakand and the Kurram Valley would undoubtedly also have reached Waziristan and the elusive quarry of the Tochi Field Force. They must surely have been encouraged in their stubbornness by the knowledge that their brothers in Islam were rushing to arms against what all saw as the increasing threat to their independence following the establishment of the Durand Line in 1893. Although it had never been the British intention to subject the tribal territories to the same administration as installed in the rest of British India, to the tribes that line of pillars running from south to north, dividing them from their kin in Afghanistan, indicated that sooner or later they would be fully subjugated to British rule.

Their fears for their future proved fertile ground for the inflammatory exhortations of their mullahs. By 1897 the supposed threat to their religion from the "infidels", and their need to defend it, was an old cry; but in urging that now was the time to strike they could call in support the rising power of Islam, as proven by the recent defeat of the Greeks at the hands of the Turks in spring 1897. Since the Sultan of the Ottoman Empire was recognised as one of the great leaders of the Mahommedan world, any victory which he achieved over unbelievers was a propaganda coup for the mullahs on the Frontier - who had attended a meeting in Kabul in May 1897 at which a Turkish representative had been present.

Soon afterwards the mullahs were exaggerating the Sultan's victory over Greece for the benefit of their credulous flock, to include the seizure from the British of the Suez Canal and of Aden, an important staging post on the route from Europe to India. They claimed that this would mean a six-month voyage for any British

3rd Rifle Brigade during a reconnaissance near Maizar. This gives an impression of the terrain through which Bunny's force had to retreat after the ambush of 10 June. (Rifle Brigade Chronicle)

reinforcements sent to counter a jehad on the Frontier – even if any could be spared, since the British would soon be under attack by Germany, France and Russia, to whom the Canal was to be leased by the Sultan; and were already distracted by fighting in Egypt. (This last was the only part of this farrago with some basis in truth, since Kitchener's reconquest of the Sudan had begun in 1896.) In short, as one report had it, "the British are at present in distressed circumstances and disheartened"[12].

It seems unlikely that the average Afridi or Mohmand tribesman of the 1890s would have had much grasp of the strategic importance of the Suez Canal, let alone that he would ever have heard of Germany or France. But given their intense attachment to independence and their religion, and their inbred warrior instincts, the fiery summons to take up arms in a holy war – pronounced by men like the Afridi mullah Sayid Akbar, the "Mad Mullah" in Swat, and the Hadda Mullah in Mohmand country – would have fallen on willing ears.

Soon after the outbreaks it was believed by some in India, and by the tribes themselves, that the Afghan Amir Abdurrahman had given his blessing to the revolt; he was said to have had second thoughts about the Durand Line. In a recent pamphlet he had proclaimed himself "King of Islam", and stressed the obligation of every true son of the faith to respond to a call for jehad; furthermore, the mullahs' meeting in Kabul could not have taken place without his permission. But when the Government of India remonstrated with him, he vehemently denied all complicity and forbade any Afghan to assist the revolt in any way.

The Amir may have had no hand in instigating the uprisings of 1897 – and indeed, subsequent events showed that he kept his word. Nevertheless, the speed at which the outbreaks further north followed the attack at Maizar, as well as the distances, and the range of often mutually hostile tribes involved – who had no faster means of communication than a horsed messenger – all suggest some concerted plan. There had been plenty of tribal outbreaks up and down the Frontier over the preceding 48 years, but never before all within a space of three months and over a frontage of nearly 200 miles. The Russians, with their advanced posts now on the Pamirs, had indeed watched the Chitral crisis of 1895 for any advantage to themselves but, with Chitral garrisoned, they were thwarted; nothing has ever indicated any direct Russian implication in the 1897 uprisings. For their motive force and planning we need look no further than the Pathans themselves – and particularly their more fanatical mullahs[13].

Just 46 days after the Waziri treachery at Maizar on 10 June the Swatis attacked far to the north at Malakand, followed 11 days later by a Mohmand threat further south near Peshawar, and in late August–early September by Afridi and Orakzai attacks on the Khyber, the Samana Range and in the Kurram Valley. For two years the whole Frontier had been quiet from north to south. Suddenly, as Kipling's Tommy exclaimed: "The Tribes is up be'ind us, and the Tribes is out in front"[14]. First it must be seen how the Swatis and Bunerwals rallied, with war-drums beating and green flags flying, to the Mad Mullah's summons to holy war.

The destruction of a village near Maizar by the 3rd Rifle Brigade and the Sappers during the punitive operations of the Tochi Field Force. At left, in a cloud of smoke and dust from an exploding charge, a watchtower can be seen collapsing. (Rifle Brigade Chronicle)

CHAPTER FOUR

War-Drums in Malakand

The game of polo originated in the East and was introduced into England in 1870 by officers of the 10th Royal Hussars. It soon became popular in the Army, both at home and abroad. On the afternoon of 26 July 1897 some officers of the Indian Army brigade garrisoning Malakand rode over to play polo at the village of Khar, half-way to the outlying fort at Chakdara ten miles away to the north-east.

For some months past there had been rumours in the garrison that the Mad Mullah was active among the people of Upper Swat, and tales of his ability to work miracles circulated in the Malakand bazaar. News of the Maizar outbreak had of course reached the authorities at Malakand; but that had occurred 200 miles away to the south-west, and was regarded as a flash in the pan. As the rumours came to be supported by more substantial reports, however, the Political Officer at Malakand, Major Deane, decided to report the possibility of impending trouble to his superiors, and the commanding officers of the garrison looked to the security of their camps. Nevertheless, so peaceful did the surrounding countryside seem, and so friendly the inhabitants, that it was difficult to take the threat seriously. By 26 July there certainly seemed no reason to cancel the polo match at Khar.

The game was played and won, much to the enjoyment of both the players and the spectators from the village. When it was over the officers rode back to their camps, leaving their *syces* (grooms) to rug up the polo ponies and tidy up the ground. As they did so the villagers moved among them, whispering: they should be gone, and quickly, for there was a great armed host coming that would sweep all before it. All would be killed. The grooms took the hint, and made off.

Back at Malakand the returning polo players found a hive of activity. While they had been away news had reached Major Deane that the Mad Mullah had indeed assembled a great following, and had entered Lower Swat at a place only 20 miles east of Malakand. Deane had immediately conferred with the garrison commander, Colonel Meiklejohn; this experienced officer, formerly of the 20th Punjabis, had seen service in four Frontier campaigns as well as the Afghan and Egyptian Wars. It was decided to telegraph at once for the Corps of Guides from their station at Mardan, 32 miles to the south. The whole Malakand garrison was then put on immediate alert.

As a further precaution Lieutenant-Colonel McRae of the 45th Sikhs was to prepare his battalion, with two companies of the 31st Punjabis, a squadron of the 11th Bengal Lancers and two mountain guns, to march out at midnight to secure the Amandara Pass five miles to the north-east, through which any advancing enemy must pass. Since the whole garrison had to be placed forthwith on a war footing, with all the consequent preparation of weapons, issuing of ammunition, rations and equipment, there was much work to be done.

Col., later Brig. Gen. Meiklejohn, commanding the Malakand garrison and subsequently 1st Brigade, Malakand Field Force; he is photographed in the dress uniform of the 20th Punjabis. (Navy & Army Illustrated)

The camps occupied by the brigade were ill-suited for defence. Commanding the Malakand Pass itself was a fort, held by 200 men of the 24th Punjabis with two 9-pounder guns, sited on a spur to the left of the road looking north. This spur ran down to a bowl some 600 yards in diameter, called the Crater; from this the road forked, north-east towards Chitral and left to the north-west. Here were located the camps of the 24th Punjabis and 45th Sikhs with, in the centre, a company of Madras Sappers and Miners, the Engineer park and the Commissariat stores and office; the whole was encircled by a line of abattis and a wire entanglement. Slightly to its north was the bazaar.

The rest of the brigade - 31st Punjabis, the cavalry

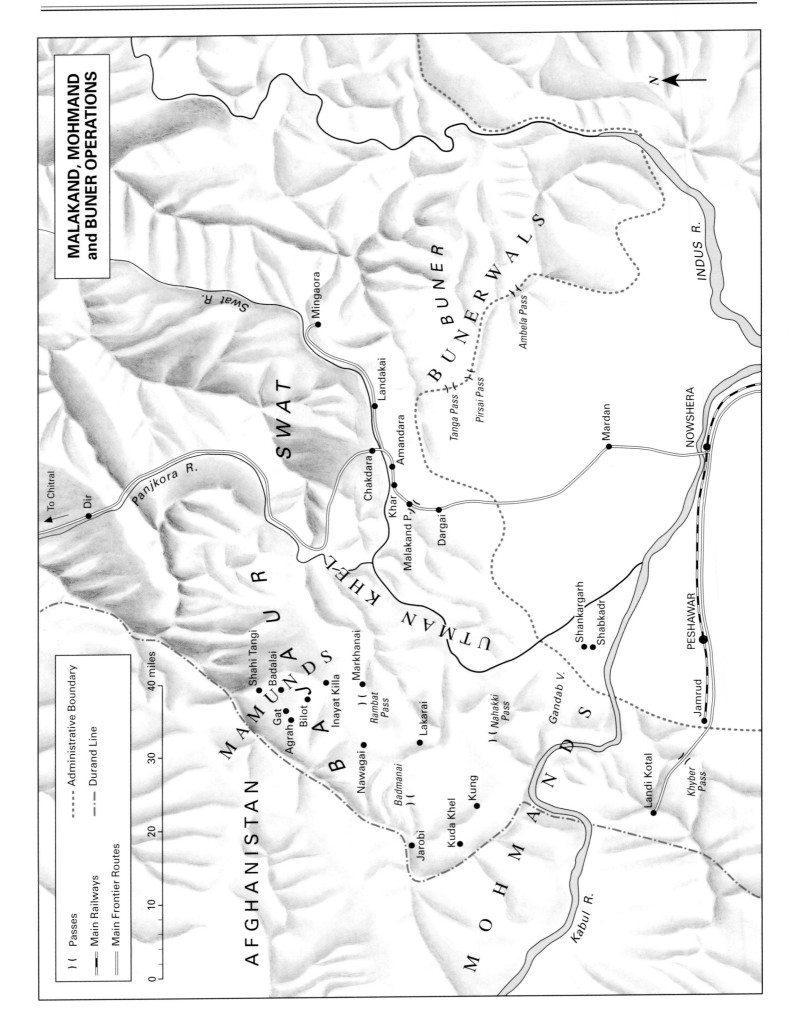

MALAKAND, MOHMAND and BUNER OPERATIONS

Passes
Main Railways
Main Frontier Routes
Administrative Boundary
Durand Line

N

To Chitral
Dir
Panjkora R.
Swat R.
Mingaora
Landakai
SWAT
Chakdara
Amandara
Khar
Malakand P.
Dargai
BUNER
BUNERWALS
Ambela Pass
Tanga Pass
Pirsai Pass
UTMAN KHEL
Mardan
NOWSHERA
INDUS R.

MAMUR
Shahi Tangi
Badalai
Gat
Agrah
Bilot
Inayat Killa
Markhanai
Rambat Pass
Lakarai
Nawagai
Badmanai
Jarobi
Kuda Khel
Kung
Nahakki Pass
Gandab V.
Shankargarh
Shabkadr
PESHAWAR
Jamrud
Landi Kotal
Khyber Pass
Kabul R.
MOHMANDS
AFGHANISTAN

40 miles
30
20
10
0

42

squadron, a mountain battery and all the transport – were encamped some 1,300 yards away up the north-west road on an area of flat, open ground known as North Camp, protected by low breastworks and abattis. Both camps were overlooked by high hills to east and west.

The location had been chosen not so much as a position to hold the Malakand Pass, important though this was as a gateway between Chitral and the Punjab, but as a base of operations from which the strategic road from Nowshera to Chitral could be controlled. Since the government had decided, following the Chitral campaign of 1895, to hold Chitral as part of the revised "forward policy" for the security of the Frontier, that road northwards from Nowshera, the rear base for any operations in the area, was a vital link. Ironically it was the road – made, maintained and guarded by the infidel British – that aroused such fears for their independence among the tribesmen whose lands it traversed. It was these fears that made them so susceptible to the urgings of the Mad Mullah that now, late on 26 July, they were advancing on the Malakand camps in their thousands, bent on slaughter, loot or, if Allah so willed, a guaranteed place in Paradise.

At 9.30p.m. the officers sat down to a late dinner, the polo players still in their polo kit, not having had time to change. A quarter of an hour later a telegram came in from Lieutenant Rattray, 45th Sikhs, commanding the two companies of his regiment garrisoning the fort at Chakdara, who had also attended the polo match. He reported that large numbers of tribesmen were advancing on Malakand. Soon afterwards the telegraph wire was cut, but a rider came galloping in with the news that the enemy had passed Khar, where the polo had been played, heading for Malakand, and that the hills to the east were swarming with tribesmen.

While the officers finished their interrupted dinner, speculating on what was to come, a bugle sounded the "General Alarm". As they rushed to their posts an unceasing fusillade of musketry began to pour into the camps from many directions. But this was to be far more than simply shooting from a safe distance. Taking advantage of the darkness, the surprise achieved, and the broken ground between the fort and the two camps, masses of sword- and knife-armed tribesmen rushed forward from the east, the north and the west, in the old Pathan style. On hearing the alarm Colonel McRae, whose 45th Sikhs had been preparing to march out at midnight, ran with Major Taylor to their guardroom close to the main road. He sent Taylor with the first handful of Sikhs to turn out towards a narrow defile on a track that ran parallel to and east of the road, through which he anticipated any attack on the camp's right flank must come. He himself followed close behind after collecting a few more men. Apart from the two officers this group numbered no more than 20, but Lieutenant Barff, the Adjutant, was calling out the rest of the battalion.

McRae's party reached the defile in the nick of time. Around the corner some thousand swordsmen were stealthily approaching, all crammed together by the narrow confines of the track, no more than five yards wide at this point. He immediately opened fire with volleys, as rapidly as his men could reload. At such close range and with such a massed target every shot told, inciting the tribesmen to a frenzy. Fired by fanaticism and the courage of their numbers they pressed forward, forcing McRae and his men to fall back, still firing. The grossly outnumbered Sikhs responded nobly to the challenge, shouting their war-cry and working

Part of the Crater, looking north from Malakand Fort and showing the Sappers and Miners' camp. (Author's collection)

The Crater camp of the 24th Punjabis, looking north. (Author's collection)

their Martinis as fast as they could.

Seeing that they were not to be moved while they lived, some tribesmen began clambering up the rock face to their left to hurl boulders down upon the Sikhs. Major Taylor was killed by a sniper, as were several sepoys, but Lieutenant Barff came up with more men who dislodged the tribesmen from the rocks from which they were beginning to descend on McRae's rear. Behind Barff came the rest of the battalion on which McRae then fell back, to take up another position to protect the right flank of the camp. This they held against repeated attacks until 2a.m., when the tribesmen melted away into the darkness.

McRae's resolute action on this flank had undoubtedly prevented the enemy from encircling Crater camp and cutting it off from the fort. This was just as well, for the former had been under the most determined and ferocious assault from a horde of tribesmen who had advanced down the main road before fanning out across the whole north front of the camp. Again, all the attacks were made by massed swordsmen hurling themselves out of the darkness without care for their lives, although parties of marksmen kept up a ceaseless fire from the surrounding high ground.

To the left front of the camp was the native bazaar and a small enclosure, known as a *serai*. Through this hundreds of looting tribesmen rampaged, slaughtering anyone who had not got away in time. Lieutenant Climo led his company of the 24th Punjabis in a bayonet charge and, after a fearful hand-to-hand struggle, drove the enemy out. They came on again, to be met with volleys which held them for a while. Soon, however, numbers broke off to their right to get round behind Climo's left; this quickly rendered his position untenable. He fell back to join the rest of his battalion and the Sapper company, all of whom were now concentrated around the Sappers' camp, the Commissariat lines and the Engineer park in the central and lowest part of the Crater.

Here Colonel Meiklejohn had taken over direct command of the defence, which was under great pressure. Wave after wave of close-packed tribesmen flooded down out of the darkness, scrambling over the wire and through the abattis, yelling and screaming while their war-drums thundered to encourage them – a daunting sight for the outnumbered troops. Yet all stood their ground, knowing their lives depended on the speed they could fire their single-shot Martinis.

Some enemy broke into the Commissariat lines, killing anyone they could find and plundering the sheds. In the hut which served as his office and accommodation the Commissariat officer, Lieutenant Manley, stood ready with Sergeant Harrington. Tribesmen smashed in the door. Manley opened fire with his revolver and was cut to pieces. Harrington knocked out his first assailant but then lost his weapon, so he flung himself against the wall, standing motionless in the pitch darkness. The tribesmen groped around for a while but, finding nothing, rushed out in search of new victims. Harrington remained in the hut and

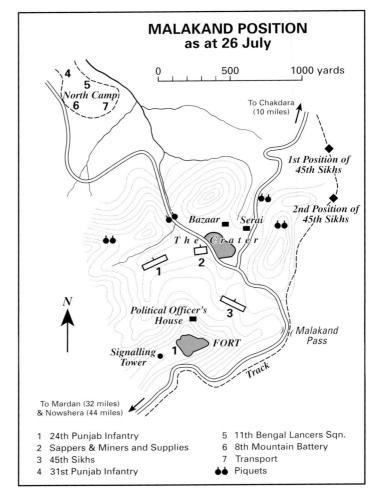

MALAKAND POSITION as at 26 July

0   500   1000 yards

To Chakdara (10 miles)

1st Position of 45th Sikhs

2nd Position of 45th Sikhs

Bazaar   Serai

The Crater

N

Political Officer's House

Malakand Pass

Signalling Tower

FORT

To Mardan (32 miles) & Nowshera (44 miles)

Track

1 24th Punjab Infantry
2 Sappers & Miners and Supplies
3 45th Sikhs
4 31st Punjab Infantry
5 11th Bengal Lancers Sqn.
6 8th Mountain Battery
7 Transport
◖◗ Piquets

survived a nerve-wracking night.

All the while enemy riflemen kept firing into the camp causing casualties, no doubt among their own people as well as the defenders. A staff officer, Major Herbert, was hit in the leg. While trying to lift him Lieutenant-Colonel Lamb, commanding the 24th Punjabis, was shot through the thigh, a

Officers prominent at Malakand on 26 July. From left: Maj. Taylor, 45th Sikhs, killed holding the defile in the first action; Lt. Costello, 24th Punjabis, awarded the VC for bringing in a wounded NCO under fire; Lt. Col. Lamb, 24th Punjabis, died of wounds. (Author's collection)

Types of the Guides Infantry. From left: sepoy, wearing the fleece-lined poshteen Frontier coat; jemadar in full dress uniform; lance-naik and havildar. (Maj.A.G.Harfield)

wound from which he later died. This gave Captain Holland command of the 24th; but he, too, was soon to be wounded, leaving Lieutenant Climo as the senior British officer of that battalion - and a tower of strength he proved to be.

Climo was among the first to join a small party of a dozen, led by Colonel Meiklejohn in person, which tried to recapture the Quarter Guard. This building, which held all the garrison's reserve ammunition, had been defended by the Sappers until they were driven out and their officer, Lieutenant Watling, severely wounded.

Meiklejohn's party was intercepted by tribesmen holding an intervening cookhouse and, losing half its strength, had to fall back. Climo carried back the wounded Captain Holland and returned with more men. A second counter-attack failed with further losses. Climo called upon his men for a third charge with the bayonet; this time they succeeded and the enemy fled, leaving 29 dead behind them, but the reserve ammunition had been removed. This, in view of the strength of the tribal forces, was a serious depletion of the garrison's ability to resist, particularly if the attacks were protracted.

At around 1a.m., during a break in the firing, the Punjabi company nearest the bazaar heard a weak cry for help, obviously from a wounded soldier some 60 yards away. The ground in front was in the fire zone of both sides and tribesmen were running hither and thither across it. Nevertheless Lieutenant Costello of the 24th and two Punjabi sepoys ran out across the open space, to find a havildar of their regiment with a gunshot wound in the shoulder and three sword cuts. Their dash had drawn fire, but Costello and his men managed to bring the NCO in to

safety. The lieutenant was later awarded the Victoria Cross, the first of the Pathan Revolt.

Although the perimeter was still holding, and indeed must have inflicted heavy losses, there was no weakening in the enemy's aggressive spirit nor any lessening of their ferocity. The noise of firing and the sight of star-shells to the north-west showed that the North Camp was also under attack. Furthermore the sound of distant drums from up the main road suggested that more tribesmen were approaching. Meiklejohn decided to send for reinforcements from the hitherto unengaged 200 men of the 24th Punjabis holding the fort.

Lieutenant Rawlins volunteered to carry the message with three sepoys. It was still dark, the ground was very broken and, although the south side of Crater had been less seriously engaged - due in part to the 45th Sikhs' stand on the right flank - there were still tribesmen lurking in the vicinity. Exercising great caution the four men began the climb up the spur to the fort, some 700 yards away. They were seen and silently followed. Suddenly, when well clear of the camp, a swordsman sprang at Rawlins and hacked him across the wrist. He managed to get off two shots with his revolver, killing his attacker, and raced for the fort with his sepoys. They got in safely, collected the reinforcements and returned to Crater.

Whether the enemy appreciated this accession to the camp's firepower or had simply had enough cannot be known. For whatever reason, at around 3.30a.m. they

The relief column from Nowshera at Dargai before climbing to Malakand - the fort is on the skyline, centre right. From a drawing by Maj.Hobday, RA, a staff officer with the column. (Author's collection)

started to carry off their dead and wounded, as was their practice, and everywhere withdrew. Their riflemen, who had come forward to the rim of the Crater from their earlier, more distant hilltops, continued firing until 4.15a.m. when they fell back to the hills, whence they kept up a sporadic sniping at long range.

As the sun came up the weary garrison could take stock. Greatly outnumbered, they had held their ground after six hours' continuous fighting in the dark; but they had lost, in British officers, one killed and two who were to die of their wounds, and three more wounded; in Indian ranks, 21 killed and 31 wounded. Much damage had been done and much looted, including the reserve ammunition. Moreover it was soon apparent that while the tribesmen had pulled back, they had not dispersed. There was more to come. Clearly this was very much more serious soldiering than the desultory and frustrating operations then being carried out in the far-off Tochi Valley.

As it was quickly learned that the North Camp had only been lightly attacked, Meiklejohn ordered out the 31st Punjabis under Major Gibbs with two guns to follow up the enemy, supported by part of the 24th Punjabis. At the same time, no word having been received from Chakdara, Captain Wright and 40 sowars of the 11th Bengal Lancers were ordered to reinforce that post. After a very hazardous ride through country infested with growing numbers of tribesmen they succeeded in reaching Chakdara, which had also been under constant attack, as will be seen later.

Meanwhile Gibbs had not advanced far before he was confronted by a large body of tribesmen, far stronger that his own force, advancing towards him; upon reporting this he was ordered to retire. Furthermore, in view of the obviously overwhelming strength of the enemy in the vicinity, Meiklejohn decided to abandon the North Camp altogether and concentrate his whole force around the Crater and fort. Much tentage and baggage had to be abandoned which was later pillaged by the tribesmen.

During the day the garrison received a welcome reinforcement in the shape of the Guides Cavalry and Infantry from Mardan. Having received the order to march to Malakand the night before, the Guides Cavalry had covered the 32 miles, in intense heat and choking dust, in

six and a half hours, arriving at 8.30a.m., the Infantry coming in ten hours later. Under difficult marching conditions this was a fine achievement, particularly as the final seven miles were entirely uphill; but the Guides had a reputation for forced marches - as they had proved 40 years before in their famous, and much longer, march to reinforce the besiegers of Delhi in the Mutiny.

They were just in time - as they had been at Delhi. An hour after the Guides Infantry's arrival the tribesmen attacked again all round the revised defences at 7.30p.m. The west side of Crater was now held by the 24th Punjabis. The right flank, between Crater and the fort, was the responsibility of the 45th Sikhs, reinforced by 100 Guides. The rest of the Guides, the 31st Punjabis and the other elements were all in the Crater camp, save for an outlying post forward, in the serai, manned by 24 men of the 31st under Subedar Syed Ahmed Shah.

Before the light faded white-robed tribesmen had been seen massing on the hills around, banners unfurled and drums throbbing, their swords and knives flashing in the setting sun's rays, while their riflemen again began to fire into the camp. The troops, just finishing their evening meal, doubled to their action stations. As darkness fell the massed swordsmen came on once more, charging the stone breastworks in the face of the Martini volleys crashing out from all sides.

At such close ranges hundreds of enemy must have fallen, killed or wounded, but most were carried off by the living before they returned again to the fight. No losses seemed to deter them. If they got into the breastworks they were bayonetted either by the sepoys holding them or by the supports held slightly in rear to deal with any breaking of the line.

Some of the fiercest fighting occurred round the loopholed mud walls of the serai. For six hours Subedar Shah and his men fought them off but all the time their number decreased. Getting close under the flanking walls, the tribesmen started to tunnel through the sun-hardened mud from both sides. Finally they broke in. With only four sepoys left the Subedar, himself wounded, ordered them to abandon the position over the rear wall. With the tribesmen momentarily distracted by their eagerness to mutilate the dead sepoys and those who could not move, the survivors managed to get away to the main line with as many wounded as they could help. All five later received the Order of Merit - the Indian VC.

On the west side the 24th Punjabis were hard pressed but held their defences, though Lieutenant Costello, who had distinguished himself the previous night, was badly wounded. At dawn, seeing no lessening of the onslaught, Lieutenant Climo led out two companies in a counter-attack - a tactic hitherto untried against this enemy. Although at first the tribesmen resisted, with rifle-fire and by rolling boulders down the hillside, the sepoys' disciplined musketry caused heavy casualties in their packed ranks, forcing them ever further back until Climo's men had driven them two miles from the camp. As some fled for shelter in a village two mountain guns opened fire, causing further casualties. Climo's bold and decisive action did not affect the enemy's longer-term resolve to continue attacking Malakand, but henceforth they were to abandon the hills nearest the camp before daylight in the hope of avoiding further counter-attacks.

To the east Colonel McRae's Sikhs and Guides beat off continual attacks along their line. Though some enemy got into their position, they did not get out again. At daybreak he too advanced to clear his front as everywhere the enemy fell back. The garrison had survived another night's intense fighting, but had sustained a further 42 casualties.

Once free of attack, the by now very tired troops set to work to improve the perimeter defences. Trees were cut down to thicken up the abattis, the breastworks were repaired, and the wire entanglement renewed and strengthened. The Swati tribes must have lost heavily during the two nights' fighting yet there was no sign of their breaking off. Indeed, as evening came and the garrison stiffened itself for another night's trial, new masses of men could be seen approaching from the east. Their dark clothing marked them as Bunerwals, who had not taken up arms in earnest since the Ambela Campaign of 1863 but who now, aware of the massive onslaughts on Malakand, saw a chance of loot and pillage too good to be missed.

They came with the night, no change of tactics, swords and knives raised to kill, supported by their riflemen, Swatis and Bunerwals together. For the former to face the steadfast sepoys' musketry and the guns' case-shot a third time the exhortations of their mullahs must have been powerful indeed, with their promises of the delights of Paradise which awaited the Faithful – and for which by now there must have been many applicants. Yet once more the thin line of sepoys, still deployed as on the 27th, held firm, aided by bonfires set alight in front; where it did not, the supports ran forward with the bayonet to restore it. Fewer casualties were suffered that night, only 15, but with three more

British officers wounded. However, the ammunition situation was becoming critical.

Fortunately the next day, the 29th, a squadron of the 11th Bengal Lancers reached Malakand from the south with a re-supply and news that the 35th Sikhs and 38th Dogras, plus more ammunition, were on the way up from Nowshera. After a gruelling march they had reached Dargai, just under ten miles away; so severe had been the conditions that the Sikhs had lost 21 dead on the march from heat stroke. Colonel Meiklejohn, confident that he could hold for another night, therefore signalled them to halt and rest.

During the day the remains of the bazaar and serai were cleared away to improve the field of fire on the front face of the camp. Where the serai had stood the Sappers laid explosive charges which could be fired by pulling on wires.

The attacks resumed that night, led in person – it was later reported – by the Mad Mullah, who had promised his followers that victory would be theirs before dawn. In the event, so effective had been the garrison's daylight preparations that the frontal assaults were unable to make headway across the open space, while the ground suddenly exploding beneath the feet of those near the serai caused much consternation. The enemy's main effort therefore became directed at the flanks, particularly against the 24th Punjabis, whose Lieutenant Costello was wounded a second time in hand-to-hand fighting, yet remained at his post.

Tired though the garrison was from the previous three nights' fighting, the repair work by day and the incessant

A picquet of Guides Infantry in a sangar *guarding the road below Malakand Fort (top left). Drawn by Maj.Hobday, RA. (Author's collection)*

long-range firing, its morale still held. During these attacks some tribesmen urged the Afridi company of the 24th to join their fellow Pathans and Moslems for a share in the plunder once Malakand fell. The Afridis made such encouraging responses that the Swatis came forward to welcome this supposed defection, only to be shot down to a man. The mullahs may have inspired the Swatis to sacrifice themselves for Allah; for the Afridis, their allegiance to the 24th Punjabis - tinged perhaps with distrust for all Swatis - proved a stronger call upon their loyalty.

On the right McRae's Sikhs withstood everything thrown against them. At around 2.30a.m. the attacks rose to a frenzied crescendo for about an hour's desperate fighting. Then they began to peter out, and finally ceased altogether. It was later learned that the Mad Mullah had been wounded - contrary to his earlier assertions that he was invulnerable - and another influential mullah killed. These losses, together with their own heavy casualties, caused the tribesmen to lose heart. The garrison, on the other hand, lost only one man killed that night and 19 wounded.

The following day, the 30th, saw little of the enemy other than removing their dead and helping their wounded. When night fell they rallied to make a last effort, though later than usual - at 9.30p.m. - and with far less fervour and determination than before. Only once, in the middle of the night when a sudden dust storm was followed by a thunder storm, did they make a serious rush, against the 45th Sikhs. McRae's men, tired but with the confidence bred of success, met them with the bayonet and sent them flying. Although some desultory sniping continued into the next day, the Mad Mullah's levies had shot their bolt against Malakand. They were not yet ready to return to their own hills, remaining out of range but within reach of Malakand; however, the nights of fanatical mass onsets against the defences were finished.

Over the five nights of savage fighting the garrison's three Indian battalions, plus their cavalry, gunners and sappers, and the Guides from the second night, had stood their ground successfully against thousands of fanatically brave assailants who did not count the cost, in a peculiarly testing form of warfare. In night-fighting so much is unseen, so much can go wrong, and a soldier's courage is tested to the limit. Yet all of them, Sikhs, Punjabis and Pathans, had remained true to their salt, standing by their British officers and fighting for the good name of their regiments. They had emerged victorious, but not without cost. Three British officers and one British NCO were dead, ten British and seven Indian officers wounded; 27

Indian NCOs and men had been killed, 126 wounded.

On the morning of 31 July the 35th Sikhs and 38th Dogras marched in from Dargai, with enough ammunition to replace the thousands of rounds that had been fired. So alarmed had the authorities in India been by the scale of the attack on Malakand that further forces had been assembled at Nowshera and were on the way. The time had come to go over to the offensive and exact retribution; but before that was done the outlying post at Chakdara had to be relieved.

* * *

There had been no communication with Chakdara since the night of 26 July when the telegraph wire was cut. On 1 August a very brief and compelling signal was received by heliograph: "Help us!" But even the two new battalions needed to rest after four days' marching in intense heat, and the garrison were exhausted after their long ordeal. None were fresh enough that day to attempt a relief which, since the enemy still lay in strength between the two posts, would involve much more than a ten-mile march. Chakdara would have to hold out for at least another day.

After the Chitral campaign a suspension bridge had been built over the River Swat, nearly a mile south of the village of Chakdara on the north bank, to carry the road from Nowshera and Malakand - which hitherto had run parallel to the river on the south bank - northwards to Chitral. Upon a rocky, isolated mound close to the north end of this bridge had been built a fort to protect it, while the south end was guarded by two blockhouses either side of an iron gate. Situated on the western and north-west faces of the mound were double-storied, loopholed stone buildings, 25 feet high, in which the garrison lived. The north-east end, which was higher with very steep sides, was surmounted by a stone-walled enclosure containing a 9-pdr. gun. On the south side were two linked stone sangars protected in front by a barbed wire entanglement, which ran on and up round the north-east summit.

To the west lay a range of hills from which one spur ran down to within some 150 yards from the mound. Further up the spur, on a knoll, was a square, raised, one-storey blockhouse tower from which signal communications with Malakand were maintained. This post was 500 yards from the fort. Though strongly built and with good fields of fire, the fort's close proximity to the nearby hills made it possible, as one observer noted, for an enemy "to look or fire right into the fort. Every open space is commanded. Every parapet is exposed"[1].

Chakdara's garrison on 26 July consisted of 180 men of the 45th Sikhs and 20 sowars of the 11th Bengal Lancers. Besides the 9-pdr. they had two Maxims, one of which was in the blockhouse at the south end of the bridge. In command was Lieutenant H.B.Rattray, aged 27, whose father, Colonel Thomas Rattray, had raised the 45th Sikhs in 1856 and whose family name the regiment had since borne as a subsidiary title. With him were another subaltern of the regiment, 2nd Lieutenant L. L. Wheatley, Surgeon-Captain Hugo, and an Assistant Political Agent,

The interior of Chakdara Fort, looking south-west towards the Swat River; the signalling tower held by 16 men under Lance-Naik Vir Singh is just visible on the hill at the extreme right, some 500 yards west of the fort. In the right foreground is the westernmost of the two barracks; at left, part of the steep hill which was surmounted by the 9-pdr. gun position. (Navy & Army Illustrated)

Chakdara Fort and the bridge over the Swat River, looking north-east. The main gate is visible in the barracks block to the left, which in July 1897 accomodated the 180-strong garrison of Rattray's Sikhs. The signalling tower was up a spur off the left of this picture; a blockhouse with one of the two Maxims stood at the south end of the bridge, off the right of the picture. Drawn by Maj.Hobday, RA. (Author's collection)

Lieutenant Minchin. Rattray had seven years' commissioned service. Wheatley, six years younger and also the son of a colonel, had been commissioned for barely a year, but had all the qualities then thought ideal for a good officer: at Wellington he had been a school prefect, a member of the VIth Form and the rugby First XV, later captaining the Sandhurst XV.

When Rattray had played polo at Khar on the 26th he had been given a warning that an attack was possible, but not probable, and had prepared his garrison accordingly. As the game ended he received a message from Wheatley that large numbers of tribesmen had been spotted advancing towards the fort; during his gallop back to Chakdara he saw some of them in the distance, but reached the fort safely.

At 10.15p.m. the sentries reported a bonfire on a hilltop, a pre-arranged signal that an attack was imminent. The "Alarm" was sounded. Soon, from the darkened hills, heavy fire was opened on the fort. Almost at once, from out of the west, came the first of many massed charges such as Malakand was then confronting. The Sikhs on the west wall shot them down till they fell back.

They came again at the north-east corner, then on the east side, and finally on the south. Each attack was shot away by disciplined Martini fire, the 9-pdr. and the Maxim in the fort. At last, some time after 4a.m., the tribesmen melted away into the darkness, leaving their riflemen to continue firing into the fort from the commanding heights.

Although the little garrison had survived the night, the dropping rifle-fire which went on throughout the day made any movement within the fort a risky undertaking. Later that morning, as mentioned earlier, Captain Wright and his 40 sowars of the 11th Bengal Lancers succeeded in reaching the fort, accompanied by a staff officer, Captain Baker. To do so

they had had to ride through country infested by tribesmen who kept up a steady if ill-aimed fire; had taken to some very difficult tracks, quite unsuitable for horses, to avoid ambushes; had swum the river – of unknown depth – twice; and had finally fought dismounted with carbines to recover their wounded until they came under the covering fire of the Maxim on the bridge. Captain Wright, as the senior officer, assumed overall command at Chakdara but, as a cavalryman, left the detailed handling of the defence to Rattray. Captain Baker set about making himself useful by devising means of protecting the sepoys from the overhead fire.

The arrival of 40 extra carbines was timely, for soon afterwards the enemy suddenly launched a massed daylight assault from the north and east. This was beaten off with heavy loss, although parties of the more fanatical *ghazis* periodically attempted to accelerate their journey to Paradise by hurling themselves at the defences, where their ambitions were rapidly accommodated by the sepoys.

A major problem for the defenders, then and throughout the siege, was the survival of the distant signallers under Lance-Naik Vir Singh in the blockhouse tower up the spur. The telegraph had been cut off the first night, leaving the heliograph as the only means of communication with the outside world, and indeed with the fort; the signaller, however, could only operate it by exposing himself at great risk. The post was entirely

Officers and men of the 45th Sikhs after the relief of Chakdara. Lt.Rattray stands at front left, with bandaged neck; 2nd Lt.Wheatley, bareheaded, stands third from left. Third from right stands Lt.Col.McRae. See also Plate C. (Rulzion Rattray)

dependent on the fort for food and water and was constantly under fire from the enemy riflemen, who also commanded the steep, winding track up to it. That first morning, the 27th, almost the entire firepower of the garrison had been required to cover the movement of six men with food and water up to the tower. Furthermore the water container in the tower had not been kept topped up and so needed daily replenishment.

Not until 11p.m. that night did the attacks resume. Thanks to the care with which Wheatley had laid the 9-pdr. and the Maxim on the most likely approaches during daylight, these were repulsed with many casualties, any tribesmen who survived the fire zones being shot down by the sepoys manning the parapets. A lull ensued. Then, just when it seemed the garrison might be able to get some much-needed rest, the enemy came on again, hurling themselves with scaling ladders at the north-east corner. Deprived of their sleep, the sepoys fired and fired until the enemy vanished once more into the night.

When daylight came it was observed that during the night stone sangars had been thrown up all round the fort some 200 yards away; these were empty, but their purpose became clear that afternoon. At 5.30p.m. a large number of enemy advanced, in small groups rather than mass, running from cover to cover until they reached the sangars, behind which they sheltered. At a given signal they all made a rush for the walls with their ladders, and thick bundles of packed grass which they threw across the wire entanglement. Again the Sikhs and sowars were ready for them and did great execution, though some reached the foot of the walls before

they were killed. After three nights' fighting not one tribesman had yet entered the fort.

During the morning of the 29th no further attacks were made. Owing to the incessant sniping from the hills work had to continue on improving the overhead cover on the walls. That afternoon and evening determined assaults were made on the signalling tower, using grass bundles in an attempt to burn down the door; as it was six feet above the ground this failed. Though closely pressed, the 16-strong garrison were as resolute as their comrades in the fort. Firing downwards at their assailants through loopholes in the raised floor, and well supported by flanking fire from the fort, they managed to hold on until after dark, when the enemy lost heart and made off with their casualties, both from the tower and the fort.

Firing continued all the next day, followed by renewed assaults that evening. Those too were beaten off eventually. Despite the losses they had sustained the enemy's numbers, far from decreasing, were actually growing as more and more tribesmen arrived from distant hills. At the start of the siege the garrison had been outnumbered by about eight to one; by 30 July it was more like fifty to one, and more could be seen approaching in the distance.

With this steadily increasing, visible evidence of the odds against them, added to the weariness caused by the constant shooting, the periodic attacks, the lack of rest, the unceasing watchfulness, all aggravated by the intense heat, lesser troops might well have yielded under the strain. Fortunately, thanks to their defences, their casualties had been light. Certainly the Sikhs and lancers found difficulty in staying awake, but their British and Indian officers drove themselves to the limit to ensure wakefulness, to encourage and to commend the gallantry and steadfastness of their sepoys and sowars. Rattray's Sikhs and the 11th Bengal

Lancers were not done for yet, grim though the outlook seemed on 31 July.

That evening the reinforced enemy launched a massive assault on the east side. Due largely to excellent shooting by the gunners on the 9-pdr. and the Maxim, as well as enfilade fire from the Maxim on the bridge, the charges were held at bay. However, a strong body of riflemen on the west side occupied a solitary building between the fort and the signal tower which had been used as a hospital. Having loopholed the walls, they kept up a constant fire at close range from early on 1 August.

It was on this day that the desperate message, "Help us", was heliographed to Malakand. The operator, Sepoy Prem Singh, had several times risked his life signalling to the fort, chiefly for water. Signalling to Malakand entailed much greater exposure, in full view of the surrounding marksmen; hence the previous lack of communication with Malakand and the stark brevity of this message. As his comrades opened rapid fire, Prem Singh climbed from the tower window, set up his heliograph and got the message through. This signaller's work was most bravely done considering, in the words of one contemporary account, "the extreme danger, the delicacy of the operation of obtaining connection with a helio, the time consumed, and the composure required"[2].

Worse was to come for the party in the tower. Their water was already low, and on this day the tribesmen surrounded them in such numbers that there was no longer a chance of their receiving any further re-supply. Always under fire, with the sun blazing down on to their confined quarters, all they could do was hold on as long as their ammunition, and their strength, lasted.

Not only were the enemy forces as a whole increasing, but their riflemen were much more numerous than earlier. In addition to those on the spur and in the hospital, more began to take up positions in nearby nullahs and other folds in the ground. By 1 August the fort was surrounded by fire and at much closer ranges than in the early stages.

No serious attack was made that night, though sniping continued to bedevil the watching garrison who, so accustomed had they become to night attacks, could not risk taking advantage of this apparent respite. Instead they had to get what rest they could at their posts while sentries scanned the darkness.

At daybreak on the 2nd the firing intensified from all

directions. Then a great mass of men – between 10,000 and 12,000, some said as many as 14,000 – bore down upon the fort in the greatest onslaught yet seen. By that day the tribal leaders must have realised that with Malakand now safe and reinforced an attempt to relieve Chakdara could not be long delayed. This huge effort, therefore, must have been a do-or-die attempt to overwhelm the fort before relief arrived.

Despite the numbers, the covering fire, the ladders and grass bundles, the defenders held them off, the guns in particular effecting much slaughter. It was touch-and-go for two hours. Suddenly a heliograph flashed from south of the river. Not long afterwards lance-points were spotted approaching at speed; and soon the riders, 11th Bengal Lancers, were clattering over the bridge followed by the Guides Cavalry. Seeing them coming and preparing to charge, the nearest of the tribesmen – always fearful of cavalry – began to run. Their sudden panic spread like a contagion, and everywhere the enemy host made off for the hills.

As soon as he saw the tide turn Lieutenant Rattray, whose fatigue must have been greater than anyone's, called for a counter-attack. Followed by ten of his Sikhs he charged the hospital, pursuing its occupants towards the river, being joined by Wheatley and Baker with more men. Returning to the fort he led another charge at an overlooked sangar. As the Sikhs bayonetted the men still holding it Rattray received a neck wound; undeterred, he cut down the man who had fired with his sword. He was later admitted to the Distinguished Service Order, for he had indeed been "the life and soul of the defence". Wheatley also received the same decoration[3]. By 8.30a.m. on 2 August Chakdara was at last relieved, after seven nights and six days of relentless assaults by overwhelming numbers.

* * *

The defence of Chakdara by six British officers and 240 Indian soldiers against up to 14,000 Pathan tribesmen must rank with that other, yet far more famous Victorian military epic, the defence of Rorke's Drift. The story of the latter has been told and retold in prose, paint and film; but who now remembers Chakdara? Certainly its defenders fought from behind stone walls, with a gun and two Maxims, rather than mealie bags and biscuit boxes. On the other hand their assailants had far more firearms and were much better shots than the Zulus. Furthermore, Chakdara had to hold out for ten times as long as Rorke's Drift before relief and, at least towards the end, was outnumbered by certainly twice the numbers facing B Company, 2/24th Foot. The two subalterns at Rorke's Drift won Victoria Crosses, as did nine others of their garrison. Indian troops, however brave, were only eligible for the Indian Order of Merit, of which seven were won at Chakdara; but their British subalterns received only the DSO.

Then again, the officers at Rorke's Drift were supported by their own countrymen whereas those at Chakdara relied upon men of a different race and religion.

Certainly Sikhs, whether of Rattray's or Probyn's (as the 11th Bengal Lancers were otherwise known), could have expected no mercy from their Moslem adversaries had they yielded, but had any been bent on escape they might have found the opportunity during darkness. None took it. Some today might call them mercenaries, on the basis of their being paid by a foreign power; that is to misunderstand the ethos of the old Indian Army. They knew that they

fought for the same Queen-Empress as their British officers; but since she was, inevitably, a somewhat remote concept, on the day the sepoys fought for the young officer who bore their regiment's name, and the sowars for their officer who was, like them, of Probyn's Horse - and right well they all did so, showing "the stuff which our Sikhs are made of"[4].

* * *

Although the Malakand garrison had been in no fit state to respond to Chakdara's plea for help on 1 August, a cavalry force had set out that morning to test the enemy strength. They had not gone far before they were opposed by large bodies of tribesmen. Although the Guides Cavalry charged more than once, the ground was too broken for effective cavalry work and soon their line of retreat became threatened. Lieutenant-Colonel Adams of the Guides, who was in command, reluctantly ordered a retirement and the squadrons went back, covering each other with dismounted fire. In view of the numbers and determination of the enemy, and because the infantry had still not sufficiently recovered from the previous week's exertions, it was decided not to persevere that day.

The problem for any relief force was the high ground around the Malakand bowl held by the enemy, particularly that which commanded the road to Chakdara; this passed through a cleft in these heights, which in turn prevented any deployment on a wide front. Such a cleft had enabled Colonel McRae to hold up the enemy advance on the first night at Malakand; so now could the tribesmen hold up a relief column going the other way.

Maj. Hobday's drawing of the Guides Cavalry (see also Plate C) and 11th Bengal Lancers reconnoitring from Malakand on 1 August. (Author's collection)

It took a fresh eye, as will be seen in the next chapter, to perceive a solution. Near this cleft was a commanding spur. Having formed up in darkness, at first light on 2 August Colonel Goldney led 250 of his 35th Sikhs and 50 of the 38th Dogras into a silent attack upon this spur. Taken by surprise, the enemy opened a hurried fire before fleeing. The way through the cleft was open.

The main column - 400 each of the 45th Sikhs, 24th Punjabis and Guides Infantry with four guns, and followed by two squadrons each of the 11th Bengal Lancers and Guides Cavalry - pressed rapidly on up the road and into the more open country beyond. Here they deployed and went straight into the attack against any enemy prepared to stand. The tribesmen, suddenly demoralised by this turn of events, began to run, mostly to the east. The cavalry squadrons came up, rode through the advancing infantry and pursued mercilessly across the flat fields on the south bank of the Swat. The infantry followed, meeting some resistance in the villages; but now, their tiredness forgotten and their morale lifted by success, they were not to be denied. The enemy was on the run and the way to Chakdara was clear.

Malakand had been held and Chakdara relieved. The Mad Mullah's great onslaught with the tribes of Swat, Buner and Bajaur had been repulsed and routed, with casualties numbered in thousands. The time for retribution had come.

CHAPTER FIVE

Blood on the Warpath

When news of the Malakand attacks first reached England the press quickly took up the story. Even in the distant Channel Islands the local daily paper, the *Jersey Evening Post*, carried a headline "Malakand Rising. Troops Ordered Up" on 29 July, only three days after the first attack. The *Illustrated London News* had earlier reported the Tochi trouble and was to devote considerable coverage to the whole Pathan Revolt but, being a weekly, could not announce the new uprising until 31 July.

Lieutenant Winston Churchill, then on home leave from the 4th Hussars in India, read of it in a newspaper at the Goodwood Race Meeting (always held in the last week of July) when the fighting at Malakand and Chakdara was at its height. Though his leave was not yet over he determined to return to India at once, by taking the overland train to Brindisi, there to catch the boat for India. However, realising from the newspaper that his regiment, then stationed at Bangalore in southern India, was not to be included in the Malakand Field Force which was about to be assembled, he telegraphed immediately to the general nominated to command it. He had met this officer the previous year while staying with Lord Patrick Beresford, and had extracted a promise from him that he would include Churchill on any Frontier expedition which might arise.

Churchill was to receive no reply until he reached Aden. The general said he had no staff vacancies but suggested Churchill join the force as a war-correspondent. After further telegraphing, and assisted by his influential mother, Churchill got himself accredited to the *Daily Telegraph*, and to the Indian paper *The Pioneer* on which Kipling had worked ten years previously. He reached Bangalore, obtained his commanding officer's permission, and took the train north, joining the Malakand Field Force on 2 September - just 32 days after leaving Goodwood Races, some 10,000 miles away.

The general who had befriended him was Sir Bindon Blood. First commissioned in the Royal Engineers in 1860, he had seen service in the Zulu War, the Second Afghan War and the Egyptian War, and more recently had taken part in the relief of Chitral as Chief of Staff. He was thus thoroughly familiar with the region around Malakand, and was a natural choice to command the Field Force which was to subjugate the rebellious tribes and restore peace to the district.

Blood was particularly proud to count among his ancestors the notorious Colonel Blood who, in the reign of Charles II, had attempted to steal the Crown Jewels, but who had been acquitted when brought to trial and had been appointed to command the King's bodyguard. Sir Bindon told Churchill that such an ancestor gave him a natural sympathy with the Pathans, and could he but tell them the story they would have been so appreciative that the Malakand Field Force would have been unnecessary!

Blood arrived at Nowshera on 31 July. Having made the arrangements for the assembly of his three brigades and their march north he went on ahead, reaching Malakand the next day. To those about to come under his command he appeared "a striking figure, formidable in his uniform, mounted, with his standard-bearer and cavalcade"[1]. It had been his fresh eye that had perceived the way to relieve Chakdara.

Two of his four-battalion brigades contained the six Indian battalions that had been engaged at Malakand, while the other six battalions marching up from Nowshera were the 22nd Punjabis, 39th Garhwal Rifles, and four British units: 1st Queen's (Royal West Surrey), 1st Buffs (East Kent), 1st Royal West Kent and 2nd Highland Light Infantry. An additional Indian battalion, 21st Punjabis, was included in the divisional troops, together with the Guides Cavalry; one squadron each of the 10th and 11th Bengal Lancers; three mountain batteries (two British) and the 10th Field Battery RA; three companies of Sappers and Miners; and three sections (one British) of a Field Hospital. Colonel Meiklejohn, who had commanded at Malakand, was given the 1st Brigade, the other two brigadiers being Jeffreys (2nd) and Wodehouse (3rd).

The march up, each man in field service order with the unaccustomed weight of 100 rounds in his pouches, was a hard initiation for the British battalions. For a start, the men found that the miles they actually marched were longer than what they had been told to expect - the milestones were placed at the Indian distance, which was nearly half again the length of an English mile. (One soldier was heard to remark that "the fool with the milestones must have been asleep in a cart and chucked one out every time he awoke".) After Mardan, marching at night, they had to cross "three

Maj.Gen.Sir Bindon Blood (leaning on gun barrel) among his staff of the Malakand Field Force. (Author's collection)

The 39th Garwhal Rifles had been 2nd Bn., 3rd Gurkha Rifles until 1890, and retained Gurkha dress. The battalion fought on the left of the 1st Queen's in the defence of the 3rd Brigade's camp at Nawagai during the night of 19 September. The photograph shows a bugler, a jemadar, a havildar and a naik. (Maj.A.G.Harfield)

rivers and six solid miles of swamp and mud. Every step was up over the knee in filth and dirt. On reaching the camp - wet, hungry, miserable and dispirited - instead of unpacking our tents and getting into bed, we received the by no means welcome intelligence that we were to form a line of defence round the camp. This we did in a drizzling soaking rain". A couple of days later, marching in daylight, "we had another river to negotiate, about three or four feet deep, and to make matters worse, the sun came out in all its brilliancy. The heat was something terrific. No one who has soldiered in other than a tropical climate can have the faintest idea what it was like, it was simply blinding but the men stuck to their march manfully"[2].

By 7 August the Malakand Field Force was ready to begin operations and reconnaissances were made up the Swat Valley. Seeing this large force on their doorstep the Lower Swatis made haste to surrender unconditionally; but rumours came in that the Upper Swatis were preparing to resist further up the valley, and were likely to be joined by the Bunerwals from the south-east. Wodehouse's 3rd Brigade was ordered to block any advance by the latter.

Heavy rains delayed any advance but on 16 August a cavalry reconnaissance located an enemy force 5,000 strong near Landakai, some eight miles from Chakdara, holding a long ridge at right angles to the river known as the "Gate of Swat". The road lay along a causeway between the south bank of the river, which was unfordable at this point, and the north end of the ridge, which ran up a spur on to high hills to the south. Having prior knowledge of this area, Sir Bindon Blood appreciated that the enemy's most likely line of retreat was up the spur into the hills rather than across the swampy rice fields behind the ridge. Ordering up Meiklejohn's 1st Brigade, with supporting cavalry and artillery, he planned his attack accordingly for the morning of 17 August.

As No.7 (British) Mountain Battery and the field battery's 12-pounders opened fire on the sangars lining the ridge, the 1st Royal West Kent skirmished forward frontally to engage the enemy's attention. The infantry advance coupled with the artillery fire - particularly the field gun shells, to which these tribesmen were unaccustomed - had a varied effect on the ridge. The

bravest spirits concentrated on engaging the West Kent firing line; the more cautious took cover in their sangars; others ran for shelter down the reverse slope. As Blood had planned, this helped his main attack.

Up into the hills to his right climbed the 24th and 31st Punjabis, supported by the 45th Sikhs and No.8 (Bengal) Mountain Battery, all under Meiklejohn. Arriving above the enemy left, they attacked down the spur to the ridge. Taken by surprise, finding their preferred escape route blocked and with their reserves wrongly posted to meet an attack along the causeway, the enemy began to break rearwards.

The West Kents now advanced rapidly to clear the ridge and link up with the flank attack; all then opened long-range fire on the fleeing tribesmen. The Sappers hurried forward to repair breaks previously made in the causeway, while the Guides Cavalry waited impatiently to ride through in pursuit.

As soon as the Sappers completed their work, which took some time, the Guides filed through leading their horses, remounted and set off across the rice fields to catch the fugitives before they could reach the distant hills. The boggy ground, however, caused the regiment to become very strung out. In the lead was Lieutenant-Colonel Adams who, with Lieutenant Maclean and a few sowars, rode at best speed towards a clump of trees from which he thought effective dismounted fire could be brought against the running tribesmen. With this group was Lieutenant Viscount Fincastle of the 16th Lancers, who was in the field as war-correspondent of *The Times*.

Riding with Captain Palmer's squadron was another officer-correspondent, Lieutenant Greaves of the Lancashire Fusiliers, for *The Times of India*. He and Palmer spotted some enemy near the foot of the hills and, reaching firmer ground, galloped ahead of the sowars and charged in amongst them. The nearest tribesmen rounded on them with swords while others, somewhat up the hill, opened fire. Greaves was shot from his saddle, and hacked as he lay on the ground. Palmer killed a standard-bearer but, raising his sword arm to strike again, had his wrist shattered by a bullet. Two sowars rode up and managed to save Palmer, but the enemy began to close in all around.

By now this mêlée had been noticed by Adams' group, who had reached the clump of trees. Maclean dismounted his men into good fire positions, then galloped off with three sowars after Adams and Fincastle, who were already dashing to the rescue. Seeing them coming the tribesmen fell back a little, opening a heavy fire. Fincastle's horse was shot and he was thrown to the ground. He ran to Greaves and, assisted by Maclean, tried to lift him on to Adams' horse. That too was shot; Greaves was hit again, which killed him, and Maclean was mortally wounded. By now, however, the carbine fire from Maclean's men was deterring the enemy from closing in again. With only two horses left and still under fire, Adams and Fincastle, with the five Guides, succeeded in bringing Greaves' body, the dying Maclean and the wounded Palmer to the safety of the trees.

Palmer and Greaves had undoubtedly behaved rashly, and had paid dearly; but the gallantry of the other three officers earned them the Victoria Cross - in Maclean's case posthumously - while the five Guides who had so bravely supported them received the Order of Merit[3].

Despite this flurry of resistance, the action at Landakai had a most salutary effect on the Upper Swatis. It was later estimated that since the uprising on 26 July the Swatis, Bunerwals and their allies had lost 4,000 dead[4]. Blood was able to advance unopposed for a further 15 miles up the valley to Mingaora, where the tribesmen came in to submit, thus completing operations in that area by 24 August. He next intended to move south-east to deal with the Bunerwals but, before he could begin, fresh outbreaks 50 miles and more to the south-west resulted in him receiving new orders.

* * *

Just over two weeks earlier, five days after the relief of Chakdara, the Mohmands – who inhabited the region north of the Kabul River and Khyber Pass – had attacked Fort Shabkadr, 15 miles north of Peshawar on the Indian side of the old administrative border. The fort held out until relieved by a column from Peshawar, which engaged the Mohmands in the vicinity.

Then, on 23 August, the day before the Swatis submitted, the Afridis began attacking the Khyber Pass, followed by further assaults, with the Orakzais, in the Kurram Valley and on the Samana Range. Thus, in the space of a fortnight, following the conclusion of operations in the north (except against the Bunerwals), the authorities were faced with serious hostilities spread over some hundred miles from north to south, to the west of Peshawar.

The Afridi-Orakzai combination, being the largest yet encountered, would require the concentration of another major field force. While it was being prepared the Mohmand region, north of the Kabul River, would have to be pacified first. The Government therefore decided to assemble a Mohmand Field Force under Brigadier-General Elles, which was to invade Mohmand territory from Shabkadr prior to linking up with Blood's Malakand Field Force coming in from the north. The Mohmand Field Force, and the Afridi-Orakzai operations, will be considered later; but this decision required Blood to advance not south-east against the Bunerwals, who would have to be dealt with later, but west across the Panjkora River into Bajaur.

Blood's starting point for this new operation was to be Nawagai in South Bajaur, some 25 miles west from Malakand as the crow flies. Wodehouse's 3rd Brigade was ordered up from watching the Bunerwals and, with Divisional Headquarters and Jeffrey's 2nd Brigade, advanced westwards across the Panjkora on 9 September, leaving Meiklejohn's 1st Brigade to guard the line of communications.

Winston Churchill, who had joined the force a week before, watched the marching troops: "There was the soldier as he appears on service. The tinsel and polish of parade had vanished. The marching figures slouched heavily along, their rifles carried at every conceivable angle, smoking and talking. Their travel-stained khaki was a study in neutral tints, hardly relieved by the warm colours of the native turbans. The superfine soldier of London or Aldershot would find much to sneer at. And yet, beneath this appearance of ease, was the iron framework of discipline and training". In the 3rd Brigade was the 1st Queen's, who had come up to the Frontier from Ambala, over 400 miles away by rail: "The men had just marched fourteen miles

with arms and ammunition, and not one had fallen out on the way. They looked strained and weary, but nothing would induce them to admit it. 'An easy march', they said, 'Should have been here long ago if the native troops had not kept halting'"[5].

On 14 September Blood and the 3rd Brigade reached Nawagai from where he intended to wheel south. Here an entrenched camp was constructed in a bare, level valley broken up by deep dry watercourses and surrounded by barren hills. The 2nd Brigade camped that night eight miles to the east at Markhanai close to the Rambat Pass, which was to be its start point for the advance south the following day. To ensure a secure start, Jeffreys sent the 1st Buffs up to the top of the pass while the rest of the brigade camped at its foot.

Both brigades were isolated in unknown country. To the immediate south lay the territory of the Utman Khel who, though they had participated in the attack on Malakand, were not expected to give trouble since they quickly surrendered a quantity of rifles. Beyond them was Mohmand country. To the north of the line reached by Blood were the Mamunds – kinsfolk of the Swatis and Bunerwals but not of the Mohmands – a people of "pestilential reputation"[6] with whom there was no intention of getting engaged.

The Mamunds, however, were well aware of what had been happening over the previous seven weeks, some of them having fought at Malakand; and they saw in the 2nd Brigade's camp at Markhanai an opportunity too good to be missed. Descending from their hills after dark but before moonrise, they took cover among the rocks and in the many nullahs that surrounded the camp, and waited.

The 2nd Brigade had marched some 20 miles that day under a very hot sun, and on arrival had had to entrench the camp – a *sine qua non* anywhere on the Frontier. All knew that the Mohmands were their objective, but as they would not be met for some days the troops hoped for a good night's rest. Once the officers were satisfied with the work and had seen the sentries posted, with one fully-accoutred section per company ready behind the parapet as an inlying picquet, they assembled for dinner.

The Guides Cavalry at Landakai, 17 August; watercolour by May Dart. This appears to show the attempt by Lt.Col.Adams and Lt.Viscount Fincastle to save Capt.Palmer and Lt.Greaves; at left Lt.Maclean and a few sowars follow their commanding officer, while the rest of Maclean's men fire from the trees at far left. See also Plate C. (National Army Museum)

Bunerwal ghazis counter-attacking the 24th Punjabis during the right flanking assault by Meiklejohn's 1st Brigade at Landakai, 17 August. Drawing by Maj.Hobday, RA, of the brigade staff. (Author's collection)

They never finished it. At 8.15p.m. three shots were fired, followed immediately by a heavy fusillade from the ground facing the side manned by the Guides Infantry, the bullets sweeping all over and into the camp. All lights were extinguished and the Guides stood to their parapet, opening fire into the darkness at the muzzle flashes. The moon had not yet risen, so the guns of No.8 (Bengal) Mountain Battery fired star-shell. Even so the well-concealed enemy presented few targets, and did not expose themselves by mounting charges. The Guides continued firing and, thanks to their entrenchment, suffered no casualties, though many of the transport animals in the centre of the camp were hit.

At about 10p.m. the enemy fire suddenly ceased and a lull ensued. Just as everyone thought they might resume their interrupted rest it began again, with war-drums throbbing in the background. Now it was the 38th Dogras' turn, on the opposite side. Here the entrenchment was lower, and though it afforded adequate protection for the firing sepoys the officers had necessarily to expose themselves as they stood to control their men's fire. In quick succession two of them, Captain Tomkins and Lieutenant Bailey, were killed, and soon afterwards Lieutenant Harrington received a mortal head wound.

On this side the enemy, mostly armed with Martinis, had crept forward to within a hundred yards of the camp. An attempt to mount a counter-attack had to be abandoned because, the moon having now risen, the soldiers became hopelessly silhouetted against the light as they rose to charge. Again the enemy made no attempt to assault the parapet, but continued to fire until at last, just before 3a.m., they all made off to their hills. They had cost the 2nd Brigade, besides the three British officers and the loss of a much-needed night's sleep, 12 casualties and no less than 98 valuable animals. The Buffs, high on the pass, had been undisturbed.

At first light the 11th Bengal Lancers' squadron was sent out. It not only confirmed that the attackers had been Mamunds, but managed to charge a party who had left it too late to get away, spearing 21 of them. As soon as the squadron started to withdraw, however, the tribesmen turned to pursue. With their carbines outranged by the Mamunds' rifles the cavalrymen became hard-pressed, and the Guides Infantry had to go out to cover them into camp.

When the news was heliographed to Blood at Nawagai, he cancelled the 2nd Brigade's advance over the Rambat Pass and ordered Jeffreys to march forthwith against the Mamunds. The Buffs were summoned down from the pass, and the whole brigade marched six miles north to Inayat Killa at the entrance to the Mamund valley. Here another, more substantial camp was established, with walls three and a half feet high, scooped-out holes for every man to rest in, and better protection for the animals. That evening, as the enemy kept up some sniping into the camp, Jeffreys planned his operation for the next day, 16 September, to destroy certain villages further up the valley. It was to be a long and memorable day for many.

* * *

The valley was some ten miles long and six across, running from south-east to north. Jeffreys divided his force into three columns: the right, of Colonel Vivian's 38th Dogras, less two companies, with some Sappers, was to attack Domodoloh, six miles from camp; the centre, under Colonel Goldney, of six companies each of his 35th Sikhs and the Buffs, Captain Cole's 11th Bengal Lancers squadron, four guns of No.8 Battery and a half-company of Sappers, was directed against Badalai and, at the head of the valley, Shahi Tangi; the left, of Major Campbell's Guides Infantry and some Sappers, was to destroy a cluster of villages on the west side. Seven companies of infantry with two guns were to guard the camp.

The advance began at 6a.m. Vivian on the right found Domodoloh too strongly held to be attacked without artillery or other support, and returned to camp. On the left the Guides soon reached their objective without opposition, and set about wrecking the houses.

In the centre the advance was led by Cole's squadron of Lancers; riding with him was Winston Churchill. After four miles' marching the Buffs wheeled off to the right to deal with Badalai, while the 35th Sikhs followed in the cavalry's wake. As the Lancers neared the head of the valley Churchill could see through his telescope, centred on a conical hill, "long lines of men clad in blue or white, each with his weapon upright beside him, squatting on the terraces. The sun threw back at intervals bright flashes of steel as other tribesmen waved their swords"[7].

It was now 7.30a.m. The Lancers rode forward until within range of the hill, dismounted at some trees, and opened carbine fire to hold the enemy's attention until the Sikhs and guns came up. As they intended, the tribesmen returned the fire for nearly an hour but, as the infantry came in sight, they began to climb away on to the higher ground behind.

Goldney sent Captain Ryder's company of the 35th against the conical hill, whence he was to protect the battalion's right flank as it ascended the long spur leading to Shahi Tangi. By now there was no sign of the enemy apart from the odd long-range shot. One company remained in reserve at the foot of the spur while two led the advance supported by the remaining two. The Sikhs' march up had been hastened once the enemy had been sighted; the day, according to Churchill who climbed with them, was "frightfully hot"[8]; and the spur was steep. Although there was very little opposition it was 11a.m. before the village, only some two miles up the spur, was finally reached and its destruction could begin. Time was pressing on with

Two of the Landakai VCs: Lt.Col.Adams, Guides Cavalry, and Lt.Viscount Fincastle, 16th Lancers. (Author's collection)

nothing yet accomplished, although there were still some eight hours of daylight remaining.

Nearly three hours before, Cole's report on the enemy strength observed had reached Jeffreys' headquarters. He signalled to Campbell to advance up the valley to protect the Sikhs' left. This the Guides did; but as they neared the head of the valley they came under heavy fire from their left front. The noise of the ensuing fire-fight induced Jeffreys to order the Buffs northwards from Badalai.

On hearing this new firing to his left rear, the commander of the Sikhs' two forward companies decided it was time to withdraw. The spur down which they were to move was not a level slope but switchbacked down over three knolls in succession, connected by saddles of open ground. No sooner had the rearward move to the first knoll begun than Churchill, watching the high ground north of the village, saw "the mountainside spring to life. Swords flashed, bright flags waved here and there. Widely-scattered white smoke puffs broke from the rugged face. From high up on the crag, white or blue figures appeared, dropping down the mountainside from ledge to ledge like monkeys down the branches of a tall tree. A shrill crying arose from many points"[9].

The last half-company to retire immediately opened fire. The enemy came on fast, firing as they came, and when their leaders took cover a hundred yards off the half-company fell back, covered by those in rear. All got away safely, cleared the first knoll, reached the second and went on down, all movement covered by fire. Churchill remained with the last party on the second knoll – Lieutenant Cassells and eight sepoys – firing at the tribesmen who had now reached the first knoll, until they heard the shouted order to move.

As they rose to run, fire struck them. Within seconds Cassells and four sepoys fell. Churchill and the other four tried to get the wounded away as the Adjutant, Lieutenant Hughes, Subedar-Major Mangol Singh and a few sepoys climbed back up to help, though fire was now coming from the flank as well. Hughes fell; four men picked him up but then, as swordsmen rushed down from the knoll, dropped him. The leading tribesmen hacked furiously at the body. Churchill fired his revolver – two misfires – then the next shot seemed to tell. Finding himself alone, he ran. Thus a great future Prime Minister saved himself for posterity.

Continually pressed by the tribesmen, and with many men unable to fire because they were carrying the wounded, the two Sikh companies somehow reached the foot of the spur; they were forced to leave their dead, who would be found horribly mutilated. As the enemy charged down the Sikhs formed up in close order, fixed bayonets, and fired a volley. The enemy halted 30 yards off, screaming and waving swords. A bugler sounded the "Charge". The Sikhs went forward steadily, bayonets advanced. The tribesmen, always less aggressive when troops attacked rather than retired, made off back up the spur. The Sikhs halted and opened fire. Churchill saw that "the crisis was over, and here, Praise be to God, were the leading files of the Buffs"[10].

Jeffreys was not prepared to allow the Mamunds the satisfaction of having driven the Sikhs from the spur. The Buffs were ordered to re-take it and destroy any part of Shahi Tangi still standing. The 35th Sikhs were to be in support and the Guides were to protect the left flank. At 1p.m. the mountain guns opened fire and the Buffs went forward.

By 3.30p.m. the task was done with no opposition other than some sniping, and the withdrawal was ordered. Then, just as had befallen the 35th Sikhs, the enemy came on in force again. Now, however, the Mamunds found their attack opposed by six companies with Lee-Metfords instead of two with Martinis, and were shot down before they could close. By 5p.m. all troops were clear of the spur, and the Buffs and Sikhs began their return march to Inayat Killa.

Meanwhile, Captain Ryder's company of the 35th Sikhs on the far right had been closely engaged and had signalled for help. They were encumbered with wounded and were running short of ammunition. Seeing their weakness the tribesmen redoubled their efforts to cut them off, firing repeatedly and, when close enough, charging with swords. On receiving Ryder's message Jeffreys ordered Campbell's Guides to disengage from the left and advance rapidly across the valley to extricate this company.

The Guides had already marched 16 miles that day and now had another four to cover. Nevertheless they did it, as only the Guides could, and not a moment too soon. The company was outnumbered and surrounded on three sides, Ryder and his other British officer were both wounded, the sepoys were exhausted and beginning to lose heart, and in many cases had only their bayonets left to fight with.

Approaching Ryder's hill the Guides deployed into line, fixed bayonets and doubled forward to the foot. There they halted and opened fire with company volleys. The concentrated impact of well-aimed .45in. bullets among the close-packed tribesmen quickly turned the tide. Havildar Ali Gul, a Guides Afridi, ran up to the Sikhs with as much ammunition as he could carry and, having distributed it, carried down a wounded Sikh officer. Other Guides rushed up to bring back more wounded. Thus freed from imminent disaster and responsibility for their casualties, Ryder's men managed to run down and reform behind the Guides.

All then began the return march to camp. However, encouraged by the now-failing light, the Mamunds returned to harass the march, which perforce became a fighting withdrawal. Elsewhere across the valley it was the same; the enemy, spread over three miles in a great half-moon formation, advanced firing at the rearguards of the Buffs and 35th Sikhs. It grew dark. Then a thunderstorm burst overhead, the lightning showing the way across the very broken ground but also illuminating, for the tribesmen, the path of the marching troops. Churchill,

Officers killed by the Mamunds. From left: Capt. Tomkins, Lt. Bailey, both 38th Dogras, at Markhanai, 14 September; Lt. Hughes, 35th Sikhs, at Shahi Tangi, 16 September. (Author's collection)

with the Buffs, saw tribesmen rushing up close to fire and yell insults. "They were answered with such taunts as the limited Pushtu of the British soldier allows and careful volleys. The men were determined, the officers cheery, the shooting accurate"[11].

When they were about two miles from camp the Mamunds decided that enough was enough and fell away, back into the night. Curiously it was then, with the tension eased, that the accumulated fatigue of 13 hours' continual marching and fighting, without food, began to tell – particularly on the younger soldiers. The last stretch, stumbling along in the pitch dark, was a most wearisome ordeal for Buffs and Sikhs alike. To cap it all, as the exhausted infantry reached camp around 9p.m., the rain, which hitherto had held off, came down in torrents. The Guides came in half an hour later with Ryder's company, their skill, endurance, experience and spirit having filled another "brilliant page in the history of the finest and most famous Frontier regiment"[12].

So ended the action of 16 September, in a sea of mud, shelterless – the tents having been struck earlier in the day – with no supper, the many wounded lying in pain in the open, everything made more chaotic by darkness and exhaustion. The troops' only consolation was that the Mamunds must also have had enough, and would not attack again that night.

That was to underestimate this "pestilential" enemy. When the rain stopped after an hour the officers set about restoring some sort of order and organising food and shelter for the men. It was quickly discovered that not all the brigade was complete, and among the missing was the brigadier, Jeffreys himself. Almost simultaneously they heard the sound of gunfire to the north-west. Clearly the Mamunds were not cowed yet.

During the evening's retirement Jeffreys had been moving with four guns of No. 8 Battery and 30 Bengal Sappers under Lieutenants Watson and Colvin, escorted by two companies of the 35th Sikhs. Concerned for the Guides' safety, he ordered a halt near the village of Bilot. Somehow, in the darkness, the Sikh companies had not received the order and marched on to camp. Shortly afterwards Corporal James Smith and 11 men of the Buffs appeared, looking for a wounded officer. When the thunderstorm broke Jeffreys decided to shelter in the village.

Unfortunately the enemy had preceded them. As the party reached Bilot, flaming bundles of dried grass were thrown out of the houses to illuminate their approach, followed by a hail of rifle-fire at very close range from two sides. The party immediately took cover in ditches and behind low walls in a rough square to protect the guns, which were hastily assembled to fire case-shot at the houses.

There now began a murderous close-quarter fire-fight. This was to last nearly four hours, as the 100-odd troops strove to hold a position little more than 25 yards square, while also being beset by mules careering about, driven frantic by the storm, the shooting and the fire-balls. The enemy could move freely about the village, though any attempt to charge withered under the rapid fire of the Buffs' Lee-Metfords.

Rather than remaining to be shot or burned Lieutenant Watson called for volunteers to charge the nearest houses. Followed by Colvin, Corporal Smith with his Buffs and some Sappers, they rushed forward with bayonets. The tribesmen retreated deeper into the maze-like village, leaving blazing grass bundles to bar the way. Watson's hand was smashed by a bullet, but this did not deter him from leading another charge; again he was wounded, more severely, and his men had to carry him back. Colvin and Corporal Smith made two more efforts to clear the nearest houses; but their numbers were too few to risk penetrating too far into the village, and they now had wounded to evacuate. Smith held the foothold gained with his men while Colvin ran back to fetch more Sappers; he then helped to carry away the wounded despite being slightly injured himself.

Within the tiny perimeter Jeffreys and the battery commander were both hit, though not severely. Lieutenant

Wynter, RA, took over the guns and continued to command them even after he too was shot, in both legs, until he fainted from loss of blood. All around the casualties were mounting and, if the enemy tried a massed rush, the end could not have been far off.

Finally, at midnight, more troops came out of the darkness. Earlier the previous evening two companies each of the Guides and the 35th Sikhs, who had been left in camp that morning, had gone out under Major Worlledge to support the retreating Guides. They had not found them and became benighted. Hearing the firing they had marched towards Bilot, and now drove the enemy out of the village. No further attacks occurred, and with the dawn came the 38th Dogras and some cavalry to escort the survivors of Bilot back to Inayat Killa.

The 24 hours' operations in the Mamund Valley had cost the 2nd Brigade 38 killed and 111 wounded, the hardest hit being the 35th Sikhs with 23 killed and 48 wounded, including one British officer dead and three severely wounded. No.8 Battery, besides 29 casualties, had also lost 31 mules. For Frontier warfare such losses called into question the success or failure of the operation. The Mamunds had been underestimated and they would have seen the withdrawal as a victory for them; against that, some of their villages had been destroyed, at least 200 of them had been killed, and they had been given a taste of British and Indian troops' fighting qualities, of which hitherto they had been ignorant.

Those qualities were later recognised by the authorities in India by the awards of three Victoria Crosses, to Lieutenants Watson and Colvin, both Royal Engineers, and Corporal Smith of the Buffs; two DSOs, to Major Campbell of the Guides and Lieutenant Wynter RA; four DCMs to men of the Buffs who had fought at Bilot; and a number of Orders of Merit to Indian ranks.

After a day of rest on the 17th, when the dead were buried (in unmarked graves to avoid later desecration), operations were resumed over the next five days to continue the destruction of the Mamund villages. The lessons of the 16th had been learned, and on each day all four battalions, supported by the guns and the Lancers protecting the flanks, were deployed against each objective. The pattern remained the same, culminating in a tribal onset as soon as the withdrawal began. However, so well was the retirement drill now practised, with all movement covered by fire, that few casualties were sustained and the enemy never succeeded in getting close. By the 23rd another four villages had been obliterated and a large stock of forage for the transport and other animals had been captured, at a cost of four killed and 24 wounded. The Mamunds seemed to be showing signs of having had enough.

* * *

These unexpected nine days' operations against the Mamunds had interrupted the prosecution of Sir Bindon Blood's prime task, to link up with Elles' field force to punish the Mohmands. On hearing of the Mamund trouble the government had wanted Blood to deploy both the 2nd and 3rd Brigades against them. He had considered this unsafe due to his situation at Nawagai.

Ten miles to his south lay the Badmanai Pass, held in strength by the Hadda Mullah and his Mohmands. Close by was the territory of the Khan of Nawagai, who thus far had remained neutral but whose intentions were uncertain.

Blood believed that if he went back to Inayat Killa with the 3rd Brigade, abandoning Nawagai, this could incite the Khan to throw in his lot with the Mohmands and Mamunds. This in turn could bring out the Utman Khel to the east; all Bajaur would be in arms, and probably Swat and Dir as well. He therefore decided to remain in his entrenched camp at Nawagai with the 3rd Brigade, trusting that his presence would sufficiently cow the local Khan, and wait for the Mohmand Field Force to make contact while Jeffreys dealt with the Mamunds.

Even so he was dangerously isolated. By 19 September the Hadda Mullah's forces lay between him and Elles, still over 20 miles to the south. The day before cavalry patrols had skirmished with groups of tribesmen advancing from Badmanai. Jeffreys' 2nd Brigade, as has been seen, was fully committed 15 miles to the north-east. The 1st Brigade, further east guarding the lines of communication, had insufficient transport to move. Furthermore Nawagai was too close for comfort to the Afghan border across which, so Jeffreys believed, assistance had come to aid the Mamunds. Blood therefore ensured the Nawagai camp was as strong as possible.

It was as well he did so. In the late afternoon of the 19th his cavalry scouts were fired on by a long line of tribesmen on the plain towards Badmanai. These were followed, towards sunset, by a host of some 3,000 making a great demonstration of hostility, though remaining safely out of range. As darkness fell the whole brigade stood to, expecting an imminent attack; but only a few forays were made, presumably to test the defences, and these were easily repelled.

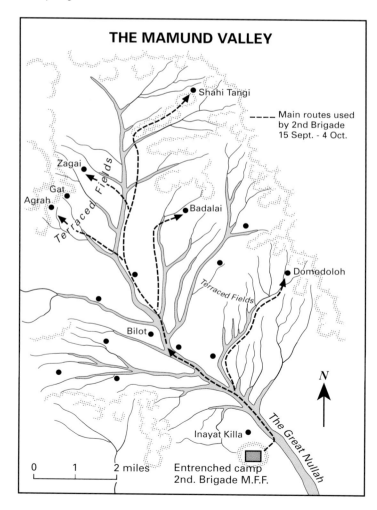

THE MAMUND VALLEY

Shahi Tangi

Main routes used by 2nd Brigade 15 Sept. - 4 Oct.

Zagai

Gat
Agrah

Badalai

Domodoloh

Bilot

Inayat Killa

The Great Nullah

0   1   2 miles

Entrenched camp 2nd. Brigade M.F.F.

N

Blood's decision to keep an eye on the Khan of Nawagai was justified the next day when the latter sent a warning that a major attack would come that night; the Khan had clearly chosen which horse to back. He further warned that the Hadda Mullah's men had been joined by a contingent of Shinwaris, who had also been promised total victory or unparalleled delights in the next world by another zealot, the Suffi Mullah. This warning was corroborated by cavalry patrols' observations during the late afternoon.

The 3rd Brigade's camp at Nawagai formed a rough square with a strong entrenched perimeter wall all round, the north and south sides being about 220 yards long, the east and west 300 yards. The whole north side and north-west angle were held by the 22nd Punjabis with, to their left and right rear respectively, No.1 (British) Mountain Battery and a squadron of 11th Bengal Lancers; between the two latter and behind the Punjabis were the British and Indian field hospitals. Half of the west and south sides were held by the 1st Queen's, the corresponding angle on the other side being the responsibility of the 39th Garhwal Rifles, whose left was prolonged by a company of Sappers, linking up with the Lancers. Behind these two battalions were the supplies and transport and, in the centre of the square, the quarters of Blood and Brigadier Wodehouse. Before last light bonfires were built at intervals 100 feet outside the perimeter, all tents were struck, and picquets posted along the edge of a deep nullah 50 yards in front of the Queens' sector.

At 8.30p.m. the bonfires were lit, the defences manned, and everyone not required on the perimeter ordered to lie down. Almost at once long-range firing began from the

The 35th Sikhs' final counter-attack at Shahi Tangi on 16 September to cover the evacuation of their casualties. This was the battalion to which Winston Churchill attached himself that day, making a narrow escape when the Mamunds followed the withdrawing unit down a steep spur in a classic demonstration of one of the Pathans' most dangerous tactics. Drawn by W.B. Wollen from a sketch by Maj. Powell, on the staff of Jeffreys' 2nd Brigade that day. (Author's collection)

surrounding heights, but most shots only found targets among the unfortunate animals. Suddenly the picquets ran in to report swordsmen in the nullah. Then began the attacks that were to last nearly six hours.

The form never varied: a preparatory fusillade, followed by groups of about 150 swordsmen rushing forward to hurl themselves at or over the defenders, backed up by much larger groups ready to exploit any weakness. For them to come again and again as they did, in the old Pathan style thought, by experienced Frontier men, to be too foolhardy against modern weapons, their belief in the promises of their mullahs must have been unquestioning. Attacks were launched without a care for death all round the perimeter, but the main effort bore increasingly upon the sector held by the 1st Queen's. If they could but break through the invisible wall of the Lee-Metfords' magazine fire, then doubtless the Indian battalions would be easier prey. But Lieutenant-Colonel Collins' West Surreys were up to the challenge, as Churchill described:

"Their fire was crushing, their discipline was admirable, and the terrible weapon with which they were armed, and its more terrible bullet, stopped every rush. When the enemy charged, the order to employ magazine fire was passed. The guns fired star-shell. These great rockets bursting into stars in the air slowly fell to the ground, shedding a pale and ghastly light on the swarming figures of the tribesmen as they ran swiftly forward. Then the popping of musketry became one intense roar. Nothing could live in front of such a fire. Valour, ferocity, fanaticism availed nothing. All were swept away. The whistles sounded, the independent fire stopped with machine-like precision, and the steady section volleys were resumed. This happened not once but a dozen times during the six hours"[13]. The Queen's lost only one man killed and three wounded.

The "terrible bullet" was the Dum-Dum, so called from the arsenal where it was made near Calcutta. Its lead nose was unjacketed, causing it to spread upon impact. The state of enemy corpses seen after this attack by a correspondent was "sufficient to show that the Lee-Metford, now that it has the Dum-Dum cartridge, is a weapon in which the soldier may have every confidence. What it hits it stops; so much so that the question of its capabilities of stopping a Ghazi rush need never more be discussed"[14].

The other faces of the square all held, having only 20 men wounded. In the centre Brigadier Wodehouse, whose headquarters had been badly shot up, received a painful wound in the leg. By 2a.m. the mullahs' promises of victory and invulnerability had proved so hollow that the tribesmen gave up, carrying off with them most of their dead and dying. It was later learned that the enemy had lost over 300 dead.

Not only had the night attack at Nawagai been decisively defeated, but so disillusioned were the tribesmen in its aftermath that most of the Hadda Mullah's host began to crumble away. The following day, the 21st, contact was made with Brigadier Elles' 1st Brigade, and Wodehouse's 3rd Brigade - now under Colonel Graves of the 39th Garhwalis - was transferred to the Mohmand Field Force. When these two brigades attacked Badmanai on the 23rd they reached the top with little loss in time to see the enemy in full flight. Blood and his headquarters returned to Inayat Killa, leaving Elles to mop up the Mohmands.

* * *

On rejoining Jeffreys, Blood found that notwithstanding the destruction of their villages the Mamunds had not yet submitted and, in particular, had not handed back rifles which they had captured on 16 September. Because of the 280 casualties sustained by the 2nd Brigade he summoned up from the 1st Brigade the 1st Royal West Kent, 31st Punjabis and No.7 (British) Mountain Battery to replace the Buffs, 35th Sikhs and No.8 Battery. When the two Kent regiments changed over, Churchill heard an old Buff tell a friend in the West Kents: "Don't go near no officers nor white stones"[15]. He also noted how the 2nd Brigade regretted the Buffs' departure, the regiment having proved that "the British infantry battalion is the backbone of every mixed brigade. They shared with the Guides Infantry one of those enviable reputations for steadiness which are so hard to gain and so easy to lose on active service"[16].

The Mamunds then sent in a deputation to enquire what terms were on offer. They were told to return the captured rifles by 29 September. Confident that Jeffreys could handle matters, Blood rode on to the Panjkora River, where he learned that he was to command the 1st Division of the Tirah Field Force then being formed to deal with the Afridis. Later it transpired that the Mamunds had been playing for time while waiting for rifles, ammunition and some reinforcements from Afghanistan, and by the 29th not one Mamund had come in to surrender. When so informed, and concerned at the possible effect on Bajaur and Dir, Blood recommended to the government that he be left to settle the whole northern region, rather than leave for his new command. This was agreed and the Tirah force's loss became the Malakand force's gain. Blood now ordered Jeffreys to advance against the Mamunds.

On 30 September the reconstituted 2nd Brigade was launched against the two fortified villages of Agrah and Gat, far off in the north-west corner of the Mamund territory, only some five miles from the Afghan border and hitherto untouched. Half a mile apart and mutually supporting, they stood on the lower slopes of steep hills with their flanks guarded by spurs covered in large rocks - "the strongest position of any yet seen"[17].

The brigade's advance could not be concealed, and before long the tribal drums could be heard beating urgently in the still air as the Mamunds massed round their standards on the spurs and cliffs behind the villages. Off to the left more were to be seen hurrying through thick scrub and boulders to outflank any advance. However, the sight of the Guides Cavalry riding forward checked them; as the cavalryman-turned-correspondent Lord Fincastle observed, "these tribesmen have the most exaggerated notion of the power of cavalry"[18].

Jeffreys ordered the Guides Infantry to clear a spur some thousand yards west of Agrah while the Royal West Kent attacked up a hill to their right, prior to encircling the village. The 31st Punjabis were to clear the low spur between the two villages before attacking Gat. The 38th Dogras were to be in reserve. Covered by the British gunners the Guides scrambled up with their usual skill and dash, their two leading companies, all Afridis and other Pathans, clearing the sangars at the top with an unstoppable, yelling charge and without losing a single man. Watching them Churchill was reminded of "a well-trained pack of hounds, for their cries, their movements, their natures are similar"[19]. They opened fire at the fleeing enemy and prepared to guard the British battalion's left flank.

The West Kents, the old "Dirty Half-Hundred"[20], must have known their performance would be measured against that of the Buffs. They made good progress up the hill but met stiffer resistance in Agrah. They fought their way through and advanced to clear some sangars beyond; behind them the Bengal Sappers set about destroying the village.

Meanwhile the 31st Punjabis on the right had been held up by very heavy fire from some huge boulders to their front and from their right. They returned the fire while orders were sent to the guns to engage the boulders and two companies of the 38th Dogras came up to clear their right. The gunfire, though accurate, could not shift the tribesmen from their cover, so Lieutenant-Colonel O'Bryen of the Punjabis ordered a charge. He had been exposing himself fearlessly, encouraging his men and directing their fire, but thereby enabling the Mamund marksmen to identify him as an important commander. Now, as his Punjabis rose to charge, he fell mortally wounded. His sepoys, who as Churchill observed "were devoted to him"[21], cleared the boulders with the bayonet but then came under renewed fire from further back and around Gat.

The night battle at Bilot, 16-17 September, drawn by W.B. Wollen from a sketch by Maj. Powell; and inset, the Bilot VCs: Lts. Watson and Colvin, RE, and Cpl. Smith, Buffs. (Author's collection)

When Jeffreys saw the Punjabis' first check he had ordered the West Kents to wheel right on to their left flank. The ground, terraced fields with high-standing crops, was infested with enemy. The leading company stormed a sangar, drove the tribesmen out but immediately came under intense fire from higher ground. Several men who had entered the sangar were hit. Lieutenant Browne-Clayton ordered others to clear the casualties out. Once it was clear he turned to follow, and was shot dead. Three men picked up the body but were forced to drop it as some Ghazis rushed them. Seeing the sangar and the body lost, Captain Styles' company counter-attacked and recovered both. However, with enemy pressure from the east increasing, Styles fell back on the rest of the battalion which had now linked up with the Punjabis.

The Guides, still holding the left spur, had come under attack again, and a widening gap had occurred to their right owing to the West Kent's right wheel, through which tribesmen were pouring down to threaten the British battalion's left rear. On the right, despite the protection afforded by the two Dogra companies, an enemy move was developing against the Punjabis' right rear. Although casualties had been inflicted on the Mamunds, Agrah destroyed and Gat shelled, the operation, rather than chastening the enemy, seemed to have attracted reinforcements from other parts of the valley - and possibly, on previous evidence, from over the border. It was mid-afternoon, the brigade was ten miles from camp, and there were 12 dead and 49 wounded to be taken back. This

would delay the march, particularly as the more lightly wounded would have to be assisted by their comrades owing to an insufficiency of stretchers and *dhoolies*. Mindful of the Mamunds' relentlessness in pursuit, Jeffreys decided it was time to go.

As the infantry companies began to cover each other back, No.7 Battery opened fire with shrapnel upon the spurs down which the inevitable follow-up started to roll. The accuracy and speed with which the British gunners worked their guns ensured a less determined pursuit than on previous occasions. Once clear of the spurs, and with the rear covered by the much-feared Guides Cavalry, the brigade was able to reach camp unharassed in daylight.

Churchill reminded his readers at home of the cost to their soldiers: "At the head of the column of dhoolies and stretchers were the bodies of the killed, each roped on to a mule. Their heads hung down one side, their legs on the other. The long black hair of Sikhs [of the 31st Punjabis], which was draggled with dust and blood, imparted a hideous aspect. At the entrance to the camp a group of surgeons - their sleeves rolled up - awaited the wounded. Two operating tables, made of medical boxes and covered with waterproof sheets, were also prepared. There is a side to warfare browner than khaki"[22]. Had the West Kent soldier, warned by his Buffs friend, witnessed this scene, he would have realised the wisdom of keeping clear of officers: out of 11 West Kent officers, eight had been hit or grazed by bullets.

On 3 October the brigade went out again to complete the destruction of Badalai, which had been started by the Buffs on 16 September before they were called away to support the 35th Sikhs. There was little opposition, and the subsequent pursuit was pounded by the screw-guns and shot down at 800 yards by the West Kent's Lee-Metfords. The Mamunds lost heavily, both in men and in heart, and made off.

Meanwhile Blood, on hearing of the Agrah action, decided to return to Inayat Killa with reinforcements and finish the Mamunds once and for all. Besides more mountain guns, cavalry, and half the 24th Punjabis, he brought the 2nd Highland Light Infantry and the 12-pounders of 10th Field Battery. By 4 October all were present. Before they could be used, however, the Mamunds sued for peace.

They had resisted for seven weeks, far longer than anyone had anticipated, but despite inflicting considerable casualties in men and animals they too had lost many men, their villages were ruined and their supplies very depleted; it was time to stop fighting and start sowing their crops. Even so they were to prevaricate over their total submission for another fortnight.

The 2nd Highland Light Infantry, the old 74th, who had been warned for service on the Frontier over two months earlier, had so far done nothing but march hither and thither between Nowshera, the borderlands of the Bunerwals, and Bajaur, which they had now reached. A sergeant recorded that "everyone was naturally impatient to test their fighting powers against such a bold and plucky foe" as the Mamunds. However, after one brief foray when they had little to do other than watch the Guides demonstrate how it was done, they learned that the Mamunds were definitely submitting. "If ever a battalion was disgusted at the turn of affairs, it was the 2nd HLI"[23] They need not have complained: their turn would come.

The Mamunds handed over the captured rifles, expressed regret, swore they had only fought because they feared annexation, and vowed to fight no more. In view of the destruction wrought upon their villages and crops and their nigh-on one thousand casualties they were spared further punishment. Their undertakings were accepted; and the Malakand Field Force marched away eastwards.

By late October, as will be seen, the Mohmands had been punished, the Tirah Field Force was entering the Afridi homeland, while in distant Tochi the submission of the Madda Khel was still awaited. The main focus of effort was now the Tirah; but there still remained the Bunerwals, whose chastisement for their part at Malakand Blood had been obliged to defer in late August. He had no intention of leaving them undisturbed as a possible focus for disaffected elements in the north.

The 1st Queen's defending their perimeter during the Mohmand night attack on 3rd Brigade's entrenched camp at Nawagai, 19 September. Watercolour by Maj.Hobday, R.A. (The Queen's Royal Surrey Regiment)

Continued on page 74

COLOUR PLATES A-D

Plate A: Pathan tribesmen

In any group photograph, of whatever tribe, the appearance of individuals will be found to vary; but Pathan dress did include certain common items. A pointed kulla or a skullcap was worn, around which was usually tied a turban (pagri or lungi). A long, loosely cut angarka smock of cotton or coarse wool, girded with a cummerbund, was worn over loose, wide-legged pyjama trousers varying in length from mid-calf to instep; another type, partig, were gathered at the ankles. Over all might be worn a poshteen, a sheepskin coat with the fleece inside, again of varying length and with long or short sleeves; a cotton or woollen chadar shawl; or both, depending on the weather. Footwear was typically chapplis, sandals of leather or plaited dried grass. The most common clothing colour was off-white, although shades of blue were noted among Afridis, Mamunds and Swatis; the Bunerwals favoured dark blue or black garments; and Waziris wore dark red or dark blue lungis. Weapons are discussed in Chapter One, which see also for photographs.

Figure A1, based on drawings by Major Hobday, RA, and Lieutenant Dixon, 16th Lancers, is a warrior of one of the northern tribes, a Mamund or Swati, ready with his dole drum to summon his comrades to action. A chora or Khyber knife, with a two-foot blade, is thrust through his cummerbund. A2, based on photographs, is one of the formidable foes of the Tirah Field Force: an Afridi wearing a poshteen but without a lungi, armed with a Martini-Henry rifle and a curved tulwar sword, his ammunition carried in a captured Indian Army pouch.

The Tochi Field Force:
B1: Captain, 2nd Battalion, Argyll and Sutherland Highlanders (Princess Louise's)

Both the British and Indian elements of the Army in India had worn khaki drill clothing for all types of field service since 1885, but with many variations between types of unit and between the two elements. This officer of Highlanders, based on photographs and contemporary drawings, wears the foreign service helmet; Scottish pattern drill frock (as the jacket was then termed); kilt of the Government tartan called "Sutherland" in this regiment; regimental sporran with the badger head peculiar to officers and sergeants; hose with garters, and khaki gaiters. He is accoutred with a Sam Browne belt with double braces to support revolver and broadsword, a haversack and a water bottle. This battalion was issued with quilted neck curtains for the helmets, and with sunglasses, but these were not always worn. The 3rd Rifle Brigade, also in Tochi, dressed as English infantry (cf. F1, G1) but with black accoutrements and puttees.

B2: Gunner, 6th (Bombay) Mountain Battery

Unlike most Indian cavalry and infantry, who wore loose blouses or kurtas in field service order, Indian gunners wore frocks similar to those of the Royal Artillery, and the latter's dark blue puttees, but with the knickerbocker trousers common to most dismounted Indian troops. This Sikh gunner, from photographs, is armed with the special mountain artillery sword suspended from a shoulder belt; the same weapon was issued to RA gunners, who were dressed similarly except for helmets and straight trousers. This man, who is also equipped with a haversack and water bottle, is preparing to sponge out the 2.5in.RML "screw-gun".

The Malakand Garrison and Field Force:
C1: Sowar, Queen's Own Corps of Guides (Cavalry), Punjab Frontier Force

This Afridi trooper, after photographs and watercolours by A.C.Lovett, wears the long, collarless cavalry kurta with shoulder chains, and regimental red cummerbund. At this date the Guides Cavalry had khaki puttees rather than the dark blue or black worn by other Indian cavalry (cf. D2); and wore this coloured pagri in place of the khaki of the Guides Infantry, with a red kulla for Mohammedan personnel. He is accoutred with pouch belt and sword belt based on the Sam Browne principle, with ammunition pouch attached. His weapons are the Martini-Henry carbine, and the three-bar-hilted sword issued to this regiment - other Indian cavalry had swords according to regimental choice. After the Malakand operations the Guides joined the Buner Field Force.

C2: Sepoy, 45th (Rattray's Sikh) Regiment, Bengal Infantry

This private soldier, from photographs, wears the Indian infantry kurta, knickerbocker trousers, puttees and native shoes. His pagri is tied over the red (or white) cloth pag in the distinctive Sikh manner. Some Sikh regiments wore a full size quoit around the turban (see H1); Rattray's had a quoit badge, though not worn in the field. All Indian troops other than Rifles had brown leather equipment, here the Indian equivalent of the British Slade-Wallace pattern; he also carries a haversack, and the circular Indian Army water bottle in a khaki cover (see E2). He is armed with the .45in. Martini-Henry rifle and 18in. sword bayonet.

The Malakand and Buner Field Forces:
D1: Private, 2nd Battalion, Highland Light Infantry (City of Glasgow Regiment)

Photographs of this battalion show the quite common practice among British infantry of sewing cartridge loops above the breast pockets of the frock; this gave the rifleman ten rounds more immediately accessible than those in the belt pouches, particularly when lying down. Below the khaki frock - of Scottish pattern, with cutaway skirts - he wears Mackenzie tartan trousers. (The 2nd KOSB, in the Tirah Field Force, were similarly dressed but with Government tartan trousers; the 1st RSF's were khaki.) By this date most British battalions had the buff leather (black for Rifles) 1888 pattern Slade-Wallace equipment with its original pouches, although this battalion and the 1st Gordons had improved 1894 pouches with the flap opening outwards instead of upwards, fastened by a strap from the back of the pouch; both patterns had an exterior cartridge loop at either end for immediate use. The Indian pattern water bottle used by British troops was square-shaped (see G1). The rifle is the .303in. Lee-Metford with 12in. sword bayonet.

D2: Rissaldar, 10th Bengal (Duke of Cambridge's Own) Lancers

This regiment, and the 11th, each had one squadron with the Malakand Field Force; the 10th's was later joined by the rest of the regiment in the Buner Field Force. This Mussulman Rajput officer, taken from a photograph, is uniformed similarly to the Guides sowar (C1) but with a collar to his kurta, and black puttees. The gold tip to his red kulla denotes commissioned rank, in addition to the insignia on his shoulder chains. Two lanyards are worn round the neck, one attached to the revolver holstered on his waist belt, the other to a whistle in the breast pocket. The sword belt has a broader cross-brace than the conventional Sam Browne; this was not worn by sowars, but they had a belt of similar width over the left shoulder for attachment of the carbine when this was not carried in its bucket attached to the saddle. The 10th Lancers sword had a pierced steel guard.

A1: Northern Pathan drummer

A2: Afridi tribesman

B2: Gunner, 6th (Bombay) Mountain Artillery Battery

B1: Captain, 2nd Battalion,
Argyll & Sutherland Highlanders

PLATE C

C1: Sowar, Guides Cavalry, Punjab Frontier Force

C2: Sepoy, 45th (Rattray's Sikh) Regiment, Bengal Infantry

D2: Rissaldar, 10th Bengal Lancers

D1: Private, 2nd Battalion, Highland Light Infantry

E1: Second Lieutenant, 2nd Battalion, Oxfordshire Light Infantry

E2: Sepoy, 20th (Punjab) Regiment, Bengal Infantry

F1: Naik, 1st Battalion,
2nd Gurkha Regiment

F2: Piper, 1st Battalion, Gordon Highlanders

G1: Sergeant, 1st Battalion, Northamptonshire Regiment

G2: Sapper, Bombay Sappers & Miners

H1: Subedar, 36th (Sikh) Regiment, Bengal Infantry

H2: Signaller, 2nd Battalion, Derbyshire Regiment

COLOUR PLATES E-H

The Mohmand Field Force:
E1: Second Lieutenant, 2nd Battalion, Oxfordshire Light Infantry

This battalion served with the 2nd Brigade and later with the Peshawar Column. Based on a photograph and a regimental officer's list of equipment carried on service, the figure represents the English infantry subaltern of 1897 (although the small button with braid loop on the collar was peculiar to this regiment). At this date captain's rank was displayed by two stars or "pips" (see Plate B1), lieutenant's by one, and second lieutenants, as here, had none. The two pouches on the Sam Browne belt contained binoculars and revolver ammunition. The cord from the second button suspended a whistle in the right breast pocket. Officers could equip themselves with a revolver of their choice as long as it would take .45in. ammunition; the Webley was a popular model. Recently commissioned officers, and perhaps some wealthier ones, would have had this new 1895 pattern sword with steel guard, but others would still have the old brass-hilted 1822 pattern with 1845 or 1892 blade. Some officers provided themselves with stout khud sticks for use when hill-climbing, or even as a substitute for the sword. Helmets purchased by officers were of a similar pattern, while those issued to the men could vary slightly in shape between battalions (cf. D1, F2, G1, H2).

E2: Sepoy, 20th (Duke of Cambridge's Own) (Punjab) Regiment, Bengal Infantry

This class-company regiment served in the 1st Brigade of the Mohmand Field Force, later transferring to the Buner Field Force. The Punjabi Mussulman illustrated gives another view of the basic service clothing and equipment seen in C2. The method of tying his pagri reflects his class (racial type), not a regimental practice; a Sikh sepoy of the 20th Punjabis would tie his turban similarly to C2. The green kulla and pagri fringe echo the green facings of this regiment's drab-coloured full dress tunics.

The Tirah Field Force:
F1: Naik, 1st Battalion, 2nd (Prince of Wales's Own) Gurkha Regiment (Sirmoor Rifles)

Although the 1/2nd used the spelling "Goorkha", their official title was as above. Apart from the Kilmarnock cap, with the regimental badge of the Prince of Wales's Feathers, this 2nd Division battalion adopted a more British style of clothing than Indian infantry, and indeed, than other Gurkha battalions: all ranks wore frocks rather than kurtas, the red collar piping reflecting the red facings of this regiment's Rifle green full dress tunics. All Gurkhas wore British-style trousers. This corporal, from a photograph, has the black leather equipment befitting a Rifle regiment; it supports pouches of a different pattern to those worn by C2, with his bayonet on the left side and the kukri peculiar to Gurkha troops behind the right hip. The circular Indian Army water bottle is slung high to clear access to the kukri. Curiously for a Rifle battalion, the 1/2nd appear to have retained the Martini-Henry's old triangular section socket bayonet rather than the sword type. The 2/4th Gurkhas had the same equipment as this battalion; the 1/3rd wore the pattern illustrated in C2, but in black. Both those battalions wore kurtas rather than frocks; the 1/3rd had black puttees, and neck curtains on their Kilmarnocks.

F2: Piper, 1st Battalion, Gordon Highlanders

This figure, from photographs, represents the six pipers who made a significant contribution to the Gordons' taking of Dargai during the 2nd Division attack of 20 October. On service the pipers were dressed as the NCOs and men, with the Scottish frock, Gordon tartan kilt, sporran with covered cantle, hose, garters and gaiters. The Gordons wore khaki covers over their white helmets, and had been issued with neck curtains, but did not wear them in Tirah. The piper's usual personal weapon was a dirk suspended from the waist belt, but photographs show that in Tirah pipers carried a sword similar to, or even the same as, the mountain artillery pattern, suspended from a shoulder belt (cf. B2). In addition they wore the Slade-Wallace equipment without pouches, to support their mess-tins and rolled gathri or "Guthrie" coats (see G1, H2), but with belt and braces blackened, as were their full dress accoutrements. The 2nd KOSB's pipers, with Royal Stuart tartan kilts, appear in a photograph with this same sword but with their home service waist belts.

G1: Sergeant, 1st Battalion, Northamptonshire Regiment

This figure from another heavily-engaged 2nd Division unit is based on eyewitness drawings by Melton Prior and the recollections of General Sir Harry Knox, who served as a regimental subaltern in Tirah. This battalion's sergeants had gold lace chevrons on their khaki frocks, its corporals having white, as in most British battalions - although KOSB and Gordons corporals followed earlier practice in wearing red chevrons. All rank chevrons were worn on the right sleeve only, and good conduct chevrons reversed above the left cuff. Sergeant's red sashes were not worn in the field. The Northamptons were not issued with helmet covers or curtains; their helmets were similar in shape to those worn by the Gordons (see F2) but stained khaki - as was their Slade-Wallace equipment, which had the 1888 pouches. The square-shaped water bottle issued to British troops in India is slung over his left shoulder, and strapped to the waist belt is the rolled gathri coat (see H2) with dulled mess-tin on top, its black cover discarded. The rifle is the Lee-Metford. Other English infantry in the campaign were of similar appearance, although the 1st Dorsets had helmet curtains.

G2: Sapper, Bombay Sappers and Miners

Sappers and Miners were the Indian equivalent of the Royal Engineers, and were vital for the efficient functioning of a field force in terrain like the Tirah. Two Bombay companies supported the 1st Division, one Madras company and some Imperial Service sappers the 2nd, and two Bengal companies the other elements of the Tirah Field Force. Like the Indian Mountain Artillery they wore frocks rather than kurtas. The Madras sappers had a special fez-type headdress, khaki puttees, and the same infantry equipment as C2. This Bombay sapper, from photographs, has the same pattern equipment as F1 but in brown leather, and the Martini-Henry rifle. Behind him is one of the invaluable mules, laden with tools for route clearance. A photograph of Bombay Pioneeers, who could assist sappers or fight as infantry, can be found in Chapter Six.

H1: Subedar, 36th (Sikh) Regiment, Bengal Infantry

This plate illustrates the cold weather clothing adopted in Tirah by Indian and British infantry. Underneath the same kind of sheepskin poshteen as worn by A2 this Sikh officer, from a photograph, wears a frock rather than his men's kurta, but the same knickerbocker trousers and puttees. His Sam Browne belt has double braces supporting his sword and revolver. The steel throwing quoit, a traditional Sikh weapon imbued with religious significance, was worn by all ranks of this regiment around the turban in addition to the regimental badge. For photographs of sepoys and British and Indian officers of this particularly distinguished regiment of the 2nd Division, see Chapters Seven and Nine.

H2: Signaller, 2nd Battalion, Derbyshire Regiment (Sherwood Foresters)

This man wears the cold weather clothing described by Captain Slessor of this 1st Division battalion. The khaki drill trousers have been replaced by the home service type in dark blue serge with a red welt. Over all is worn the gathri or Guthrie coat of khaki serge lined with grey flannel; this was usually worn over the Slade-Wallace equipment to avoid having to lengthen the waist belt. The Derbys stained their equipment - which had the 1888 pouches - by soaking it in tea. Like the 1st Northamptons (see G1) and 2nd KOSB, they used a brown leather water bottle sling to suspend the Indian pattern container, instead of the cloth sling shown on F2 and also used by the 1st Dorsets. This signaller is using a 2ft.-square flag to send a message in Morse code, the dots and dashes being made with short and long waves of the flag. For Semaphore two flags were used; and for signalling over four miles' distance a 3ft.-square flag was needed. Behind him is other signalling equipment including the much-used heliograph. For a photograph of this battalion without gathris see Chapter Two.

Continued from page 63

The mountainous western border of Buner lay some 20 miles east of the Malakand–Mardan road and was pierced by three passes - from north to south Tanga, Pirsai and Ambela, the latter where heavy fighting had occurred in 1863. Blood planned to force the Tanga, then to wheel right through the territory and come out at Ambela. The new Buner Field Force was to consist of Meiklejohn's 1st Brigade and Jeffreys' 2nd Brigade plus divisional troops. Most of the force had been with him in Bajaur, but there were some new additions, and the 2nd HLI were now to get their longed-for chance against the same enemy whom their sister battalion, the 71st, had fought in 1863. To give time for the force to concentrate and to amass the necessary supplies and transport, the Bunerwals were told they had a month to submit or face the consequences.

While the HLI waited they played football against the West Kents, and the officers held a gymkhana and "rode to hounds" after jackal. One evening they put on a "Grand Musical Jirgah", with "Sniping Strictly Prohibited" during the reels, songs and other entertainments. Major Hobday sang *Ting-a-ling-ling* "with gusto"; Lance-Corporal Munn recited, "in true elocutionary style", *The Execution of Montrose*; while Corporal Godfrey was cheered to the echo

for his rendering of *He has never been the same man since*[24]. They only attended the English regiments' Christmas celebrations as spectators, but came into their own at Hogmanay in the peculiarly Scottish fashion. This was ill-timed, for the very next day Blood ordered the advance which, for the HLI, was a "kill-or-cure" march of 13 miles.

It was now clear that the Bunerwals would fight, and reconnaissance revealed that they were holding all three passes. The main attack, by the 1st Brigade on the Tanga, was to be assisted to the south by the Guides Infantry and 21st Punjabis clearing a way over the Pirsai for the cavalry to go through and threaten the enemy's line of retreat from the Tanga; and to the north by the 20th Punjabis turning the enemy's right.

As the latter moved off to the left on the morning of 7 January 1898 the 10th Field Battery opened fire at 2,200 yards against the clusters of standards marking the Bunerwals' positions on the crest, 600 yards long and 1,800 feet above the start line. Once the 12-pounders got the range the Buffs and 3rd Bombay Light Infantry extended to begin long-range volleys at 1,500 yards, under cover of which Nos.7 and 8 Mountain Batteries also got into action. Meanwhile the four assault battalions - West Kents on the right, HLI on the left, 16th Rajputs and 31st

Sketch, allegedly by an HLI officer, of the 2nd Highland Light Infantry attacking the Tanga Pass, 7 January 1898. See also Plate D. (The Highland Light Infantry)

12-pounder gun of 10th Field Battery RA on the march to Inayat Killa - a drawing by S. Begg from a photograph taken by the battery commander, which illustrates the limits placed on the mobility of field artillery in Frontier terrain. (Author's collection)

Punjabis in the centre - had been marching up the three miles from their camps. At midday, when the 20th Punjabis' flank move was well developed, the assault began.

Lance-Corporal Munn - the reciter of *Montrose* - later described the HLI's attack: "The command 'Fix Bayonets' was given and every man sprang eagerly to his feet. The enemy's standards were fluttering in the breeze far above us and the shells from the batteries flew screaming over our heads. The pass from the bottom does not look so steep as it really is. Before we had gone far, however, we found we were in for an exceedingly stiff climb. Soon we began to enter the fire zone, it being not only frontal but also from the left; but as the attack developed the firing from the left ceased, as the enemy positions were rushed and captured by the 20th PI. The farther we advanced upward the hotter the fire became, and the enemy now began to let loose immense boulders which came thundering down the hillside.

"Nothing could have been finer than the way all responded to the call made on them. Soon the enemy were seen to be in full retreat. Their position had become untenable from the moment the 20th PI had turned their flank. Now, scrambling up the last few yards, we all advanced together. One of the enemy came rushing down the slope, shouting and brandishing his sword. But our bullets soon accounted for him and a few minutes later we had all reached the crest of the pass, raising a cheer as we saw the enemy fast disappearing down the opposite slope"[25].

Another soldier, Private Boyle, remembered how, despite the steepness and difficulty of the climb, the pipers played *The Campbells are Coming* throughout, and must still have had enough "puff" at the top because "our pipers played, we gave a cheer, then we fell out to eat our bully beef and biscuits and have a good drink from our water bottles"[26].

By 2p.m. all battalions were on the crest and the Bunerwals were flying too fast to pursue, except with rifle-fire. After a much-needed rest the force advanced some two miles where it linked up with the cavalry from Pirsai, who had faced more resistance from the terrain than from the enemy.

Indeed, so formidable had been the force deployed that the Bunerwals seemed to have lost heart and, had Blood been able to continue his advance straightaway, the whole expedition could have been completed in a few days. As it was, he had to halt until the pass could be made practicable for mule traffic to bring up supplies and the

wherewithal for his men to exist, particularly at night when it was freezing cold. The troops had assaulted in very light order so, until the mules got through three days later, they had to find what shelter and subsistence they could in the local villages.

Eventually the force advanced in two columns, traversing the whole of Buner and meeting no resistance, only submissions, until they joined up with Jeffreys, who had been sent during the halt to secure the Ambela Pass. As the force withdrew through this pass the 2nd HLI halted where the 71st had fought and died 35 years before. The pipers played a tribute to their memory; and Corporal Munn no doubt spoke for all when he wrote: "I think most of us felt a glow of satisfaction as we stood there, remembering we had helped to avenge the deaths of our gallant 71st comrades"[27]. The two battalions of the Highland Light Infantry may still have called themselves 71st and 74th but they were, after all, now one regiment, and this act of remembrance was a token of the regimental spirit that inspired the British infantry.

* * *

So ended Sir Bindon Blood's successful six months' campaign with the Malakand and Buner Field Forces. From the Ambela Pass to the Afghan border 80 miles to the west, he had put down and punished all the uprisings in the northern region of the Pathan Revolt. Never again, while the British ruled India, would these tribes take up arms against them. Perhaps, as Blood received their submissions, he told their chiefs the story of his famous ancestor....

Men of the 1st Royal West Kents during the enforced halt after the Tanga Pass assault. Several wear knitted balaclavas rolled up as caps; two pose with Pathan tulwar swords; and note the 1882 Valise equipment still carried by this battalion. (Kent County Archive)

CHAPTER SIX

The Mohmand Dog

The pacification of the Bunerwals in January 1898 was nearly the final act of the Pathan Revolt, though the Afridis were still in arms south of the Khyber after five months' fighting. That campaign is yet to come; first the rest of the Mohmand uprising, which immediately preceded the Afridi insurrection and was touched upon in the last chapter, must be considered by returning in time to early August 1897.

The Mohmand lands straddled the Durand Line. On the Afghan side was a village called Hadda, from which hailed a mullah named Najb-ud-din, "a priest of great age and peculiar holiness"[1]. Some time beforehand he had quarrelled with the Amir, who had banished him from Afghanistan; but he craftily remained on close terms with the general commanding the Afghan forces in the east of that country from his new abode at Jarobi, just over the British side of the Line in tribal territory. Despite its remoteness his influence, always hostile to British power, became widespread. His attempts to hinder the Chitral Relief Expedition had been less than successful; but since then his urging of holy war had found a more receptive audience, particularly once the Swatis began their attack on Malakand. The Mohmands, whose barren, inhospitable hills and valleys yielded little, found the Hadda Mullah's eloquent promises of plunder or paradise too compelling to resist. Yet more Pathan children would find themselves fatherless to assuage an old priest's thirst for infidel blood.

On the north bank of the Kabul River, three miles inside the administrative border and therefore outside tribal territory, and 15 miles due north of the great British cantonment at Peshawar, stood the large fort of Shabkadr, built many years before by the Sikhs as a bulwark against the Mohmands, whose lands lay to the west between the Kabul River and Bajaur. Its 50-feet-high walls had once, in 1864, held a garrison of 1,800 troops at a time when the Mohmands, thinking to take advantage of British preoccupation with the Ambela operations, had advanced against it. They had been routed beneath its walls by a combination of the 3rd Rifle Brigade's musketry and a magnificent charge by the 7th Hussars. This had kept them quiet for 15 years until they attempted to capitalise upon the Second Afghan War, only to suffer such casualties that they had not ventured from their own lands since. In 1897 Shabkadr was garrisoned by a mere 50 Border Police whose task was to send early warning to Peshawar of any incursion from the west.

Close by Shabkadr Fort stood the village of Shankargarh, inhabited chiefly by Hindu merchants and moneylenders who made a good living out of the Pathan tribesmen either side of the border. With the quick ear of their ilk they had learned of imminent danger, and on the morning of 7 August 1897 they came clamouring to the fort for sanctuary. That afternoon, at 4p.m., some 4,000 Mohmands descended upon this village, butchered anyone they found and set it ablaze. They then turned their attention to the fort but, without artillery, were unable to make any impression on its massive walls or its defenders. The Border Police, having signalled the raid to Peshawar, were able to hold on without loss despite rifle-fire continuing for most of the night.

At Peshawar a column was formed under Colonel Woon of the 20th Punjabis from his regiment, two squadrons of the 13th Bengal Lancers, two companies of the 1st Somerset Light Infantry, and four Royal Artillery field guns. These marched through the night, their approach to the fort persuading the Mohmands to fall back to some low hills out of range, where they were joined by more of their clansmen.

At daybreak on 9 August, although the visible enemy outnumbered his force, Woon decided to attack. However, as the infantry advanced more enemy appeared and soon threatened to outflank the frontage of the Punjabis and the Somersets, thereby endangering their rear. With only some 700 rifles available and with the guns not yet in action (they had been delayed crossing some difficult ground), Woon converted his attack into a retirement on Shabkadr. As always when troops fell back, the tribesmen promptly came down from the hills in a long line to harry the withdrawal.

"There seemed to be no end of them", a soldier of the Somersets' F Company later wrote in a letter home, "the Artillery came into action and they sent our two companies to guard the left flank and rear about 600 yards away so we had to alter our position. Just then Major Lumb got shot through the neck and Sergeant White got killed and we had to take four men back wounded. Then we had to fight for all our worth, we could hear nothing only the continual roar of rifles and big guns going off. Whilst we were taking up a position on a high bank the Enemy pressed us and we lost some more men"[2].

At this moment Brigadier-General Elles arrived from Peshawar. Seeing that the Mohmands had advanced onto level ground, he ordered the 12-pounders to open fire at the enemy left while the 13th Bengal Lancers rode rapidly via a ravine to the same flank. As soon as the cavalry were in position the infantry bugles blew "Cease Fire". Then the Lancers' two squadrons, led by Major Anderson, charged the length of the enemy line from right to left, over a mile and a half's distance. However brave and skilful on the hills, Pathans would never face cavalry on the flat. Broken almost on the same spot as their forefathers had been by the 7th Hussars, the Mohmands fled for the slopes.

When the fight was over the Somerset soldier already quoted (No.3345 "Fred") realised all too horribly what Kipling had forecast could befall *The Young British Soldier* if "wounded and left on Afghanistan's plains": "Two men got left behind somehow. I don't know how it happened, nobody missed them till the roll was called at night when they didn't answer their names. They sent the Cavalry over the battlefield again and found them cut and quartered. They did not know how to seperate [sic] them. They had to put them in one blanket and sew them up. We buried them that night under the fort walls with everything on just as they fell. Not a prayer book in the fort".

Realising the lowering effect of this incident in what for most of the Somersets had been their first action, Elles called the two companies together and gave them a few bracing words about dying for Queen and Country and how he hoped they would do their duty in the future as they had done it that day. Nevertheless, when the rest of the battalion arrived the next day, "they were deeply cut up when they heard how the enemy had served those two men of ours". Nor did Elles' words do much to cheer the Somersets the night after the action, which was "miserable and we could hear the groans of the wounded and men with fever and sunstroke were lying all over the place. We couldn't sleep although we were tired out and we couldn't get nothing to eat, only what the Native soldiers gave us"[3].

Over the next few days, being uncertain where and when the Mohmands might strike next, Elles increased the force at Shabkadr to a strength of 2,500 and arranged for the reinforcement of the Peshawar garrison to replace units sent out to the fort. Wise though these precautions were, no further fighting ensued for two reasons: first, because the whole area round Peshawar was deluged by five days of exceptionally heavy rain; and second, because the Mohmands seemed to have disappeared completely, except for distant picquets guarding, but not advancing from, the passes into their territory.

It was learned that as a result of the rains agriculture became a more pressing necessity for the Mohmands than fighting and that, in any case, the Hadda Mullah's prestige and credibility had been somewhat dented by the defeat on 9 August. A story out of the hills gained currency to the effect that, when he sought the congratulations of the Mad Mullah of Swat for his attack on Shabkadr, the latter, enraged, replied: "Dog! You have done nothing!"[4].

However lacklustre the Hadda Mullah's efforts had been compared with the week-long onslaught upon Malakand

and Chakdara, Elles was nevertheless determined to exact retribution for this incursion into British territory, and sought permission to do so. Before he could receive it the Afridi-Orakzai uprising broke out on the Khyber and southwards. The Government of India, realising that this would require a much larger force than any hitherto deployed, which would take at least a month to prepare, decided that punishment of the Mohmands - estimated to take no longer than that - must be completed before the much greater undertaking against the Afridis began. Authorisation for the formation of the Mohmand Field Force, of two brigades plus divisional troops, was therefore given and orders issued for its advance to link up with the Malakand Field Force, as described in the last chapter.

* * *

By 14 September the force was concentrated near Shabkadr. In Brigadier-General Westmacott's 1st Brigade, besides the 20th Punjabis and the newly-arrived 2nd/1st Gurkha Rifles, were the 1st Somersets - not as fit for a campaign as they might have been, having earlier suffered much from malaria which had been aggravated by their rain-sodden wait at Shabkadr. The 2nd Brigade of Brigadier-General Macgregor included the 37th Dogras, 9th Gurkhas, and 2nd Oxfordshire Light Infantry - known always by themselves, and by most of the Army, as "the 52nd", to distance themselves from their 1st Battalion, formerly the 43rd. To Lionel James, Reuter's Special Correspondent, they looked "in condition and it was impossible not to notice their workmanlike appearance and that eagerness which betokens confidence in the ranks both in themselves and their officers"[5].

James' assessment was borne out by the battalion's arrangements for camping kit. Warned that officers' and soldiers' kit would be restricted to 40lbs. and 15lbs. respectively, and that no tents would be transported, a quantity of little bamboo posts and ridge-poles had been prepared. "Three poles with four bits of jointed ridge-pole and four waterproof sheets make a shelter for six men to sleep under. This would keep out a great deal of rain, and with blankets thrown over the top it formed a very fair shelter against the sun"[6].

The 13th Bengal Lancers charging the Mohmands at Shabkadr, 9 August; watercolour by Maj.Hobday, R.A. (National Army Museum)

Officers of the 2nd Oxfordshire Light Infantry - still generally known in 1897 as "the 52nd" - with Brig. Gen. Macgregor (hands on knees). See also Plate E. (Navy & Army Illustrated)

Among the divisional troops were the 13th Bengal Lancers and the 28th Bombay Pioneers; two mountain batteries (one British); three Maxim guns, one manned by the 16th Lancers, the other two by men of the 1st Devons under Lieutenant Logan; and the 1st Patiala Infantry, an Imperial Service battalion officered entirely by Indians and commanded by Sir Pertab Singh - "this splendid Indian prince", as Churchill called him[7].

The force advanced, with Westmacott's 1st Brigade leading, on 15 September, the day after Sir Bindon Blood had reached Nawagai. Some 50 miles of hitherto unknown country separated the two forces, with possibly as many as 19,000 Mohmands somewhere in between. No opposition was met that day except for a few shots fired at the advance guard; but the march, 20 miles up the Gandab Valley in intense heat and in an increasingly arid terrain, was a severe trial. This was particularly true in the final thousand-foot climb up to the Mohmand plateau, where the track became no more than "a stairway of boulders up which the transport literally had to be hauled - great stepping-stones more like the ascent of the Egyptian pyramids than anything else"[8]. The effort told especially upon the sickly Somersets who, their water-bottles long since emptied, were seen offering whatever money they had to the drivers of the mules bearing the water-skins.

Thereafter the marching became a little easier, with the best routes forward reconnoitred by cavalry patrols, and on the fourth day contact was made by heliograph with Blood's force from the top of the Nahakki Pass. Furthermore the Lower Mohmands, uneasy about being caught in the pincer movement, had begun to seek terms and, on the 19th - the day the Hadda Mullah's men at Badmanai were preparing to attack Blood's camp - they made complete submission.

From the Nahakki Pass the track forked, north-west to the Hadda Mullah's lair at Jarobi and north to Lakarai and Nawagai. Information was received that the Hadda Mullah (whose setback at Shabkadr had not, after all, entirely impaired his power to attract followers) had detached some 3,000 men to block the former route, but that the other was

clear. Leaving the 2nd Brigade to guard this pass at Nahakki, a vital point for his eventual withdrawal southwards, Elles pushed on to Lakarai where, as seen previously, he met Blood on the 21st and received under his command Graves' (formerly Wodehouse's) 3rd Brigade. All was now set for the capture of the Badmanai Pass from those who still adhered to the Hadda Mullah after their bruising experience at Nawagai the night before, and thereafter for running the "dog" to earth in his secluded bolt-hole at Jarobi.

Although signs of defiance from the hilltops above the pass and some night-firing into the camps suggested that the Mohmands were preparing to resist strongly, in the event the taking of Badmanai on the 22nd proved more of a stiff hill-climb. Both brigades attacked but only two battalions of Westmacott's brigade on the left had any fighting. The 20th Punjabis, supported by the 1st Gurkhas - both of whose agility, marksmanship and fieldcraft equalled that of any tribesman on the hill - cleared the enemy from every successive position, each higher than the last. When they forced a group of tribesmen into the open these were speedily and effectively engaged by Lieutenant Logan's Maxims or the guns of No.3 (British) Mountain Battery. The Hadda Mullah may have been a persuasive orator but he was not the man for any last-ditch stand. When he fled so did the Mohmands, and the pass was won.

Particularly prominent in this attack had been the Afridi company of the 20th Punjabis which, despite having been on picquet all the previous night and not having had time for rest or even food, had shown great dash and enthusiasm in the early stages of the attack when the resistance was at its strongest. Not only had they cleared the way for the following companies; but considering the fact that their fellow-tribesmen to the south had been in arms against the British for a month by this date, this demonstration of reliability and loyalty to their regiment deserved - and received - much commendation.

Three days later Elles and Westmacott's brigade reached the Jarobi Valley, a most picturesque and fertile change from the desolate countryside they had passed through, surrounded by very steep, high hills and approached only through a narrow gorge. Curiously the Mohmands had taken no advantage of these natural defences to their holy leader's sanctuary, and the troops' entrance to the valley was unopposed. Nevertheless Westmacott took the precaution of leaving the Somersets with some mountain guns to guard the gorge and sent picquets up the heights on either side.

Although it seemed at first as if the Hadda Mullah had been unable to prevail any longer upon the Mohmands' faith and loyalty, he obviously still had influence upon the elements. As soon as the Sappers began their work of destruction thunder and lightning burst over the valley, followed by rain and hail impelled by a "bitter wind which chilled all to the bone"[9]. Unpleasant though this was, it did not deter the Moslem sepoys of the 20th Punjabis. Two companies soon found and entered a very narrow defile which led to the Mullah's "City and Mosque" (according to "Fred" of the Somersets), but more prosaically described by a gunner major as "a few mud hovels enclosed by a small wall"[10].

Nor were the sepoys deterred by the rifle-fire which suddenly blazed down from the precipitous cliffs on either side. Led by a subedar, they charged through the defile to a clearing where stood the Mullah's mosque. From it there charged out a band of swordsmen, screaming furiously. The subedar killed two with his sword, the sepoys despatched the rest with bullet and bayonet. Of the "dog" who had sent so many to their deaths there was, of course, no sign. It was suspected that he had fled over the Afghan border, only a mile or so away.

The firing from the heights continued, however, and half the 1st Gurkhas were sent forward to cover the Punjabis' withdrawal. Since, despite the continuing storm, all the dwellings in the valley were now ablaze and the day was drawing on, Elles ordered the evacuation of the area. Seeing the rearward moves begin the tribesmen grew bolder

and followed up, but were held off by steady volleys from the 28th Bombay Pioneers, who were extended as a rearguard through which the forward battalions fell back. Supported by the screw-guns all got clear through the gorge held by the Somersets, and camp was made beyond it. The day's operations had cost the Punjabis, Pioneers and Sappers some 25 casualties. The Somersets, on the other hand, had had an uneventful day, tersely summed up by F Company's letter-writer: "We reached the place and blowed it up and burned everything we could and came back again"[11].

    *   *   *

After the attack on the Badmanai Pass, Graves' 3rd Brigade had returned to its former camping ground. While the Jarobi operation was taking place it had a skirmish in some hostile villages to the west, just inside the Afghan border. In one of the houses the 1st Queen's found a letter from the Hadda Mullah's Afghan general friend which confirmed earlier suspicions that rifles and ammunition had been despatched across the border. This brigade then began its march out of the area, back to Peshawar via the Nahakki Pass where the 2nd Brigade had remained throughout the foregoing manoeuvres.

This latter brigade had so far seen no action and, where the 2nd Oxfordshire Light Infantry were concerned, "very sick every one got of it. There was absolutely nothing to do and the sun was hot, till, on the 25th a heavy storm of wind and rain came on, which made things still more unpleasant"[12]. Obviously the Hadda Mullah's baleful

No.3 (RA) Mountain Battery, part of the Mohmand Field Force, prepare their 2.5in.RML guns to fire. Note the mounted officer; and the majority of the battery mules held by the drivers well back from the gun line. (Navy & Army Illustrated)

Sketch of the bivouacs of the 2nd Oxfordshire Light Infantry by 2/Lt. Salkeld of the battalion. For the Mohmand expedition tents were replaced, for lightness on the march, by an issue of short bamboo stakes and jointed ridge-poles; with four waterproof sheets or blankets these made a shelter against rain or sun for six men. (Oxfordshire Light Infantry Chronicle)

influence was even reaching out to the skies over Nahakki. However, on the next day the 52nd, with three squadrons of the 13th Bengal Lancers, were ordered to march north-westwards up the Jarobi track as escort to a convoy of 300 camels loaded with rations for Westmacott's brigade, prior to supporting Elles' next move. He planned to return from Jarobi to Nahakki by this route, so that his whole march would have eventually encircled the disaffected region, thus bringing the Upper Mohmands to submission. He left his last camp near the Jarobi gorge on 26 September

and advanced south-eastwards to link up with the 52nd, destroying villages and watchtowers on the way. This, coming on top of the casualties and reverses inflicted on the Mohmands at Nawagai, Badmanai and Jarobi, had the desired effect and deputations started to come in to seek terms. Only one group, the Kuda Khel, proved less submissive, issuing a formal challenge to a fight. This Elles accepted on 27 September.

The 52nd, with a valiant record in the Napoleonic Wars and in the Mutiny but with no action to boast of since, were at last to get their chance to add to their laurels.

A sketch, after Lionel James of Reuters, showing Elles's force reaching the top of the Mohmand plateau, after a final 1,000-foot climb up "a stairway of boulders up which the transport literally had to be hauled - great stepping-stones more like the ascent of the Egyptian pyramids than anything else." (The Graphic)

Having safely escorted the camel convoy to the village of Kung, 12 miles from Nahakki, they received orders to advance the following morning towards the Kuda Khel's valley, eight miles distant, with one squadron of Lancers. By 8a.m. the valley was in sight and the cavalry advance guard came under fire from some houses.

Ahead of them the 52nd saw a village straggling for some 1,300 yards up a valley, about half a mile wide, enclosed at the head and on either side by steep, bare, rocky hills. Part of Westmacott's brigade was already in action, driving the tribesmen from the nearest houses back to the upper part of the village. As the 52nd approached, No.5 (Bombay) Mountain Battery were firing at the top houses and the sangars which crowned the hills behind, and the 2/1st Gurkhas were about to advance up the right side of the valley. The 52nd deployed for attack up the left side with three companies in the firing line, two in support, and three in reserve - a textbook attack formation.

"Our firing line opened fire on the top houses," recalled B Company's commander, Captain Davies, who was in support, "and we advanced up to about the middle of the village, when we were ordered to halt. Here we came under fire from men on the hills, at a range of 1,000 yards or more. They must have had good rifles and been good shots, as most of their bullets dropped somewhere near the firing line and supports. We got very good cover behind the banks which divided the terraced fields we were advancing over and no one was actually damaged"[13]. The 52nd's leading companies fired volleys in return, supported by Lieutenant Logan's Devon-manned Maxims, and after a while the enemy fire ceased.

Meanwhile the Gurkhas had scrambled up a hill above the village, where they had four wounded, and the 28th Pioneers and Sappers had begun the destruction of the houses and watchtowers. One company of Pioneers was sent up a hill to assist the Gurkhas in holding off the enemy, who had fallen back to further heights, while the demolition work went on unimpeded.

By midday the village was in flames. Three companies of the 52nd were extended as rearguard, with the Maxims and mountain guns ready for action behind them, to cover the withdrawal of the troops on the high ground. When the Pioneer company was halfway down the tribesmen predictably reappeared in pursuit. The 52nd's B Company opened fire with volleys at 800 yards, which were thickened up by the guns and "the irritating rattle"[14] of the Maxims firing over the infantrymen's heads. So effective was this fire

Lt.Logan's Maxim gun detachment of the 1st Devons, which gave effective support to the 20th Punjabis and 1st Gurkhas at Badmanai on 22 September. (Navy & Army Illustrated)

Below left: Camel convoy cresting the Nahakki Pass, guarded by a picquet of the 9th Gurkhas; drawing by W.B.Wollen from a photograph. (Author's collection)

The destruction of the Haddah Mullah's mosque at Jarobi during a thunderstorm on 25 September. Although fired on from the heights the 20th Punjabis forced the defile, and after the destruction of the buildings withdrew - supported by the 1st Gurkhas and 28th Bombay Pioneers - without serious opposition on the valley floor. Drawing by Maj.Hobday, RA. (Author's collection)

that it held the enemy high on the hills, thereby enabling the Pioneers and, a little later, the Gurkhas to fall back without loss through the rearguard. As the 52nd went back in turn they were fired at but not pursued, and the last they saw of the enemy was "men standing on top of the hill waving their guns and yelling"[15]. Doubtless the sight of the retreating troops enabled the Kuda Khel to convince themselves they had won, but they had no homes to sleep in that night.

So ended the 52nd's first action for 40 years. The Kuda Khel had not proved as formidable an enemy as the sepoy mutineers at Delhi, and the 52nd's only losses had been a perforated water-bottle and a severed shoulder-strap. They had, however, gone straight into action after an hour and a half's approach march, on no breakfast but a cup of tea and a slice of bread, and the way they had performed what was required of them had fully justified Lionel James' first assessment of the battalion. Indeed the performance of all Westmacott's force that day had been a well-nigh perfect demonstration of how such an operation should be conducted, and at a total cost of only five wounded.

Elles and the 1st Brigade, with the 52nd, marched on to Kung and the much-needed rations. After a day's rest, the circuit through the Mohmand country was completed by the return to Nahakki and the 2nd Brigade. There was still some enemy sniping into camps at night and periodic firing at rearguards and picquets, but the Mohmand campaign was virtually over. Fines in rifles, swords and cash were levied upon the various clans who had been in arms and agreed by their elders. The Atmanzai, for instance, to the east of the Nahakki-Lakarai road, whose territory had not been marched through during the advance, agreed to hand over 100 guns, 100 swords, and 1,000 rupees after being visited by the 2nd Brigade on 30 September. In a fortnight's operations Elles' troops had completed their task of bringing the Mohmands to book for their raid on Shabkadr.

By the first week of October most of the Mohmand Field Force's three brigades were back at Peshawar, ready for re-deployment to, or in support of, the Tirah Field Force. There were two exceptions. The 20th Punjabis, whose Afridi element had earned especial praise for their conduct at Badmanai and Jarobi, were despatched to the Buner Field Force to avoid what was felt would be an unfair test of their loyalty were they to be pitted against their fellow-tribesmen in the Tirah. (Their continued good work at the Tanga Pass has been noted in the previous chapter.) The 1st Somerset Light Infantry, who had had a less than rewarding experience against the Mohmands, had hoped for better things but, as "Fred" explained in his concluding sentences to his mother, "half the regiment's sick with malarial fever and ague. We was for the Tirah but the regiment's too sick for it"[16].

The Mohmand campaign, by dint of its brief duration and lack of incident, makes for dull reading compared with other episodes of the Pathan Revolt. The Mohmands, perhaps reflecting the poverty of their arid territories, seem a somewhat colourless and unenterprising tribe compared with some other Pathans. On the other hand the campaign accomplished the aim of punishing the attack on Shabkadr - "the most severe slap in the face" the Government of India had received in 30 years[17], since it was the only aggression during the whole Revolt in British, rather than tribal, territory. It had been achieved at only slight cost to

the troops involved, no more than four killed and 25 wounded. Furthermore it had demonstrated the length and strength of the government's arm by marching at will a force of all arms through territory hitherto unvisited by government forces; this, incidentally, provided much topographical intelligence that was to prove useful eleven years later[18]. It was in any case essential, in the wider context of the Revolt, to quell all resistance in this area north of the Khyber and the Kabul River before the major campaign to the south began – the bringing to heel of the powerful Afridi-Orakzai combination.

Sepoys, Indian officers and havildar of the 28th Bombay Pioneers, the rearguard at Jarobi; both service and full dress are illustrated. Note the pick and shovel slung on the soldiers' backs in leather cases. (Maj.A.G.Harfield)

CHAPTER SEVEN

Khyber, Kohat and Kurram

"The jaunty, vain, light-hearted, reckless young Afridi appeals irresistibly for, like Saul of Israel, they are 'choice young men and goodly', if dirty". So thought Sir George Macmunn, who had seen plenty of them, when writing about sources of likely recruits for the Indian Army[1]. A Gurkha subedar with much experience of Frontier warfare was once asked how he rated Afridis as soldiers compared with Sikhs. He replied that "he liked the Sikhs better, but would sooner have Afridis with him at a pinch than any other breed of men in India"[2]. This account has already described examples of the gallantry and enthusiasm with which Afridi sepoys in regiments like the Guides and 20th Punjabis could respond to whatever was required of them.

There was, however, another side to the always ambivalent Afridi character. In Bajaur a group of Afridi sepoys deserted one night with their rifles from the 24th Punjabis - the same regiment whose Afridis had earlier enticed the Swatis to their doom at Malakand by pretending to be disloyal. During the attacks in the Khyber about to be related, one Afridi father, a subedar, was in a fort with one of his sons beside him, while his other two were outside among the attackers. In a later, greater war two Afridi brothers went to France in 1914 with a Frontier Force regiment. One deserted, received the Iron Cross from the Germans, and was sent home to make trouble on the Frontier. The other became the fourth Indian Army soldier to win the Victoria Cross and never swerved from his loyalty. This mixture of volatility and valour was a very distinctive Afridi characteristic.

In August 1897 it was the former quality that suddenly surfaced. The Afridis had given much trouble on the lines of communication during the Second Afghan War; but for the 16 years prior to the great Pathan Rising, though feuding amongst themselves as was their wont, they had remained peaceful, thanks to the tutelage of Sir Robert Warburton and the receipt of a handsome annual subsidy (87,000 rupees). It was they who, besides sending their young men to the Indian Army, had officered and manned Warburton's local levies, the Khyber Rifles, which garrisoned the forts along the Khyber Pass. These posts, from Ali Masjid at the Peshawar end to Landi Kotal on the Afghan border, safeguarded all traffic between India and Afghanistan. In 1897 it was fondly hoped that this formidable and powerful people, with nearly 27,000 fighting men and the most fertile lands of any tribe, would repay Warburton's trust in them.

This optimism failed to take into account the Afridis' natural bellicosity and greed, not to mention the inflammatory preaching of yet another mullah, Sayid Akbar of Waran - who, it was later proved, had been in conspiratorial correspondence with the Hadda Mullah. Fully aware of the risings to the north, the Afridis hatched

Men of the Khyber Rifles, who garrisoned the forts overwhelmed by the Afridis in August. (Author's collection)

a plan with the Orakzais for a joint attack: by the latter upon the British posts along the Samana Range guarding the Kohat-Kurram road through the Miranzai valley, while the Afridis themselves attacked the forts in the Khyber.

The senior British officer in the Khyber was Captain Barton, once of the Guides Cavalry, a man thoroughly familiar with the Pathan character and language who combined the duties of Assistant Political Officer at Landi Kotal with command of the Khyber Rifles. When first notified of the Mohmand attack on Shabkadr on 7 August he immediately took the wise precautions of strengthening his garrisons, arranging stockpiles of 14 days' water and supplies, and building up an ammunition reserve of 50,000 rounds at Landi Kotal. His foresight was rapidly justified by reports of a 10,000-strong force of Afridis advancing on the Khyber. This news he signalled to his superior Sir Richard Udny, the Commissioner at Peshawar, together with a request for four companies of Regular infantry with two guns as a back-up for the Khyber Rifles.

Udny ordered him to report at once in person to Fort Jamrud, seven miles from Peshawar at the mouth of the Khyber. Believing he had three days before the Afridis attacked, Barton rode down in haste, only to be told on arrival that he was to remain at Jamrud. Furthermore, although there were some 12,000 troops of all arms at Peshawar, not one man or gun was ordered out to support the Khyber Rifles, now in effect abandoned to their fate. For poor Barton, forbidden to return to the men he trusted and who trusted him, Udny's ruling - even if it was for his own safety - was "gall and wormwood beyond belief"[3].

Three days later, on 23 August, the Afridis attacked as he had forecast. Ali Masjid fell quickly, making little resistance. The 40 defenders of Fort Maude, three miles into the Pass from Jamrud, did what they could against

Fort Ali Masjid, at the Peshawar end of the Khyber Pass, after its eventual re-occupation, showing the damage done by the Afridis. (Lt.Col.P.J.Mercer)

overwhelming force before managing to escape under cover of some long-range gunfire from the mouth of the pass. As they reached safety at Jamrud they spat on the ground as they marched past the inactive British troops.

The larger garrison of 370 men at Landi Kotal, first attacked at noon on the 24th, put up a spirited defence throughout the day and night, due largely to the example and efforts of their native officers. Subedar Jawas Khan was a particular tower of strength, but the following morning, after he was wounded and Subedar Mursil killed, the loyalty of many sepoys began to falter. Greetings were exchanged with their fellow-tribesmen beyond the walls, and eventually some opened the gates, allowing the attackers to pour in. Part of the garrison immediately joined in the looting (including all Barton's belongings) and destruction of the fort; others handed over their arms and were allowed to go free. A few, Pathans but non-Afridis, fought their way out under a subedar and down the pass, eventually reaching Jamrud. How the unfortunate Barton greeted these survivors is not known, but it must have been a horribly painful encounter.

Thus were all the Khyber forts lost and destroyed. A quantity of Martinis and the ammunition reserve at Landi Kotal passed into Afridi hands. The same hands now controlled the whole Khyber Pass and would continue to do so for four months. In three days the Afridis had inflicted a shaming blow upon the prestige and authority of the Government of India which, despite Barton's clear warning, had done nothing to avert it.

The sight of the Khyber Rifles survivors at Jamrud caused much frustration among the leashed-in Peshawar garrison. Winston Churchill recorded that the "Politicals" were always unpopular with the Army, which regarded them as frequently guilty of "shilly-shallying, doing everything you possibly can before you shoot"[4]. In this case, apart from Barton's ignored warning, nothing of any kind had been done to save the forts and the pass. It was not surprising that the troops at Peshawar nicknamed the Commissioner as "Udny the Unready"[5].

*   *   *

There were, however, some compensations. Rather than exploiting their triumph straightaway, and despite the exhortations of their mullahs, the Afridis decided first to return to their homes with their loot and their casualties. Furthermore, the less combative and more cautious Orakzais had delayed their part in the joint plan for a simultaneous strike on the Samana posts, waiting to see how the Afridis had fared. Fortunately this gave time to deploy troops on the Kohat-Kurram line ready to support those posts, under the overall command of Major-General Yeatman-Biggs.

The Orakzais made no move until 26 August when they appeared on the crest of the Ublan Pass, some six miles north-west of Kohat, having overcome a small post manned by local levies. Before they could develop any further attack a small force of the 2nd Punjab Infantry (PFF), two companies of the 1st Royal Scots Fusiliers, 9th Field Battery RA and a squadron of cavalry moved out at dawn from

Watercolour by J.McNeill of 1st Royal Scots Fusiliers on picquet duty in a sangar; note the kilted piper, and the fact that all ranks wear khaki trousers rather than tartan trews. (Author's collection)

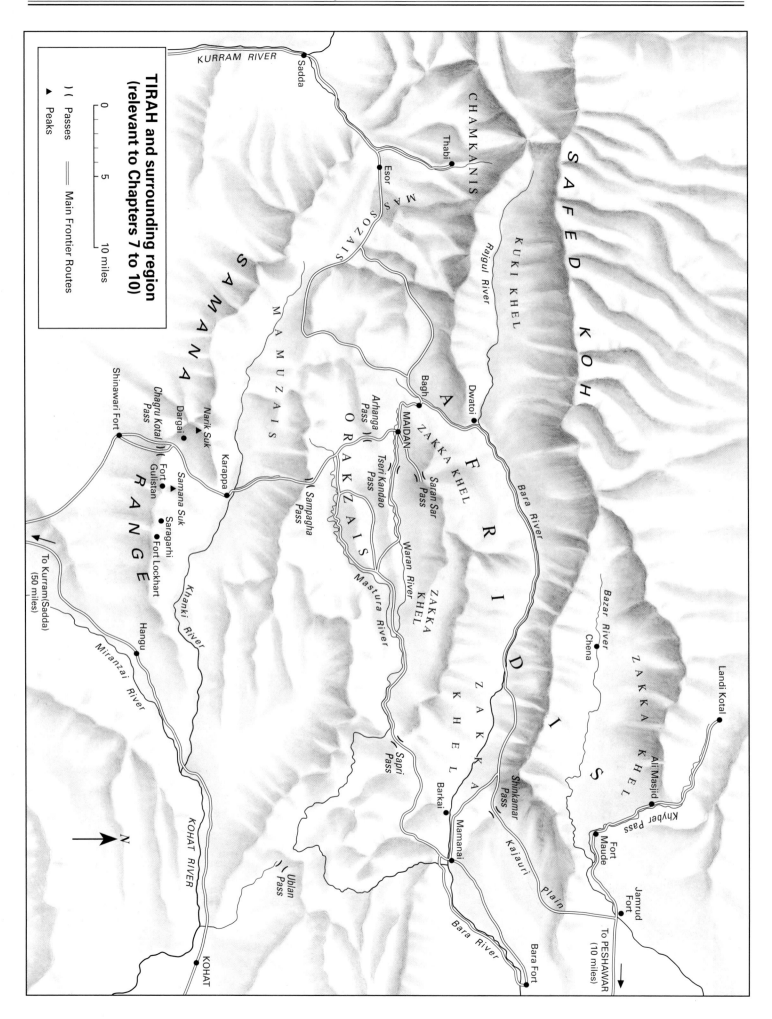

TIRAH and surrounding region (relevant to Chapters 7 to 10)

)(Passes
▲ Peaks
—— Main Frontier Routes

0 5 10 miles

N

Fort Gulistan, photographed after its relief. Note the terraced hillside, giving attackers excellent cover close to the walls. (Maj. T. C. S. Knox)

Kohat and attacked the pass. It was extremely hot, with no water anywhere in sight, and the infantry faced a very steep climb. Nevertheless the field guns' covering fire enabled them to reach the summit with only two dead - one of them, a Fusilier, from heat apoplexy.

Then, as a Scots Fusilier officer rather sourly recalled: "After a good look round, the bugles sounded the retire, the battery limbered up and went home, whilst the infantry had to disentangle themselves"[6]. Sweltering under the blazing sun, with most water-bottles now empty, the Scots Fusiliers heard the bugles' command with relief; but almost at once, as the more experienced Punjabis may have expected, they came under a heavy fire. No longer pinned down by the battery's shells, the Orakzais sprang to life with the usual Pathan tactic of harrying retreating troops, seriously wounding two Scots Fusilier officers and causing several casualties among the Punjabis. Fortunately they did not pursue far and the troops eventually reached the road at the bottom, so exhausted by heat and thirst that the lucky find of a pond, however unhygienic, had to be exploited before they could march back to Kohat. Inconclusive and unsatisfactory though this engagement had been, it had deterred this thrust by the Orakzais, who soon turned their attention elsewhere.

Meanwhile some Border Police posts further along the Samana Range had come under attack from other Orakzais. These were driven off by a force under Colonel Richardson which had been pre-positioned at Hangu, 24 miles west of

Kohat. No sooner was this done than Richardson's force had to march much further west to Sadda in the Kurram Valley, 65 miles away, from where reports had been received of a combined Afridi-Orakzai force of 3,000 advancing to attack posts held by the Kurram Militia (a body similar to the Khyber Rifles).

The first Kurram post was attacked on 1 September, two days after Richardson had started from Hangu. Though garrisoned by only 20 men under a havildar - an Afridi, as it happened - it held out manfully throughout the day and well into the night until help arrived from Sadda, whereupon the attackers pulled back. On the following day news of Richardson's approach both cheered the Militia and discouraged the Afridis, who dispersed without further attacks even though the relief column was still three days' march away. Apart from a night attack made on Richardson's camp at Sadda - and easily repulsed - 11 days after his arrival, the Kurram Valley thereafter remained quiet. The focus of enemy activity shifted away eastwards, back on the Samana Range.

After their rebuff at the eastern end of the range in late August, the Orakzais made no further effort in that area until 10 September when, joined by some Afridis, they were spotted moving eastwards down the Khanki Valley on the north side of the range. After Richardson's departure for the Kurram, Yeatman-Biggs' remaining troops between Kohat and Hangu had been reinforced. He at once moved out to check this new advance and succeeded in doing so on the 11th; but again the acute shortage of water in the region, added to the excessive heat, prevented any follow-up and he had to return to Hangu the next day. His enemy, however, growing in strength until they mustered some 10,000 men,

Types of the 36th Sikhs, defenders of the Samana forts: jemadar, havildar, sepoy in poshteen, bugler. See also Plate H. (Maj.A.G.Harfield)

had found, as they thought, an easier prey.

* * *

Where the Samana Range rose to about 6,500 feet, some ten miles north-west of Hangu as the crow flies, were two forts, the nearest to Hangu being known as Lockhart, the other, four miles westwards, as Gulistan. Communications from one to the other were maintained by a signalling post sited at Saragarhi midway between them. East of Lockhart, guarding the track up from Hangu, were three smaller picquet posts. These important positions, looking out over Orakzai territory to the north, with the vital Kohat-Kurram road to their south, were the responsibility of a Regular Indian battalion: Lieutenant-Colonel Haughton's 36th Sikhs. This was a relatively new regiment, raised only in 1887; and neither it nor its commander had been in action before. Haughton, then aged 45, had been born of parents with distinguished Indian service on both sides; standing six feet six inches tall, he appeared "strong and valiant, a man to be depended on and trusted", yet with a modest and kindly demeanour[7]. He was well educated in his profession, particularly in Frontier matters; and his Sikhs were noticeably tall, strong men, not one being under five feet eight inches in height.

Haughton and his headquarters were in Fort Lockhart with 168 men, while another 102 sepoys with three Sikh officers were spread between the three picquets to the east. He also had a dozen sick men from the 2nd Royal Irish Regiment, who had collapsed from heat during Yeatman-Biggs' operation on the 11th and had been left at Lockhart rather than carrying them back to Hangu. Gulistan was garrisoned by 175 men under Major Des Voeux, with a subaltern of only a year's service, 2nd Lieutenant Pratt, and Surgeon-Captain Prall. In the latter's sick-bay was another officer, Lieutenant Blair, who had been dangerously wounded in some skirmishing a fortnight before. There were also some non-combatants. Since all had been quiet during the weeks preceding the Orakzai rising, Mrs Des Voeux, her three children all under nine years old, and their nursemaid Miss Teresa McGrath had been allowed to join her husband in Gulistan. Now, in early September, it was too unsafe to evacuate them - and in any case Mrs Des Voeux was shortly to give birth again; so in Gulistan they would have to remain, come what may.

Prior to Yeatman-Biggs' sortie from Hangu on 11 September, Gulistan had been fired on by Orakzais on 28 August and, more seriously, on 3-4 September; but when Haughton had come over from Lockhart in support the Orakzais had lost heart and had tried nothing since. Now, on 12 September, as Yeatman-Biggs' column slaked their thirst at Hangu, the Orakzais, reinforced and stiffened by Afridis, swarmed up once more in much greater numbers against Gulistan and Saragarhi, cutting them off from each other and from Fort Lockhart.

The signalling post at Saragarhi, ill-sited for defence (being surrounded by much dead ground), was garrisoned by no more than 20 Sikhs under Havildar Ishar Singh. These brave men defended their post against continual attack for seven and a half hours, and maintained signal contact with Fort Lockhart throughout. With thousands of tribesmen swarming between there was no chance of

The ruins of the Saragarhi signalling post, defended to the last by Havildar Ishar Singh and his 20 men. Fort Lockhart is on the skyline, left centre. (Maj.A.C.Yate)

Haughton getting through to help, and in any case his other posts to the east were also under attack. He tried to create a diversion by sending out his Adjutant with the sick Royal Irish soldiers to open long-range fire with their superior Lee-Metfords from a point closer to Saragarhi; but against so many their volleys had no effect, and he had to recall them.

At about 3p.m. a heliograph message was received from Saragarhi that their ammunition was running low. Haughton felt that he must make some attempt to help his valiant little garrison in their desperate situation. Leaving some 80 Sikhs and the Royal Irish to hold the fort, he led out the remainder. Advancing with great care across the intervening mile and a half, he and his men had got just under half way when they saw a great mass of tribesmen surging up and over the walls. They were too late. In a letter to his wife the next day Haughton expressed his feelings: "Yesterday was a terrible day, for I saw twenty-one of our gallant men slaughtered at Saragarhi, and was unable to do anything to prevent it"[8].

All the while the havildar's devoted men had been manning the walls, two Afridis, concealed from them by a dead angle, had been undermining the base. When they succeeded in breaching it the whole wall collapsed, enabling the attackers to pour in. The Sikhs fell back to make a last stand in their barrack-room until they were all killed. The last man to die was burned alive and all the corpses mutilated. Of these 21 men of the 36th Sikhs a newspaper report later stated: "They behaved with splendid courage and there is perhaps no more touching instance of inflexible devotion to duty than this in the whole narrative of frontier fighting"[9].

While this drama was unfolding Gulistan had also been under heavy attack, and its assailants were now joined by most of those from Saragarhi. Gulistan, more a fortified post than a proper fort, was rectangular in shape, with stone walls 12 to 15 feet high surrounding the garrison's single-storey living accommodation, with loopholed bastions at diagonally opposite corners; attached to the west wall was an enclosure or hornwork with much lower walls.

To Major Des Voeux's concern for the security of his post was added his dismay at having been unable to assist Saragarhi, and his natural anxiety for his heavily-pregnant wife and young family, who faced an unspeakable fate should Gulistan fall. He was, however, most loyally supported by all his garrison and not least by Miss McGrath, whose bravery and devotion to the wounded endeared her to all. Mrs Des Voeux did what she could in this regard but her efforts were limited by her condition.

Survivors of the Gulistan sortie party pose with the captured Afridi standards for a photograph by Lt.Col.Haughton. They greeted the relief force by parading these trophies at the gate. (Maj.A.C.Yate)

Elated by the fall of Saragarhi, the attackers became yet more aggressive the next day, increasing their fire and pushing forward a body of about 200 into some dead ground close to the north-west corner of the hornwork. Though this rush was spotted, fire could not be brought to bear upon them. Havildar Kala Singh and 16 sepoys volunteered to make a sortie. Leaving the fort by the southern gateway, they approached stealthily along the outside of the hornwork's south wall. When 20 yards from the concealed enemy they charged with fixed bayonets. So intense was the enemy fire which greeted them that they had to take cover, firing back at point-blank range. Then Colour-Havildar Sunder Singh, with another 12 sepoys, scrambled over the hornwork wall to their aid, and both parties sprang at the enemy. Big, strong Sikhs at the charge with bayonets were not to be denied and the enemy suddenly bolted, leaving behind three standards which were brought back triumphantly to the fort. Throughout the sortie covering fire had been kept up from the main wall; nevertheless 16 of the 30 Sikhs were wounded, some so seriously that they later died. One of these was Havildar Kala Singh, and another Sepoy Wariam Singh, whose bravery had been notable on 3 September.

This sortie greatly cheered the spirits of the garrison as well as disheartening that section of the besiegers whose standards had been captured – so much so, it was later learned, that they had gone home. Even so plenty remained, surrounding Gulistan with constant fire and cutting it off, by sheer numbers, from any chance of relief from Fort Lockhart all through the rest of the day and night. Not until 8a.m. on the 14th, when gunfire was heard to the east, could the tireless Des Voeux and his stalwart Sikhs begin to hope that help might not be far off.

At Hangu Yeatman-Biggs had learned earlier of the fall of Saragarhi and the attack on Gulistan but, although concerned for the latter's safety, he also had to consider a possible threat to Hangu from more tribesmen between him and Fort Lockhart. Furthermore, to reach Gulistan he had to amass sufficient water carriage to support an opposed and possibly prolonged advance across these parched hills.

However, he did send four guns of 9th Field Battery RA, escorted by five squadrons of cavalry, down the Kurram road to a point south-west of Gulistan to open fire at its besiegers on the evening of the 13th. The range was too long to be effective, but the sound of the guns heartened the defenders and may have induced the tribesmen to believe – as he intended – that any relief force would come from that direction rather than the approach he planned, from the east via Lockhart.

Defenders of Fort Gulistan. From left, front: the seriously wounded Lt.Blair, caught in the Gulistan sick-bay by the attacks of 12-14 September; Maj.Des Voeux; 2/Lt.Pratt. Rear, Surgeon-Capt.Prall and two Indian officers of the 36th Sikhs. (Maj.A.G.Harfield)

Having left Hangu in the early hours of the 14th, he attacked the enemy force (estimated at 4,000 strong) lying to the east of Fort Lockhart at daybreak. Covered by mountain guns and the long-range rifle-fire of the 2nd Royal Irish, the 1/3rd Gurkhas, supported by the 1/2nd, went up with their usual dash, driving the enemy off the heights, into the volleys of 30 Sikhs and the dozen Royal Irish sent out by Haughton from Lockhart to support the attack. The relief column passed Haughton's three picquets, which had managed to hold out, and found its way clear to the fort. From here Saragarhi could be seen, still with enemy in the vicinity. As soon as the mountain guns opened up on them they dispersed at such speed that by the time the infantry, now headed by Haughton and his garrison, reached the desolate remains of the post not a tribesman was to be found - only the dishonoured corpses of the Sikhs who had held it so devotedly.

Advancing once more they soon sighted Gulistan, still holding out but still surrounded by enemy. Again the guns went into action, while every one of Des Voeux's men who could stand lined the walls to open rapid fire with the last of their ammunition. The besiegers sensed their time was up. The 36th Sikhs had proved more redoubtable foes than they had bargained for and, as always with Pathans, discretion was the better part of valour. By the time Haughton and Yeatman-Biggs' infantry reached the fort they had no work to do except to open a few long-range volleys at the fleeing enemy and greet the defenders. "Blackened with gunpowder, worn out with forty-eight hours of continual toil and stress, many bandaged and blood-stained, the garrison still preserved a brave front. Drawn up in the gateway were the survivors of the sortie with the three standards they had captured"[10]. The Samana Range, from Gulistan to the east above Hangu, was now clear of the Afridi-Orakzai combination.

Colonel Haughton, of whom the last has by no means been heard, and his 36th Sikhs, splendid in their baptism of fire, had held their ground, thereby later earning a battle honour unique to them in the British and Indian Armies: Samana. No less than 56 Indian Orders of Merit (3rd Class) were awarded to Indian ranks of the garrison. Miss Teresa McGrath had more than earned her Indian Frontier Medal and the Royal Red Cross, later presented to her by Queen Victoria in person.

Two of her charges, then aged eight and two, later went to Wellington and Sandhurst, the elder following his father into the 36th Sikhs; both were to fall in the Great War. No doubt both boys, and their mother, would have agreed wholeheartedly with Colonel Haughton's letter to his wife, in which he said, "Teresa has just been splendid" while "Dr Prall has worked like a horse, or like a whole team of horses"; he further hoped that the doctor, 2nd Lieutenant Pratt and Major Des Voeux "will be well rewarded"[11].

In the event Des Voeux was only mentioned in despatches and promoted to lieutenant-colonel the following year - though he was also awarded a brevet-colonelcy which must have assisted his ascent to the higher ranks, since by 1908 he was a lieutenant-general and received the KCB three years later just before his death, aged only 58. He was also presented with a fourth child by his brave wife, who had endured a most hazardous confinement.

Only Miss Des Voeux, aged six, seemed not wholly to share in the general enthusiasm for Gulistan's commander. Confiding to a war-correspondent with the relief column that she had seen her father actually give a skulking Afridi a second chance before firing at him, she pronounced indignantly: "Daddy should have shotted him *at once!*"[12]

CHAPTER EIGHT

The Heights of Dargai

While fighting was raging around the Samana forts, Colonel Ian Hamilton, lately of the Gordon Highlanders, who had survived the Afghan War unscathed only to have his wrist shattered by a Boer bullet on Majuba Hill, was aboard a P & O steamer bound for Bombay. He had been on leave in England but, on hearing of the Afridi uprising, had cut it short, determined to return at once at his own expense in the hope of obtaining a command in the coming campaign. One morning on deck he passed a fellow-passenger who, looking up from his book, waved it at him with the words "Hulloa, Hannibal!" - an allusion to the book they had earlier discussed, about the Second Punic War. The friendly greeting struck Hamilton as "a good augury"[1], since the student of Roman history was none other than Lieutenant-General Sir William Lockhart, recently recalled from sick leave at home to form and command the Tirah Field Force for the chastisement of the Afridis and Orakzais.

This officer, then aged 56 and the fourth son of a Lanarkshire clergyman, had been first gazetted to the 44th Bengal Infantry during the Mutiny; when that regiment was disarmed Lockhart had been attached to the 5th (Northumberland) Fusiliers during their operations in Oudh. Having gained his first experience of active soldiering at an early age, he had since seen much service. Except for staff appointments in the Abyssinian Expedition of 1868 and the Afghan War, and command of a brigade in Burma in 1886, all of it had been on the Frontier, from Hazara in the north to Waziristan (only two years previously) in the south.

In 1890 Lockhart had been appointed to command the Punjab Frontier Force, and in the following year he had commanded an expedition in the very area where fighting was now taking place - the Miranzai Valley. With both command and staff experience, together with first-hand knowledge of his intended area of operations, he was thus well-qualified for the task in hand. He had not yet, however, fully recovered his health.

It was estimated that the Afridis and Orakzais could muster a combined strength of up to 50,000 fighting men to defend the 900 square miles of their homelands. Moreover their aggression in the Khyber and on the Samana Range demanded swift and decisive punishment to restore British prestige and authority in both Indian and Afghan eyes, as well as along the Frontier. The force committed, therefore, had to be large and well-found enough to achieve this.

The main striking force for the Tirah was to consist of two divisions, each of two infantry brigades, each in turn of two British and two Indian or Gurkha battalions with two field hospitals. There was also to be a special force, 120 strong, of Gurkha Scouts, carefully selected and trained from the 3rd and 5th Gurkhas[2]. Each division was also to have two cavalry squadrons, three mountain batteries, a battalion of Pioneers, two companies of Sappers and Miners, one Imperial Service battalion, and an extra field hospital; the 2nd Division also had the 16th Lancers' Maxim detachment - the only British cavalry representatives in the whole force.

In addition there was to be an all-arms force with

Gen. Sir William Lockhart (seated second from right) with his personal staff including (seated right) Sir Richard Udny as Chief Political Officer - see Chapter Seven. (L. James)

Maxim gun detachment of the 16th Lancers, attached to the 2nd Division of the Tirah Field Force. (Author's collection)

logistic units to hold the line of communication and support the main force; a reserve brigade stationed at Rawalpindi; an all-arms brigade, or column, based on Peshawar; and another all-arms brigade, known as the Kurram Moveable Column, based on the line Hangu-Sadda.

In infantry alone this deployment required 36 battalions - 12 British, 17 Indian or Gurkha, four Pioneer and three Imperial Service (nearly three times as many as were employed in the whole Zulu War of 1879). The other arms would provide six cavalry regiments, two field and eight mountain batteries, and seven engineer companies. The whole totalled 34,506, of which 1,010 were British officers and 10,882 British soldiers, together with a further 19,934 non-combatants - the largest force ever employed on the Frontier.

Of the 16 battalions in the two divisions, there were those like the 1st Queen's, 36th Sikhs, and the three Gurkha battalions (2/1st, 1/2nd and 1/3rd) which had been in action during the various operations of the preceding months, or had been on the fringe of those operations, like the 1st Gordon Highlanders and 1st Devons. On the other hand there were some from farther afield, like the 2nd Derbyshire from Bareilly in Oudh, and the 1st Dorsets and 1st Northamptonshire from even further south where, as the former's historian observed, "it was hardly easy to give the troops the special training required for the very different conditions of the Frontier"[3]. When the Derbys first did a practice attack after arriving in the theatre of operations, Captain Slessor "realised very forcibly that the pretty little manoeuvres and formations of the parade ground or ordinary field day on the plains have mostly to be chucked overboard when it comes to scrambling about hills like the side of a house"[4].

Furthermore, some men in the Dorsets and Northamptons contracted cholera during the journey north, from which a few died; this required the battalions' confinement in a cholera camp for ten days - hardly conducive to getting fit for long, arduous marches and hill-climbing. The 2nd Derbys were spared cholera, but the day after their first long march "was spent comparing the pulpy condition of our feet"[5]. Colonel Haughton of the 36th Sikhs, met in the last chapter, thought that while "the King's Own Scottish Borderers and the Gordons had benefited much from the Chitral campaign", he was "very much struck with the unfitness to march of most British regiments at the beginning of the campaign"[6].

All the British battalions were full of enthusiasm at being included in the Field Force. When the Derbys, having reached Rawalpindi, were quartered on the Duke of Cornwall's Light Infantry, the latter told them they had only come up for fatigue duty when the DCLI took the field. As the Derbys marched out the next day to join the Field Force some of them were overheard "begging the DCLI, in simple but kindly terms, to be of good cheer as 'we were only a fatigue party and not really going away'"[7]. But such jibes, however enthusiastic, were not sufficient substitute for fitness and training in hill fighting.

Indifferent health was not confined to the lower ranks. General Lockhart's has already been mentioned, and an early casualty among the senior ranks was his shipboard companion Ian Hamilton. His "good augury" had indeed come true, presenting him with command of the 1st Brigade of the 1st Division. Sadly, before he could lead it into action he fell from his horse and broke a leg. His command was given to Brigadier-General Hart, who had won the VC in the Afghan War. Dysentery claimed a victim in Major-General Yeatman-Biggs shortly after exchanging his duties on the Kohat-Kurram line for command of the 2nd Division.

His brigadiers were Kempster and, fresh from his chastening of the Mohmands, Westmacott. The other brigadier in the 1st Division was Gaselee; his and Hart's commander in that division was Major-General Penn Symons, who had led the 2nd Brigade in the Tochi Field Force (and who two years later would be the first senior officer killed in action in the initial battle of the Boer War at Talana Hill). Hamilton, before his accident, had much looked forward to serving under him as he had great respect for Symons' abilities; but he believed that, because "Lockhart does not like him and is so much guided by his personal inclinations", the 1st Division would be relegated to second place, "at any rate until he realises that we are better than he thinks"[8].

Lockhart's aim was to establish his force as quickly as

possible in the Tirah Maidan, the very heart of the Afridi-Orakzai homelands which, as the tribes frequently boasted, was concealed, like Moslem women in purdah, behind a curtain "which has never been drawn aside"[9]. To tear this curtain aside would, it was felt, have great moral effect upon the tribes, while the presence of a large force within such an inaccessible and hitherto unpenetrated region would convince them of the sense in submitting sooner rather than later. Another factor persuading Lockhart to go straight for the heart, rather than adopting a more cautious approach, was the need to get in and out of such an area – where even the valleys were 6,000 feet up – before the snows blocked the passes.

There were two possible approaches: from the north, using Peshawar as the base of operations, or from the south via Kohat. Peshawar had the advantage of being a railhead, at which all the necessary resources for the expedition could be easily accumulated and the troops concentrated prior to advancing and establishing the line of communication westwards. However, once tribal territory was reached that route was both unknown and over difficult mountain tracks.

The nearest railhead to Kohat was 31 miles away at Khushulgarh (as mentioned in Chapter Three), but a good road connected the two and continued westwards, south of the Samana Range, as the Kohat-Kurram route. Off this, some 12 miles after Hangu, a side road branched up to Shinawari Fort underneath the range and only five miles from Fort Gulistan as the crow flies. Shinawari had been attacked earlier by the Orakzais, who had got away with the rifles of the small police garrison and 56,000 rounds, but the fort was not seriously damaged. From it a track ran up and over the range at the Chagru Kotal, and thence proceeded more or less due north across the Khanki Valley, through the Sampagha and Arhanga Passes, into the Tirah Maidan.

Though considerably further from a railhead than the Peshawar approach, this offered better roads for a large force, at least as far as Shinawari; its right flank from Kohat onwards was guarded by the Samana posts and forts up to Gulistan; and the region was more familiar, having been traversed in part during Lockhart's Miranzai operations in 1891. Furthermore an advance from this side would penetrate first the Orakzai territory, whose tribesmen were thought more likely to submit than the more redoubtable Afridis to their north.

Lockhart therefore issued orders for a concentration at Kohat, an advance to Shinawari, followed by the main thrust northwards into Tirah. Once the latter began it would have the Kurram Moveable Column on its left or west flank, and the Peshawar Column available to its right or east.

* * *

From the railhead at Khushulgarh to Shinawari was some 80 miles, or seven days' marching. To supply and maintain a force of two divisions with food, water, ammunition, medical supplies and all the necessities for functioning in the field over that distance, followed by an opposed advance of at least another 20 miles and subsequent operations, would require the amassing of huge quantities of supplies and the assembly of sufficient transport animals to carry it all.

Loads were calculated in *maunds*, one of which equalled 80lbs; and baggage animals were classed as 1 ½-maund (which was a donkey's load); 2-maund (mules, ponies or pack-bullocks); or 5-maund (camels). Carts could be used on the Kohat road but once the force entered enemy territory only pack animals would suffice. The two divisions for the Tirah required 29,440 two-maund animals (or more if donkeys had to be used) and 13,370 five-maund: 42,810 animals in all. Since the reserve formations had to be similarly equipped, and since some of the earlier field forces were still in the field, the difficulties of finding such a number, with drivers, were considerable.

There was also the matter of their quality. Since the Army in India maintained a very small scale of its own transport, much had to be hired from Indian contractors even in peacetime. The numbers of men and animals required for an arduous and dangerous campaign in Afridi country would undoubtedly enrich many contractors – but what too many produced were reluctant, inexperienced and indisciplined drivers, below-standard animals, and inadequate pack equipment: "the scourings of the countryside with the dregs of the bazaars in charge"[10].

Then again, it was one thing to assemble this mass of transport and supplies but quite another to organise and control it for the advance. Officers and NCOs were detached from other units in India and appointed to transport duties but, however willing, they were neither trained nor experienced in such work, which was unappealing to the average officer. A gunner captain who found himself so detailed heard from his father, an old officer, who wrote: "I don't much like this Carter Paterson business you are doing"[11].

A British infantry battalion had 105 pack-mules for so-called "obligatory" stores, which marched in the following order: the reserve ammunition of 239 rounds of "Dum-Dum Special" per man (each man also carrying 100 rounds in his pouches), water, signalling equipment, entrenching tools, stretchers, cooking kit and greatcoats. In addition it had a number of mules or other animals to carry the battalion's baggage, the number being calculated on the scale of one mule for every field officer, or three regimental officers, or six soldiers (eight in Indian regiments). Since no British battalion advanced initially from Shinawari with more than 700 all ranks, this scale produced about another 120 mule loads. Had tents been carried this number would have been much higher, but these, and a battalion's other baggage, were all left at Shinawari under rear parties to be

1st Gordon Highlanders marching towards Tirah; in the left background is a halted pack-mule convoy. (Author's collection)

forwarded on later.

What kit was carried on the baggage animals may have varied slightly between battalions. An important consideration for commanding officers was the likelihood of encountering very cold weather before the campaign was over, for which the usual marching dress of khaki cotton drill with sun helmets and puttees would be inadequate, even though backed up by the greatcoats carried on the "obligatory" mules. Some winter kit had been issued at Kohat, but the final choice of what to take into Tirah was not made until just before battalions left Shinawari.

In 2nd Derbyshire, for example, each man was to have carried for him: a waterproof sheet, three blankets, a cardigan, a woollen "Balaclava helmet" or nightcap, his home service blue serge trousers, mitts, spare flannel shirt, socks and boots. On the man was his Slade-Wallace equipment with 100 rounds, his haversack for the day's rations and any small requirements he could cram in, water-bottle, mess-tin and, strapped to the back of the waistbelt below the latter, a rolled-up Guthrie or "*gathri*" jacket. This single-breasted garment, part of the winter kit issued at Kohat, was made of thick khaki serge lined with grey flannel, with two large flapped pockets in front, and reached to about mid-thigh; it was cut generously enough to be worn over the equipment or, if the waistbelt was lengthened, under it.

The Derbys discarded the shiny black covers of their mess-tins as useless, and dulled the tin to prevent its shining in the sun. They also washed all the pipeclay out of their belts, straps and pouches and stained them a "muddy-looking brown by being soaked in tea"[12]. Indian regiments with their more serviceable brown or black leather equipment had no need of such measures, but sensible commanders of other British battalions would have emulated the Derbys in preparing their men to take the field.

Throughout most of September and early October the Commissariat and Transport Departments pursued their onerous task of collecting the wherewithal to fight and despatching it up the line of communication to Shinawari.

At the same time the fighting units marched into Kohat and were pushed on to the same place as they arrived. A mountain gunner saw "the roads in every direction full with gathering troops, Highlanders, Gurkhas, Sikhs eager to avenge Saragarhi, long lines of Indian cavalry, their lances standing high above the acrid dust they stirred. By the side of the roads strings of laden camels padded on beside the troops, the jinkety-jink of the mountain guns, the skirling of the pipes, the haunting lilt of '*Zakhmi dil*' played on *dole* and *sarnai*, all contributed to the wild excitement and romance of the scene"[13].

As the long, dusty columns of men, guns and animals tramped westwards, always keeping a wary eye to their right in case the Orakzais came over the hills, a proclamation from Lockhart was on its way to all the tribal sections of the Tirah. It explained that due to their treachery in August and September all their subsidies were forfeit, and that he was going to enter and traverse all their territory with a large force. This was not open to negotiation; but no damage would be done if they did not resist. They were to send their deputations to him once he reached the centre of their territories to hear his terms for their submission and reparation.

By the middle of October this uncompromising statement would have reached the tribes, and the means to enforce it were poised at Shinawari in the shape of the complete 2nd Division; as Hamilton had forecast, the 1st Division was still at least a day's march back down the Kohat road, although the order of march may have been determined more by Yeatman-Biggs' familiarity with the terrain than Lockhart's possible aversion to Symons.

* * *

The great advance, which was planned to begin on 20 October, had as its first objective the village of Karappa in the Khanki Valley, six miles beyond the Samana Range. To reach it there were two tracks: a minor one from Fort Gulistan via the Talia spur, and a slightly better one to the west from Shinawari over the Chagru Kotal. Both were so indifferent that the Sappers had been working hard to improve them, but those on the Kotal had been constantly

English infantry on the march near Kohat with mule and camel transport. (Author's collection)

harassed by long-range firing from a high point further west called Narik Suk and, to the south of it, the village of Dargai[14]. This was perched on top of a precipitous cliff, 1,100 feet above - and 1,800 yards as the bullet flies from - the Kotal; and the flight of those bullets clearly indicated that Lockhart's proclamation had been ignored.

The 1st Northamptons had been camped around Forts Lockhart and Gulistan since 25 September, thus acquiring at least a "feel" of the Frontier after their five-year sojourn in South India. From 11 October they had been sent out daily with No.9 (British) Mountain Battery to give long-range covering fire to the working parties from a north-south ridge called Samana Suk, midway between the Kotal and Gulistan. However the range, at 3,200 yards, was too great for effective rifle-fire - even from one of the best shooting regiments in the Army[15] - and almost up to the maximum range of the mountain guns; and in any case the enemy were too well-protected in sangars and behind rocks. Obviously their position would seriously imperil the advance over the Kotal on 20 October; so the 2nd Division was ordered to clear them on the 18th.

Leaving Shinawari at 4a.m., Kempster's 3rd Brigade began a long and difficult flanking march and climb to the west, in order eventually to attack the Dargai position from its rear while the enemy's attention was held by Westmacott's 4th Brigade attacking frontally from Chagru Kotal, covered by Nos.9 and 5 (Bombay) Mountain Batteries. As Yeatman-Biggs was still laid low with dysentery, Lockhart gave command of the attack to Lieutenant-General Sir Power Palmer, hitherto commanding the line of communications, who elected to accompany Kempster: the flank attack was conceived as the main effort, since it was thought that the vulnerability of the frontal approach would permit no more than a holding action. Lockhart and his staff took up a position of observation on Samana Suk.

The approach facing Westmacott's men was formidable indeed, in more ways than one. The enemy atop their cliff had excellent cover, both from view and from fire, due to their sangars and the huge rocks along the crest. These

A sketch by the correspondent Melton Prior of the veiw from Shinawari towards the Dargai Heights (centre skyline), Chagru Kotal (right centre, under smoke cloud), and Samana Suk (right hand peak). (Author's collection)

positions commanded the head of the only track, which was very rough, narrow, and zig-zagged diagonally up the cliff face, although its base, at the foot of the cliff, was invisible from the top due to the gradient. This point could only be reached by following another track from Chagru Kotal, which initially ran westwards through the small village of Mamu Khan, along a narrow ridge or spur for some 1,500 yards; this was in full view of the crest, although some cover could be obtained by moving along its southern side. However, between the end of this spur, after it had bent northwards, and the foot of the cliff where the zig-zag track started, there was an open space or saddle some 200 yards long by 30 yards wide, bounded on the west side by a perpendicular rock-face jutting out from the main cliff and slanting down to a precipitous fall to the east. Apart from a rocky outcrop halfway across it was quite devoid of cover, and was within only 200-250 yards range of rifles on the crest. Its slant was such that later, when a man was hit crossing it, he rolled over and over until he disappeared over the east side.

Westmacott's attack was to be led by the 1/3rd Gurkhas, supported by the 2nd King's Own Scottish Borderers, with the Northamptons in reserve. (His fourth battalion, the 36th Sikhs, was still garrisoning the Samana forts.) Having marched up from Shinawari after Kempster's brigade had left, Westmacott reached the southern end of the Chagru Kotal at 7a.m. and halted out of range to allow time for the flanking movement to develop. At 9a.m. the 1/3rd Gurkhas advanced and took cover in Mamu Khan while the mountain guns went into action, firing over their heads at the heights, and the Borderers got into fire positions to cover the Gurkhas' further advance.

As the Orakzais started firing down at the spur Corporal McKeown of the Borderers, commanding a section, gave the order to open fire with volleys at 750 yards: "The

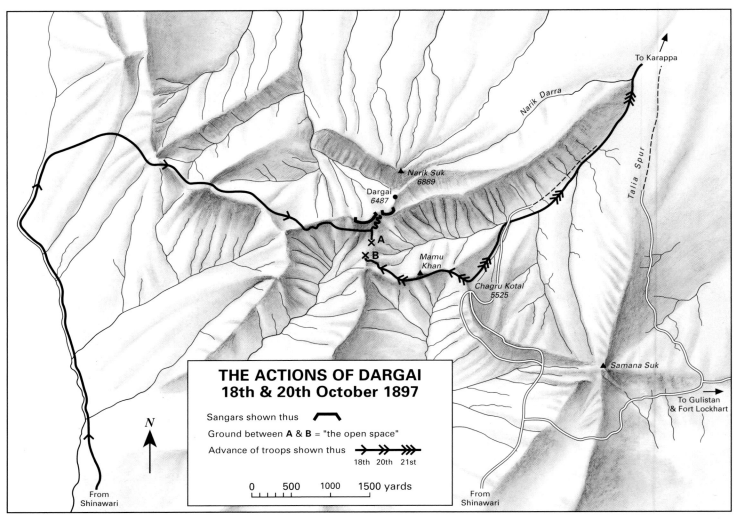

THE ACTIONS OF DARGAI
18th & 20th October 1897

Sangars shown thus

Ground between **A** & **B** = "the open space"

Advance of troops shown thus
18th   20th   21st

0   500   1000   1500 yards

enemy's fire coming over our heads made me a little excited, but I gave the commands all right except the command 'Fire' which I gave too quick for the first two volleys, the men not having enough time to aim. After these two volleys I was all right, I had 16 men and each fired 19 rounds, myself and men were calm and collected and having the right distance we scattered the enemy"[16].

Once the gunfire and rifle volleys began to take effect the Gurkhas moved forward from Mamu Khan, below the east-west spur, towards the ledge which marked the beginning of the open space and behind which they formed up, being at this point in dead ground from the crest. By noon, though there was still no sign nor sound of Kempster's flank attack, they were told to go.

"Over the brow we rushed by successive companies, the appearance of each being greeted with a shower of bullets", wrote Captain Ormsby afterwards. Having raced across the fire-swept space, each company found cover at the foot of the cliff from where, after a brief pause to get their breath, they began the steep ascent. Hard on the heels of the last Gurkha company came the Borderers, "trying hard to catch us up, but we had a good start on them and kept the lead, though they were very nearly on even terms with us at the finish". Corporal McKeown recalled, "we could not run, we didn't go up at ordinary walking pace, we were tumbling all over the place".

However, despite the steepness of the climb and the natural strength of the enemy position, so effective had been the covering fire and so determined the assault that the Orakzais would not face the kukris and bayonets coming up

at them. Before the leading company reached the top, "the hearts of the enemy failed them and they bolted. A little after midday, exhausted but well content, we gained the crest. We got in a few volleys at the scattered figures scurrying down the slopes, and then sat down for a welcome rest"[17].

When Lieutenant Beynon, "with revolver in one hand and alpenstock in the other"[18], led the 1/3rd Gurkhas over the crest, one reason for the Orakzais' sudden departure became apparent - the sight of Kempster's Gurkha Scouts leading his brigade only a mile away. Kempster had been delayed by terrain so difficult that he had had to return his mountain battery and mule-borne hospital to Shinawari, escorted by the 1st Dorsets. Although he had been unable to deliver his attack before midday, the approaching threat to their rear must undoubtedly have unnerved the Orakzais and accelerated their retreat. Nevertheless Westmacott's men could not have known of this, and to have captured such a strong and so difficult a position so quickly, and with no more than a score of casualties, reflected, in the view of one eyewitness, "great credit on all engaged in it, and testifying to their endurance as well as to their pluck"[19].

So much so that the Northamptons in reserve had had nothing to do except practise their hill-climbing with a walk up to Dargai - and then another walk down again, to rejoin No.9 Battery on the Samana Suk. This was to conform with a decision then taken by Lockhart, which was to have the most serious results and was to be much questioned.

By early afternoon the Dargai Heights were securely

held by both brigades of the 2nd Division, the Orakzais had fled, and the route forward over the Chagru Kotal to Karappa had been made safe for the advance on the 20th - all as planned. Lockhart's immediate aim was to establish both his divisions in the Khanki Valley prior to forcing the Sampagha and Arhanga Passes, led by the 2nd Division. The 1st Division was still marching up from Hangu and was not due to advance from Shinawari until the 22nd. To hold until then the Dargai Heights, and a line of communication thereto from Shinawari, would require most of the 2nd Division remaining where it was. This it was not equipped to do, having gone out for only a one-day operation since it was believed that, once the Orakzais had been driven off, they would not return. Retention of Dargai would also render null and void a deception plan intended to delude the enemy as to Lockhart's chosen line of advance. In any case it was understood that there was insufficient water in the vicinity to sustain a holding force. Lockhart therefore signalled for the position to be evacuated. Westmacott at least was so astonished that he immediately questioned the order with Sir Power Palmer, who confirmed it and told him to lead off down with his brigade.

However valid Lockhart's reasons for his decision, they failed to take account of the Afridis who, it was thought, were fully occupied preparing the Sampagha Pass for defence. Unfortunately several thousand of them in the Khanki Valley, hearing the sound of the guns, had been hastening up to Dargai, rallying the Orakzais on their way.

Westmacott's brigade had begun its descent, encumbered with dhoolies carrying the wounded, at 2.30p.m., leaving B and H Companies of the Borderers as rearguard. Kempster had started to follow two hours later, when the appearance of the returning tribesmen forced him to convert an unimpeded retirement into a fighting withdrawal against heavy odds on ground favouring the enemy. He therefore took the two Borderers' companies under his command.

Leaving the 15th Sikhs to hold the head of the zig-zag track, Kempster sent five companies of the 1st Gordon Highlanders, with the remaining Borderers, to take up positions around the open space to cover the Sikhs coming down, while the mountain batteries on the Chagru Kotal opened fire on the tribesmen now thronging the heights. Despite the gunfire and the Sikhs' volleys the tribesmen followed up the withdrawal, firing through the now gathering dusk which, before long, forced the gunners to cease fire. The Gordons' and Borderers' rearguards were soon under fire; Major Jennings-Bramly of the former was killed and several men wounded.

Once the last Sikh company was safely through, three Gordons' companies and the Borderers fell back to a new position. When they were ready, the last two companies, now under fire from several directions, thinned out one after the other. Though severely pressed, the Gordons remained very calm as they returned fire. When only Captain Kerr and one half-company remained some hitherto unseen enemy tried a surprise rush against their rear from just 30 yards away. Though momentarily confused, "Kerr's men stood steady and shot six within a few yards of their bayonets, when to their great relief the others turned and ran"[20].

It was now almost dark, and the enemy fortunately made no further attempt to pursue. The men had been marching and climbing since 4a.m. that morning, with a stiff fight at the end; and they still had another eight miles to cover, carrying their dead and wounded, before they reached camp at Shinawari. The plight of the wounded on jolting stretchers borne by tired men over the rough ground was painful indeed, and it was not until 11p.m. that the exhausted rearguard got in. The order to abandon the heights, so splendidly cleared earlier in the day, had been carried out successfully but at a cost of seven killed and 35 wounded, of which nearly half belonged to the Gordons. Many must have wondered whether these casualties, and the 21 suffered by the 4th Brigade, had been justified by the day's operations.

With only one day left before his planned advance on the 20th, Lockhart had intended that the 2nd Division should spend it sending out working and covering parties to continue improving the Chagru Kotal-Karappa track; this activity would also, it was thought, deter the enemy from re-occupying the Dargai Heights, since they would fear being cut off once the force reached Karappa. However Yeatman-Biggs, who had resumed his command, believed his division needed a rest and kept his men in camp. When news of this reached Lockhart, it was followed by the even more unpalatable information that the tribesmen were now holding Dargai in great strength.

Signal traffic between the divisional and force commanders intensified. To avoid the Dargai threat to his left flank, Yeatman-Biggs said he would advance on Karappa from Gulistan, via the eastern side of the Samana Suk and Talia - the easterly track. Lockhart replied that that track was quite inadequate, the ground wooded and broken, inviting ambushes from the enemy, who could easily descend from Dargai. He ordered Yeatman-Biggs to stick to the Chagru Kotal route, as once over the other side he could threaten the enemy rear via a defile running down from Narik Suk; but he accepted that the 2nd Division would at least have to contain the enemy on Dargai. To this end, Yeatman-Biggs would have attached to his command from the 1st Division the 2nd Derbyshire, 3rd Sikhs, and No.1 (Kohat) Mountain Battery. The Northamptons, 36th Sikhs, and No.9 Battery would remain on Samana Suk to guard his right flank and give long-range fire support if needed.

No.9 (RA) Mountain Batterry manhandling its "screw-guns" into position; with the 5th (Bombay), this battery provided fire support for the assault on Dargai of 18 October. (Author's collection)

Lt. Col. Dixon (centre of three offficers) poses with his sergeants of the 2nd King's Own Scottish Borderers, who followed hard on the heels of the 1/3rd Gurkhas in the successful assault against the Orakzais holding Dargai Heights on 18 October. (Navy & Army Illustrated)

This gave Yeatman-Biggs no choice of route; and to pass a division, with all its baggage train, over the Kotal and down into the Khanki Valley within 1,500 yards' range of the Dargai Heights would, he decided, require rather more than containment of the latter. He therefore ordered Kempster's brigade to assault the Heights from the Chagru Kotal the following morning, using the same route as on the 18th. Thus the work was all to be done again, but with the enemy now in far greater strength.

* * *

At 10 a.m. on the 20th three mountain batteries opened fire and the 3rd Brigade advanced. Leading were the 3rd Gurkha Scouts just ahead of Lieutenant-Colonel Travers' 1/2nd Goorkhas[21], with the 1st Dorsets in support and the 2nd Derbyshire in reserve. The 1st Gordons were to fire long-range volleys from around Mamu Khan, and the 3rd Sikhs were escort to the guns on Chagru Kotal. The 15th Sikhs were attached to the 4th Brigade. The second assault on Dargai had begun.

When the Gurkha Scouts had progressed about half a mile westwards along the Mamu Khan spur the tribesmen started to fire down, but to little effect owing to the protection afforded by the spur – as had happened on the 18th. By 11a.m. the Scouts and the 1/2nd were poised behind the ledge fronting on to the open space, with the Dorsets and Derbys closed up behind under cover among the rocks, while the Gordons, a little further back, were adding their volleys to the gunfire. The Derbys, unable to see anything from where they crouched, opened their haversacks for a bite at their bully beef and biscuits, having had nothing since 5a.m.

When Travers was confident his men were ready he asked the nearest Dorset companies to give covering fire, and ordered Lieutenant Tillard and the Scouts forward. They scrambled over the ledge, into an immediate hail of bullets as they raced across the open ground. Several fell, but Tillard and the others reached safety on the far side, looking back for the 1/2nd. Led by Travers in person two companies were already moving at best speed. The intensity of the fire had increased and, though Travers, two captains and some

riflemen reached Tillard, many failed to cross the space.

Major Judge led the next rush; he was shot in the eye as he started yet continued, only to be shot dead as he reached cover, leaving more dead and wounded behind him. When Travers saw Captain Robbins emerge with more men, "I was yelling myself hoarse to stop them, but they could not hear and we could not go back"[22]. Robbins came on, men fell, he was hit in the foot, then limped back – to stop the others, according to Travers, to bring on more men, according to Tillard - but was wounded again, this time mortally.

In ten minutes the Scouts and 1/2nd Goorkhas had sustained 71 casualties. Some had reached their colonel among the rocks at the foot of the cliff; others had run back to the shelter of the ledge where they "squatted, officerless, dogged and sullen, thirsting to revenge the slaughter of their comrades"[23]. Above them thousands of the best-armed, most martial tribesmen of the Frontier, relatively immune from the covering fire among the great rocks and strongly-built sangars, were concentrating their fire from several directions, at the most lethal ranges of 200-300 yards, upon this fatal strip of rock and stone. Had it not been for the Goorkhas' speed and agility over this bad, slanting ground the casualties could have been even worse. But for the time being the 1/2nd had shot their bolt.

Now it was the Dorsets' turn. They were not natural hillmen like Gurkhas or Afridis. Two months before they had been living a peacetime routine in a sleepy South India cantonment. They had not even seen action on the 18th. Their first four companies, A-D, had been firing to support the 1/2nd but had seen how ineffective their volleys had been. The other four had heard the fire and seen the casualties. Nevertheless "Primus in Indis" was their ancient motto[24]; and over the ledge clambered Captain Arnold's E Company by sections.

Arnold was hit at once and most of the leading section went down. A few got across, some reached the half-way rocks. Among them was Private Vickery, a Somerset man aged 24. Seeing a wounded comrade lying in the open with bullets falling around him, he ran back through the rain of fire, picked him up and carried him back towards the ledge. Although the slightest movement across that exposed space attracted an instant and concentrated fusillade, he managed to reach cover with his burden quite unscathed himself, and saved the other man's life.

F Company's first section tried; only one officer reached the far side and the other sections fell back behind the ledge. Meanwhile, for Travers among the rocks at the cliff's foot, "watching each rush and knowing what must happen was a terrible experience"[25]. G Company went next, but for men in action for the first time, well knowing how their comrades had fared and hearing the constant musketry raining down, it was a most daunting test. Only one officer and some 20 men got anywhere and that was into the nearest cover.

By now the Dorsets' A to D Companies in the firing line were running short of ammunition. Three mule-loads were sent up from below, but the animals took fright and fell over the side of the narrow path taking their loads with them. As the 2nd Derbys had now pressed forward, their A and C Companies were ordered to relieve the Dorsets in the firing line, while Captain Smith's E Company was to move up alongside the Dorsets' H Company in the hope that two companies going over the ledge together would stand a better chance than the section rushes tried hitherto – not that this had served the Goorkhas any better.

Moreover this was easier ordered than executed, due to the mass of men huddled together, with the wounded, under the ledge, through which the two fresh companies had to force their way. Instead, therefore, of a double-company rush all together, they emerged in handfuls which offered easy pickings for the enemy marksmen.

Of the Dorsets, only two officers and some men dashed right across or reached the half-way rocks. Captain Smith and Lieutenant Pennell charged out with a few Derbys but all went down except Pennell. He, seeing his captain no longer with him, ran back through the fire to try to get him into cover; but Smith was too big a man for him to lift and, seeing some Dorsets lying around, he called for them to help. One said: "We're all wounded, sir, except those that are dead"[26]. Despite his acute danger Pennell continued to try to drag Smith back until, realising that his captain was already dead, he left him and raced down to the ledge. Tillard, who had seen this from the cliff's foot, found it "hard to understand how he escaped untouched as at the time he was the only man moving on the dangerous zone and had all the Afridi rifles directed at him"[27].

After a second Derby attempt had failed their colonel, Dowse, suggested to the Dorsets' colonel, Piercy, that he move his men back so that the other Derby companies could try a rush in mass. To this Piercy would not agree; nor would he allow his other four companies, A–D, to try, despite their captains' pleas to do so. So the blockage remained at the ledge – Goorkhas, Dorsets and Derbys all intermingled and disheartened. Any movement over the ledge drew instant retaliation; the wounded in the open lay helpless; while "from the heights above the exultant enemy waved his wretched rags of standards and yelled defiance"[28].

It was now 2p.m., four hours after the attack had first started. News of its failure had already been signalled back to Kempster and Yeatman-Biggs, who had ordered the Gordon Highlanders forward from Mamu Khan, followed by the 3rd Sikhs. By now the Gordons were a few hundred yards below the ledge where they received a signal ordering them to attack with the 3rd Sikhs; the Goorkhas and Derbys were to be in support, the Dorsets in reserve. The three latter battalions were to move aside or back to clear the way. All the mountain batteries, which had been firing intermittently hitherto, were to put down a concentrated bombardment for three minutes just before the Gordons went over.

The Gordons had an advantage over the English battalions, having fought over this very ground on the 18th, though going the other way. Even so it cannot have been encouraging to watch – as they had over the previous hours – the mournful procession of dead and wounded being carried down from the ledge, or to hear the comments of the discouraged English soldiers as they filed back out of the way. Still, the Gordons were veterans of Chitral; some of their older men, like their Lieutenant-Colonel H.H.Mathias, had fought the Dervishes on the Nile in 1884; and they had their casualties of the 18th to avenge. Above all they were Highlanders – even if their Sergeant-Major had a more natural affinity with the Dorsets, being a Wiltshireman enlisted at Dorchester[29] – and as such they would have to show the English battalions how the work should be done.

Captain Slessor of the Derbys watched the kilts swinging past him: "Up they came, a long, thin string of men with stern, set faces, stumbling, scrambling up the steep in a frenzy of courage not to be gainsaid, amid

Conspicuous in the assault against the Afridis at Dargai, 20 October - from left top: Lt.Col.Mathias, 1st Gordons; Maj.Judge, 1/2nd Goorkhas; Lt.Lamont, 1st Gordons; Pte.Vickery VC, 1st Dorsets; Lt.Pennell VC, 2nd Derbyshire; Piper Findlater VC, 1st Gordons. (Author's collection)

occasional spasmodic gasps from the pipes and cheers from any who had breath to utter, a sight for those who witnessed it to remember all their lives"[30].

In the ground below the ledge, now cleared by the other battalions, Lieutenant-Colonel Mathias closed his companies up ready to go. Not for them the failed double-company, company or section rushes; this time it was to be a battalion rush, with another - the 3rd Sikhs, a veteran Frontier Force battalion - close behind. The English infantry and Goorkhas took up firing positions wherever they could find them, ready to support the Gordons. The batteries opened up, all 24 guns firing together, deluging the heights with shells as the Highlanders prepared themselves.

The guns ceased. Colonel Mathias called out: "Highlanders! The General says the position is to be taken at all costs. The Gordons will take it!"[31] The bugle blew, the pipers struck up *Cock o' the North*, and Mathias, with Major Macbean on his right and Lieutenant Gordon on his left, led over the ledge with his Highlanders cheering close behind.

As soon as they appeared, the tribesmen once again poured their fire down regardless of the volleys from the English battalions and the 1/2nd. Lieutenant Lamont and two men were killed immediately. Macbean fell shot through the thigh, but dragged himself to a boulder and cheered the men on. Others went down wounded, among them four more officers including Lieutenant Dingwall, who was hit four times. Private Lawson, a Northumbrian, ran to him, picked him up and carried him to cover; he turned back, was struck twice, but reached the fallen Private Macmillan and brought him to safety. Piper Findlater was shot through both feet but crawled to a rock, propped himself up against it and, despite the bullets falling around him, continued to play *Cock o' the North* to encourage his comrades.

All the while the Afridis fired as fast as they could reload, for they were witnessing something they had not seen before that day. Though inevitably they were still inflicting casualties, the speed and impetus of a whole battalion charging together was carrying it across the killing ground where so many had failed or fallen. Close behind came the 3rd Sikhs and with them, in no sort of order, Goorkhas, Derbys and Dorsets, all with their spirits lifted by the Gordons' great rush.

Reaching the rocks at the foot of the cliff, where those who had got across earlier had waited for so long, the leading Gordons paused for breath before scaling the zig-zag path up which none that day had even begun to climb. Tillard of the Gurkha Scouts, who had been there for some three hours, wrote later: "The scene makes me shake with excitement even now. The Gordons, pipers playing and men cheering, never stopped or wavered although many of them were down. It was one wild continuous rush of men all eager to get at the enemy. The sight was magnificent and the excitement so intense that I for one, although I was shouting at the top of my voice, felt the tears springing up into my eyes and could not keep them back"[32].

Then on the Gordons went, up the path with everyone joining in, vying with each other to reach the top. Had the Afridis held the head of the narrow track they could still have inflicted great loss and even held up the Gordons' climb; but now their fire began to waver and die away in the face of the mass of men scrambling up towards them. A few last shots, then silence save for the pipes and the cheering. By the time the leading troops - among them Tillard, his orderly Naik Hastbir, and Lieutenant Cowie of the Dorsets - gained the crest not an Afridi, not an Orakzai was to be seen except in the distance. All had fled. Dargai was won.

A remarkable photograph of corporals of the 1st Gordons and naiks of the 1/2nd Goorkhas posing together after the taking of Dargai, emphasising a bond of comradeship between the two battalions which was unusual between British and Indian Army soldiers. (The Gurkha Museum)

As Mathias, who had led his Highlanders so gallantly, breasted the last rise somewhat out of breath, he remarked to an NCO: "Stiff climb, eh, Mackie? Not quite...so young...as I was...you know". Giving his commanding officer a comradely slap on the back, the Colour-Sergeant replied: "Never mind, sir! Ye're gaun vara strong for an auld man!"[33] Seeing, no doubt with some pride, what he and his men had achieved and hearing them cheering him, and the other regiments cheering them, he asked for a signaller. Sergeant Cursley of the Derbys stepped forward with a signal flag. Mathias told him to inform the brigade and divisional commanders down on the Chagru Kotal that the Dargai Heights were cleared.

The second capture of Dargai, opening the way forward for the whole Tirah Field Force, had not been without cost. The Gordons had lost one officer and two men killed, six officers and 35 men wounded. The 1/2nd Goorkhas had the heaviest losses - two officers and 16 men killed, 49 wounded; the 3rd Sikhs, three killed, one officer and 16 men wounded; the 2nd Derbys, one officer and three men killed, eight wounded; the 1st Dorsets - the hardest-hit British battalion - nine killed, two officers and 39 men wounded; and the Gurkha Scouts, two killed and two wounded - 197 casualties in all, more than three times as many as had been sustained during the first capture and withdrawal on the 18th.

It was after 3p.m. by the time Dargai was taken, too late to begin any further movement towards Karappa. This time there was no question of evacuating the Heights before the interrupted advance could be re-commenced. The 1/2nd Goorkhas and Dorsets were positioned for the night around Dargai and the Derbys on the Narik Suk, being later relieved by the 30th Punjabis of the 1st Division. The other battalions descended to spend a cold, cheerless night around Chagru Kotal, with little food or water, as the transport animals' move up from Shinawari had been blocked by the long delay at the Kotal. During the descent the Gordons volunteered to carry down the dead and wounded of the 1/2nd Goorkhas and the Dorsets, an act of kindness which particularly cemented a bond of friendship with the former regiment (first formed in the Afghan War when the Gordons' 2nd Battalion, then the 92nd, had served alongside the 2nd Goorkhas at Kandahar).

* * *

After the 1st Gordons had undergone their annual inspection between the Chitral and Tirah campaigns, the inspecting officer had observed that their officers were "an exceptionally nice set; the warrant and non-commissioned officers seem to be very efficient, and the privates have an admirable physique" - a revealing insight into a Victorian general's priorities[34]. At Dargai the lower ranks had undoubtedly justified that verdict, while their officers could be said to have displayed fine leadership and great gallantry - though of course prevented by their "niceness" from making any such claim themselves. They were, however, more than ready to recommend their men for bravery awards. Seven NCOs later received the Distinguished Conduct Medal, including Colour-Sergeant Mackie and Lance-Corporal Milne, who had led the pipers and been shot in the chest; and the Victoria Cross went to Private Lawson and Piper Findlater for the deeds already described. VCs were also awarded to Lieutenant Pennell of the Derbys and Private Vickery of the Dorsets. Lockhart recommended Colonel Mathias for the VC but he was debarred by a War Office ruling that commanding officers were ineligible. Then as now, they see things differently in Whitehall.

*Robert Gibb's 1909 painting of Dargai, showing the Gordons and
3rd Sikhs reaching the 1/2nd Goorkhas at the cliff foot after rushing
the fire-swept open ground. This is one of the best reconstructions of
the action, although not accurate in all details: the Gordons did not
wear helmet curtains on 20 October, and their pouches should be the
1894 - not 1888 - pattern. See also Plate F. (Sotheby's)*

The Gordons' storming of Dargai exemplified the best
kind of regimental pride and spirit. Had they not succeeded,
Yeatman-Biggs would have been guilty of ignoring the
well-known principle of war that one should never reinforce
failure, while Lockhart would have had to recast his plan of
advance. Certainly they had benefited from knowing the
ground and from much better co-ordinated fire support than
the earlier attempts had been given. Furthermore the enemy,
after four hours' firing, may have been running short of
ammunition, hence their surprising failure to dispute the
final climb up the zig-zag track - though to have done so
would have required them to leave the rocks which hitherto
had shielded them so effectively. Then again, after
successfully halting the earlier "penny-packet" attempts to
cross the danger zone, they may have become confused, even
unnerved, by Mathias' decision to swarm across in mass.
Nevertheless the fact remained that the Gordons had
converted defeat into victory.

When news of Dargai reached home, in that year of
Queen Victoria's Diamond Jubilee, it aroused enormous
public enthusiasm, not only in Britain but throughout the
Empire, such as no other action of the Pathan Revolt had
attracted hitherto. Writers and journalists, poets and
versifiers, artists and illustrators, all rushed to assuage the
public's appetite. That the heroes of the hour were
Highlanders - always great favourites with the public - was an
added bonus to their efforts. Two paintings of the action
would be exhibited at the Royal Academy in 1898 - both, in
one officer's view, "impossible"[35]. Mathias' brief but
compelling exhortation to his men became almost household
words - if in several variations. When the wounded Findlater
VC returned home he was feted as a national hero after being
decorated by the Queen, appearing at the Royal Tournament
- and even on the stage of the Alhambra Music Hall.

In military circles such commercialisation of a soldier's

bravery was felt to be contrary to the customs of the service.
Moreover, while not denying the great credit due to the
Gordons - the Commander-in-Chief, Lord Wolseley, sent
them a personal telegram of congratulation - some officers
felt that in the general enthusiasm sight had been lost of the
part played by the other battalions, particularly the two
which had taken Dargai in the first attack on the 18th. In
the cloakroom of the Army and Navy Club in London,
always prone to the inadvertent misappropriation of
umbrellas, a notice bearing a waggish play on Mathias'
famous words appeared one day: "Do not leave your
umbrella in this Club. The Gordons will take it!"[36]

It would have amused any KOSB, Dorset or Derby
officer who saw it - perhaps even a Gordon; but the
national mood would have responded more warmly to that
balladeer of Imperial themes, Henry Newbolt:

"There are bullets by the hundred buzzing in the air;
There are bonny lads lying on the hillside bare;
But the Gordons know what the Gordons dare
When they hear the pipers playing!"[37]

*Dorsets and Gordons burying their dead at Shinawari after the
second taking of Dargai. Note the helmet curtains (left); and (centre
background) the Gordon wearing his sporran pushed round to the
back, as often seen in photographs of Highlanders labouring.
(Author's collection)*

CHAPTER NINE

The Scouring of Tirah

To the public at home the victory at Dargai may have seemed to be the end of the Tirah campaign. For the men in the field, however, it was only the beginning. Furthermore, the fact that the two days' fighting at Dargai had cost more casualties than had been sustained during the four-day defence of Malakand, and nearly as many as the Mamunds had inflicted on Jeffreys' brigade over three weeks, might have portended a much greater butcher's bill to come than had been presented in the whole Revolt so far.

Had Lockhart been in more robust health and able to exercise a closer control over events from the 18th onwards than had been possible from his headquarters at Fort Lockhart (selected as being more beneficial for his health than Shinawari), those events might have taken a less costly turn. Nevertheless, for the immediate future, with both divisions concentrated around Karappa by 27 October, he was able to claim that "the enemy's defeat was rendered more complete and decisive by their being encouraged to hold on to the last and the movement of the troops, baggage and supplies from Shinawari to Karappa was almost unmolested"[1].

The advance to Karappa, led by the 2nd Division, had begun on 21 October, a day later than planned, and the following week was occupied with closing up the rest of the force and reconnoitring forward towards the Sampagha Pass. The move of the baggage train proved particularly time-consuming due to the bad tracks and the indifferent quality of the beasts and their drivers. Although the enemy had not contested the advance, the concentration of such a large and mainly stationary force around Karappa presented a worthwhile target for night sniping and the daytime harassment of small foraging parties.

After the loss of 22 casualties on the 25th, this marauding was countered by positioning company-strength picquets, well defended, on the highest surrounding hilltops to deny them to the tribesmen, who were always sensitive to any firing from above them. Small parties of Gurkha Scouts were also sent out, barefooted and in plain clothes with only their kukris, rifles and a few rounds, to stalk the snipers. These measures, plus the digging-in or stonewalling of sleeping and living areas, greatly reduced the casualties and were adopted in all future camping sites.

By late on 27 October all was ready for the thrust through the two gateways into Tirah, the Sampagha and Arhanga Passes. The advance to Karappa might have been almost unmolested; but from the evidence of sangar-building and enemy activity around Sampagha, only some six miles away, serious resistance as well as stiff climbing lay ahead.

To ensure that he had his force well in hand for the attack, Lockhart devoted the 28th to a move forward of three miles. This was protected by the 1st Northamptons and Haughton's 36th Sikhs moving out before dawn to seize

Men of the 1st Dorsets watching a flank. Most wear the additional quilted curtain attached round their helmets. (Authors's collection)

a prominent hill which commanded the line of advance and was known to be occupied by the enemy during daylight. So effectively was this done that the two battalions reached the top before dawn and before the tribesmen re-occupied it. The latter then opened fire from another hill 900 yards away and a fire-fight continued for most of the day, but the main force was able to advance without interference and made ready to attack the the Sampagha the next day, with the 1st Division leading.

* * *

The summit of the pass was 7,000 feet up; it was approached by a valley three-quarters of a mile wide and guarded on either flank by spurs running down from the main ridge. At 5a.m. Hart's 1st Brigade went forward, the 1st Devons up the right spur, the 2/1st Gurkhas up the left, while the 2nd Derbys seized a prominent knoll on which the Division's three mountain batteries were to be positioned, ready to support the main attack by Gaselee's 2nd Brigade. All was done in darkness, in complete silence and with total success.

With daylight the guns arrived, followed by Lockhart, "clad in a long brown ulster"[2] and accompanied by his staff with some war correspondents. Among them was a veteran of many campaigns, Melton Prior of the *Illustrated London News*, who proceeded to sketch the scene after the guns opened fire at 7.30a.m. at 1,850 yards' range against some strong sangars on the lower slopes of the Sampagha[3]. Slessor of the Derbys, whose men were protecting the gun positions, was impressed by the "beautiful precision" with which the shells struck the sangars, but doubted how much damage they actually achieved as the tribesmen endured the bombardment for at least 20 minutes. When they did make a run for it, though shells burst in their midst, "only very rarely was a man seen to drop". Slessor believed they were

No.8 (RA) Mountain Battery shelling enemy sangars along the heights flanking the Arhanga Pass, 31 October; the mouth of the pass is left of the burning building.
Sketch by Melton Prior. (Author's collection)

driven from their defences more by the Devons' rifle-fire from their left flank.[4]

Meanwhile the 2nd Brigade, led by the 1st Queen's – old hands from Malakand – and the 2/4th Gurkhas, had been climbing to the attack supported by the 2nd Yorkshire[5] and 3rd Sikhs. As they neared the forward sangars, now abandoned, the 2nd Division's mountain batteries, which had followed up, began firing at the sangars around the summit of the pass. By 9.45a.m. the Queen's had captured the dip in the ridge over which the pass ran against little opposition, though some enemy still held the higher ground on either side. However, when the other three battalions moved against them they too decamped, and the Sampagha was in Lockhart's hands.

Westmacott's 4th Brigade had been coming up, and he now sent the 36th Sikhs on against a further ridge overlooking the Mastura Valley beyond, with the King's Own Scottish Borderers in support. The enemy thereon started firing, but the combination of a very rapid advance by the Sikhs and very accurate covering volleys from the Borderers enabled Haughton to be the first man to look into the Mastura Valley, with only one sepoy killed and three wounded. By 11.30a.m. all fighting was over and the enemy – who turned out to be all Orakzais – were in full flight across the valley. Despite all forebodings of another Dargai, the first gateway had been forced with the loss of only 24 casualties, of which four were killed, including Captain De Butts, who was shot while reconnoitring the best place for his guns of 5th (Bombay) Battery – "a great loss to the force"[6].

As the troops descended into the Mastura Valley all were astonished at its fertility, "a Garden of Eden in comparison with the barren inhospitable country" elsewhere[7]. Again there was much delay in getting the baggage train forward, so most had to spend a very cold night without blankets or greatcoats and many British soldiers, who had already consumed their day's rations, would have gone hungry had it not been for the generosity of Sikhs and Gurkhas who shared theirs.

Equally astonishing had been the ease, against all expectations, with which the Sampagha had been forced. Lockhart determined to exploit this – and to prevent any

"scorched earth" action by the tribesmen – by attacking the Arhanga Pass without delay. The next day had to be spent getting the baggage and supplies over the Sampagha into Mastura, where they were to be guarded by the 1st Brigade, while the other three prepared to attack on the 31st.

In the event hardly any resistance was encountered. Westmacott's men seized a gun position, three massed batteries opened fire, all three brigades advanced, and by 11a.m. the Yorkshires were on the crest; only two men were wounded. That evening the Field Force, less the 1st Brigade which was to remain in Mastura, was encamped at Maidan in the heart of the Tirah. The purdah curtain had been torn aside. Lockhart had proved to the Afridis and Orakzais that he was as good as his proclamation; would they now submit?

The Afridis had flinched from another Dargai, but they soon showed their hand as guerrillas. The very evening the camp was established at Maidan they ambushed a long, straggling convoy of baggage animals escorted by the 15th Sikhs after dark. The Sikhs managed to save the ammunition mules, but much else was lost and many muleteers were butchered. The next evening another convoy from Arhanga was passing through a village within a mile of the camp. Suddenly Afridis leapt from the roofs into the midst of it, killing three of the escort from 1st Queen's, wounding others, capturing 11,000 rounds of Lee-Metford ammunition, and dispersing some 70 baggage animals carrying nearly half the battalion's kit. The 60-strong escort had been spread over the mile-long convoy, but close to the attack was Lance-Corporal Simpson with a dozen men. He at once charged the nearest tribesmen with fixed bayonets, killing or driving them off. He then doubled his men up the hillside to fire volleys down into the houses. When the enemy tried to get above him he changed position, continuing to fire.

Meanwhile Lieutenant Bulwer of the Northamptons, on picquet nearby, heard the firing and hurried his 30 men down to Simpson's aid. They found the village burning, loose mules careering about, and Queen's and Afridis fighting hand-to-hand. Bulwer's men charged in with bayonets and drove the enemy off; their only casualty was Sergeant Anderson who, well to the fore, was hit twice, later losing his arm but gaining the DCM. Once the firing

The Sampagha Pass: wounded men in dhoolies. The pass was taken from the Orakzais on 29 October for the loss of only four dead and 20 wounded. (Author's collection)

Melton Prior's impression of L/Cpl. Simpson, 1st Queen's, defending the baggage convoy during the major ambush of 1 November; Simpson was promoted sergeant for his conduct. (Author's collection)

What Lt.Col.Haughton, 36th Sikhs, called his "dog kennel" (below) - sleeping quarters in the field, constructed from a tent with overhead cover from a pole and grass roof, and piled stone walls as protection from night sniping into the camp, a favourite passtime of the Pathans. (Maj.A.C.Yate)

ceased the Northamptons carried the Queen's casualties back to camp, commending Simpson to his colonel, who promoted him to sergeant.

Later that evening another 60 Northamptons under Major Compton were returning from picquetting near Arhanga when they too were fired on and surrounded near where the 15th Sikhs had been ambushed. The enemy "kept up a desultory fire and continual howling"[8] but were eventually driven off by good shooting and without loss.

During the first week at Maidan, taken up with surveying – since the issued maps were virtually blank – and foraging, the enemy continued these harassing tactics as well as frequent sniping into the camps. The counter-measures of picquetting and the Gurkha Scouts' fighting patrols remained in force, but the odd shot still found a target, particularly among officers – who were always recognisable to Afridis familiar with the Army from their accoutrements. Captain Sullivan of the 36th Sikhs was hit within an hour of his arriving in camp from England; and on the same evening Lieutenant Giffard became the Northamptons' first fatality.

This battalion, "the old 48th of Peninsular fame" as one officer-correspondent called it[9], had not so far seen much fighting apart from the night actions of 1 November. Writing to a brother officer about Anderson's amputation and the Queen's losses, Lieutenant Norman hoped "our prolonged immunity will continue"[10]. This was just before Giffard was killed on the 6th, and three days later his hopes were to be further dashed.

By now there were indications that the Orakzais, whose territory had been traversed by the recent advance, were contemplating submission. Few signs had come from the Afridis and one clan in particular, the Zakka Khel, was thought to be responsible for the current harassment. A small force under Westmacott had already made its presence felt at Bagh, west of Maidan, a known centre of Afridi intrigue where the mullah Sayid Akbar had planned the uprising. The Zakka Khel lands, however, lay to the east, over the high pass of Saran Sar, 9,500 feet up. It was to reconnoitre this pass and the country beyond that Lockhart

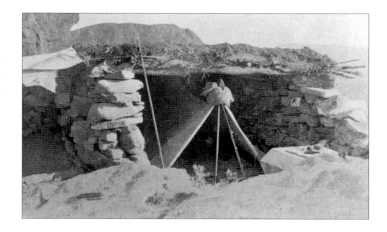

ordered Westmacott to take out a force drawn from the 3rd and 4th Brigades on 9 November. It was to consist of two mountain batteries, a company of Sappers, the 15th and 36th Sikhs, 1st Dorsets and 1st Northamptons.

* * *

The Northamptons had been commanded for three years by Lieutenant-Colonel Chaytor, first commissioned 30 years earlier. Among his majors were two who had fought Zulus and Boers: Hill, who held the Victoria Cross, and Compton, a Staff College graduate. This was Chaytor's first campaign, and in several photographs he seems a less commanding figure than his second-in-command Major Fraser. Nevertheless, as a lieutenant he had been judged competent enough to be Adjutant, a most responsible post, and after commanding the joint Northamptons-36th Sikhs operation on 28 October - with the redoubtable Haughton under his orders - he had received Lockhart's commendation. Since reaching Maidan, however, as Lieutenant Norman humourously observed, "the colonel's guts are out of gear"[11].

On 9 November it fell to Chaytor to seize Saran Sar with his left or north flank guarded by the Dorsets, his right by the 36th Sikhs. Leaving camp at 7.30a.m the Northamptons began the four-mile approach by advancing eastwards up a steep-sided nullah before extending for the

Officers of the 1st Northamptonshire in January 1898. Lt.Col.Chaytor is seated centre, between the second-in-command Maj.Fraser (in helmet) and Maj.Hill VC. Others mentioned in the text are standing: Capt.Parkin, G Coy.(left), Lts.Bulwer and Norman (fourth and sixth from left). Maj.Compton is absent from this group. (Maj.T.C.S.Knox)

final climb to Saran Sar, covered by the guns. They and the Dorsets encountered some slight opposition but by 11 a.m. Chaytor's men had occupied the pass, with three companies to cover the survey parties while the other five were deployed to their left, or north, to watch a wooded slope some 900 yards away, on which tribesmen could be heard but not seen. This slope should have been occupied by the Dorsets, but they had been delayed.

By 12.15p.m. the surveys had been completed. Westmacott was about to order the withdrawal when Lockhart and his staff appeared to have lunch and a look around. This postponed the retirement until after 2 p.m., leaving only three and a half hours to reach camp before dusk. The 36th Sikhs withdrew first to an intermediate position, followed by the three Northamptons companies on the pass, leaving the other five as rearguard under Major Compton, who opened fire on the vacated position to prevent its occupation.

Once the others were ready to cover him Compton began to thin out from his right, sending back A and B Companies 700 yards. These were then fired on from the north, where it was thought the Dorsets still were, but their answering volleys enabled the final three companies to start doubling away. The last to move was Captain Parkin's G Company. They covered 200 yards, then came under heavy fire from the ridge they had just left, to which the tribesmen had rushed forward from the wooded slope. Several men fell; being without stretchers, the company took cover and fired back until help could arrive. In this suddenly perilous situation Sergeant Lennon's reputation and example as a marksman had a very steadying effect upon the younger

soldiers facing their baptism of fire.

Men from the rearward companies came climbing back with stretchers. G Company's ten wounded required four men per stretcher, plus another one or two to carry the rifles, thereby depleting the firing strength; nevertheless the company finally got down the hill in good order to rejoin the rest of the battalion.

Meanwhile the 36th Sikhs, having seen the first three Northampton companies taking up covering positions, had begun to retire but, learning of G Company's difficulty, quickly re-occupied their former position to cover the whole English battalion's move back towards the head of the nullah up which it had advanced that morning. Seeing the Northamptons complete, Haughton recommenced his retirement to protect the south flank, about 1,400 yards from the nullah. To the north the Dorsets, whose H Company had rendered assistance to Parkin's withdrawal, had been fired on from their open flank but had continued their march towards camp.

Chaytor, presuming the Dorsets were still guarding his right, told his leading five companies to move on down the nullah to Maidan. Unfortunately the wounded were not with them, but escorted by the last three companies. As these filed down with the stretchers and dhoolies beneath the steep banks, moving on either side, the sun was setting and there were still another three miles to go. Speed was necessarily limited to that of the bearer parties.

Suddenly an intense, rapid fire rained down upon them from above at point-blank range. Lieutenant Waddell was killed immediately and several men hit. The Afridis, masters of their ground and seeing that the Northamptons' flanks were no longer closely protected, had waited until Chaytor's men were well into the nullah and then, using its intersecting gullies, had raced into position above the slow-moving companies with the wounded. Some were using magazine rifles and their smokeless powder made them difficult to spot.

Since the banks were too steep to climb, the Northamptons could only volley back from either side of the nullah's bed; and the number of effective rifles constantly decreased owing to the growing need for men to carry the casualties. Such men, closely grouped round the stretchers, became prime targets for the Afridis, so that the wretched casualties were often tipped out on to the rocks. Lieutenant Trent, shot in the thigh by a Dum-Dum, suffered this fate when his stretcher broke; but his bearers repaired it while the bullets fell around them, one man having a button shot off his jacket and two others through his clothes; miraculously he, and Trent, survived.

Every effort was made to save the wounded. Corporal Gray picked up the 6ft.2in. Sergeant Litchfield, whose knee was shattered, and carried him away. Sergeant Guy, who had distinguished himself in the night action of 1 November, went back to look for Colour-Sergeant Hull, who had been shot through both ankles, and got him into a dhoolie. Despite the slow, painful and hazardous struggle down this bullet-swept death-trap, not a casualty was left behind.

Meanwhile Major Compton had hurried after the Dorsets. He reached their rearguard, which turned back, but they were too far away to bring immediate help. Fortunately this came from the other flank. Aware of what had happened, Haughton sent across some of his Sikhs who relieved the pressure on the Northamptons, allowing them to get clear. Major Fraser remained in the nullah to the last to make sure all his Northamptons were through. However, in the dark and confusion he did not realise until the roll was called back in camp that 2nd Lieutenant Macintire, Colour-Sergeant Luck and 12 men were missing. Their bodies were found next day and it seemed clear that, having been cut off, they had fought to the end rather than leave their wounded. As Compton wrote later: "All honour to their memory"[12].

The retirement from Saran Sar cost the Northamptons two officers and 20 men killed, one officer and 29 wounded, of whom two later died. Much had gone wrong: the delayed start, the lack of liaison with the Dorsets, the choice of the false security of the nullah for the return, the leaving of the wounded with the rearguard. Part could be ascribed to the Northamptons' - and Dorsets' - inexperience in Frontier warfare. When the wounded Trent reached England he told the story to a brother officer, who afterwards wrote in his diary "Colonel Chaytor does not appear to have done at all well and managed to make everything uncomfortable for them all round"[13]. Chaytor was later placed on half-pay. Nevertheless one officer-correspondent present, when recording Westmacott's praise for the Northamptons' "pluck and coolness" in rescuing their casualties, called it "a display of heroism and devotion worthy of a regiment that fought at Albuera"[14].

The Zakka Khel Afridis had to be taught a lesson; and two days later Gaselee's 2nd Brigade, with the 1/3rd Gurkhas, climbed up to Saran Sar. When the retirement began at noon that day the 3rd Gurkhas abandoned their positions so rapidly that the enemy came on apace - only to run straight into a very accurate and costly cross-fire from the Queen's and 2/4th Gurkhas carefully positioned in rear. Gaselee's men sustained only three casualties.

* * *

On the same day Orakzai deputations arrived at Maidan to hear the terms for their submission. These were fines in rifles and money, restoration of all stolen property, forfeiture of subsidies and formal surrender; they were given a fortnight to comply. Since there was to be no annexation of their territory, their consequent relief seemed likely to outweigh their unwillingness to pay these penalties, though difficulties could be expected over apportioning these between the rival Gar and Samil factions of the tribe. However, the mood in camp was generally hopeful and there were indications that at least some of the Afridi clans were disposed to submission.

Any optimism over the Orakzais received a setback two days later in the Mastura Valley, where the 1st Brigade had remained guarding the line of communication from Shinawari. Major Smith-Dorrien of the 2nd Derbys - famous as one of the few survivors of Isandlwana in Zululand in January 1879 - took out a foraging party with five companies of different battalions. As the forage was

From a group photograph of the 1st Northamptons' G Half-Company at Secunderabad in 1896: from left, Sgt.Litchfield, wounded at Saran Sar on 9 November; Sgt.Lennon, noted for his marksmanship during the action; L/Cpl.Gray, awarded the DCM for rescuing Sgt.Litchfield; and Cpl.Goffey, killed. (Author's collection)

being loaded the 2/1st Gurkha and Devon companies came under heavy and enveloping attack. The forage animals were got away and the forward companies withdrew covered by the Derbys' E Company, Smith-Dorrien handling his small force as skilfully as he was later to command II Corps at Le Cateau in 1914. Subsequently it transpired that this was the Orakzais' last effort, and in any case had probably been instigated by the Afridis.

Though some Afridi clans were wavering the Zakka Khel were still showing their teeth. On 13 November Kempster's 3rd Brigade marched due east into the Waran Valley over the Tseri Kandao Pass, where the invaluable 36th Sikhs, attached for the operation, were posted as a midway link between Kempster and Maidan. The track east of the pass wound through deep, steep-sided gulleys flanked by high hills, some of them wooded; all movement therefore required the most careful picquetting. Thus protected, the advance and the subsequent two days' foraging and reconnaissance met only slight opposition, mostly from long range. In one encounter the Dorsets successfully emulated the Gurkhas' retirement from Saran Sar on the 11th. The mullah Sayid Akbar's house was destroyed, but not before incriminating correspondence had been found therein.

Trouble began, as always, with the withdrawal. The main body and baggage set off at 9a.m. on 16 November for the Tseri Kandao, where the 15th Sikhs replaced the 36th, who fell back to a covering position. Apart from some long-range sniping all went smoothly until 1p.m. when the rearguard - Colonel Travers' 1/2nd Goorkhas with one

The last stand of 2/Lt.Macintire and his 13 Northamptons at Saran Sar, 9 November; drawn by Frank Dadd from a sketch by Lt.Brown, 1/3rd Gurkhas, who found the bodies next day. See also Plate G. (The Northamptonshire Regiment Museum)

company each of the Dorsets and Gordons plus five guns - having seen the main body well up the pass, began to follow. Then the enemy, making every use of the tangled terrain, came on in strength, particularly on the flank. Though suffering casualties the rearguard fell back steadily but, with the constant climbing up and down to hold commanding positions, it was 3p.m. by the time they came under the protection of the 15th Sikhs on the pass, and all were exhausted. In the final moments of their retreat Lieutenant Wylie, a great favourite in the 2nd Goorkhas, was shot through the head only seconds after Travers had warned him to be more careful. His best friend Captain Macintyre braved a merciless fire to rescue his body.

Colonel Abbott's 15th Sikhs quickly came under intense pressure from close range, the Afridis at one point even attempting a sword charge, though this was shot away. However, so closely were the Sikhs engaged and so many their wounded, including Abbott himself and a captain, that instead of thinning out they had no choice but to hold their ground and signal for help.

With his quick tactical perception Haughton, further back, had anticipated their need and was already climbing up with two 36th companies, while Major Des Voeux was following with the other three plus two under-strength Dorset companies, the latter only totalling some 40 men. Haughton's timely intervention stabilised the 15th Sikhs and so checked the enemy assault that he was able to re-start the withdrawal, which he conducted without further loss or interference.

The light had been failing, and by the time they reached the foot of the pass it was quite dark. As they marched west firing hit them from in front and both flanks, the heaviest fusillade coming from houses straight ahead. Haughton immediately ordered all Sikhs and Dorsets to fix bayonets and led a charge at the houses. These they cleared in short

Three of the Northamptons who died with Macintire on 9 November: C/Sgt.Luck, seated in front of Pte.Underwood; and the young Drummer Little. Pet dogs are often seen in such photographs.(Author's collection)

order. Then, being encumbered with wounded, Haughton decided to occupy the houses for the night, while Des Voeux took up position in some ruins about a hundred yards away. They managed to construct some hasty defences; but the enemy went on shooting from the darkness, killing Captain Lewarne of the 15th and wounding Lieutenant Munn of the 36th, as well as numbers of sepoys. It was freezing cold and the few Dorsets, who had no protective clothing, could only be kept warm by allowing them to lie down in relays near some warm embers where an Afridi fire had burned earlier.

They survived the night and when dawn broke, after improvising stretchers for the wounded with rifles and puttees, they set off for Maidan pursued by only a few shots. Before long they met Gaselee's brigade coming to their rescue, and reached camp without further incident. Haughton's leadership and initiative had prevented a potential calamity. Lieutenant Cowie of the Dorsets believed: "We all owe our lives to his determination"[15]. However, neither he nor Haughton had been able to save

some of the Dorsets from a fate similar to that of Macintire's party of Northamptons on 9 November.

It transpired from survivors that two young officers attached from other regiments - Lieutenants Hales and Crooke - and some 30 Dorsets had started with Des Voeux, but had somehow become separated from him and set off for camp. In the dark they had taken separate paths. Hales had been killed but a sergeant had led that party to safety. The other had blundered into a nullah where they had been ambushed. Among them was Private Vickery, one of the Dargai heroes. Attacked by three Afridis he shot one, bayonetted another, then, having difficulty withdrawing his bayonet, hurled a rock at the third before disengaging his rifle and clubbing him with the butt. Though wounded, he collected another injured comrade and found his way through the night to safety. Crooke and 12 men were found butchered next day, their Lee-Metfords stolen.

* * *

After Gaselee's brigade had cleared determined but scattered opposition from a new camping ground at Bagh, the entire

force moved there on 18 November. Lockhart's next reconnaissance was the route from Bagh to Dwatoi seven miles to the north-east, from where access could be gained to the Bara Valley, which led back to Peshawar. With part of Westmacott's brigade he set out on the 22nd, Haughton's redoubtable 36th Sikhs now the inevitable choice for rearguard.

Most of this route, hitherto unsurveyed, proved to be no more than a stony path following a streambed two feet deep in icy water, twisting through a deep, narrow gorge with precipitous heights on either side. Before Westmacott's men could venture into such a potential death-trap the heights had to be secured, on one side by the 2nd Yorkshires, on the other by the 1/2nd Goorkhas.

This was done, but not without loss. Lieutenant Jones, recently joined from England and temporarily commanding his Yorkshire company, encountered a galling fire from some concealed tribesmen about 200 yards away. Unable to spot them he called for a few volunteers and went forward. Having identified the position he ordered his men to keep the tribesmen's heads down, while he, Corporal Brunton and Private Dangerfield reconnoitred a route to outflank it. They were spotted, fired on, and ran to some rocks within yards of the enemy, whose fire they returned. As Jones emptied his revolver he was killed, just managing to shout back to his covering party: "Charge, men, charge!" Brunton was then hit but Dangerfield stood his ground, firing as rapidly as he could until the others came up. Lieutenant Watson followed with the rest of the company and was badly wounded, but they cleared the position. Dangerfield later received the DCM for protecting Jones' body at great risk to himself. For three days and two bitterly

cold nights the flanking battalions held the heights, enduring the first night without food or blankets due to difficulties in getting any up to them.

Led by the 1/3rd Gurkhas, Westmacott's men made their laborious and sometimes contested way through the gorge, taking ten hours to cover the seven miles to Dwatoi. Here the terrain opened out, and the 28th Pioneers and Scottish Borderers had a quick fight to clear the camping ground. Every man, from Lockhart down to the youngest soldier, all soaked to the waist from the stream, faced a cheerless, freezing night without food, blankets or greatcoats. The baggage train had been so delayed by the track's obstacles that Haughton decided to halt it in the gorge for the night under his regiment's protection. Any attempt to light fires immediately attracted long-range sniping.

The next day the Pioneers and Sappers went back to improve the pathway, the baggage came in, some hostile villages were destroyed and the surveys made, all harassed by occasional firing. In the afternoon two companies of the Borderers had to retake an inadvertently unpicquetted hill upon which the tribesmen held on so long that the officers were within revolver range during the final assault.

By dint of a very early start on the 24th – in such cold that spray splashed up from the steam froze in the men's moustaches and the animals' tails – the withdrawal was under way before the Afridis realised it. When they did, they followed up hard and the 36th Sikhs, again on rearguard despite having only reached Dwatoi at dusk the previous evening, bore the brunt. As always Haughton proved a master of his profession, spotting the most favourable positions, deploying his companies to the best

Left: *Northamptons awarded the Distinguished Conduct Medal. From left: Sgt.Anderson (1 November), Sgt.Guy (9 November), Cpl.Chambers (1 November). In each case their second medal is the India Medal 1895-1902, with clasps for "Punjab Frontier" and "Tirah". (Maj.T.C.S.Knox)*

Above: *Officers of the 2nd Derbyshire, several of them wearing the "Guthrie" winter coat. Standing third from right, holding a staff, is Maj.Smith-Dorrien, the Isandlwana survivor who commanded the foraging expedition attacked in the Mastura Valley on 13 November. (Lt.Col.P.J.Mercer)*

advantage, forever anticipating rather than responding to danger. At one point his men caught some tribesmen between two fires and had the rare satisfaction of counting enemy corpses.

By this means, and still flanked by the two battalions high above, the return to Bagh was completed by 5p.m. without further casualties except in the 36th Sikhs, who lost one sepoy killed and Captain Venour and 13 men wounded. The whole enterprise, which had cost seven killed and 35 wounded, had nevertheless inflicted retribution on the Afridis and gained much topographical intelligence for further movements.

* * *

The Field Force had so far made its presence felt in the south, to the east, and some way to the north-east. Now it was the west's turn, where dwelt Mamuzais, Massozais and Chamkannis. Ever since Lockhart's first proclamation these clans had adopted an intransigent attitude, especially the latter who, on 7 November, had cut off and killed 36 men of the Kapurthala Imperial Service battalion with Colonel Hill's Kurram Moveable Column. This had been reconnoitring a route into Chamkanni country from Sadda, preparatory to co-operating with Lockhart in the operation now planned.

On 26 November Gaselee's brigade with one battery began its march to Massozai country, followed a day later by Lockhart with another battery, 2nd Yorkshire, 1/2nd Goorkhas and four companies of 1st Royal Scots Fusiliers. These had just joined the 2nd Division, less the RSF Maxims which had been with the Kurram Column since 1 October; these guns had had a good shoot during Hill's action of the 7th, covering the 1/5th Gurkhas' retirement.

Gaselee's column met some resistance at the first pass. The most determined came from a sangar full of enemy which Lieutenant Engledue of the Queen's attacked with his 20 men in a masterly display of minor tactics more typical of 1939-45 than of the late 1890s. Ordering half his men to put down covering fire, he worked his way round with the remainder in dead ground to a flank, then charged with the bayonet. Six tribesmen were killed in the sangar and all their rifles taken - a rare feat against Pathans.

Once over the pass the force marched south-west. The advance suffered the usual night-time discomforts due to bad tracks delaying the baggage, aggravated by occasional sniping; but on the 29th the Massozai, seeing the troops in force in their country, submitted. The next day contact was made at Esor with Hill's column, which had left Sadda on the 29th marching north-east, and the Mamuzai also submitted. There only remained the recalcitrant Chamkannis to punish.

Their centre lay at Thabi, seven miles to the north, which Hill was ordered to destroy on 1 December. He had two Indian battalions, two of Gurkhas, some dismounted cavalry, a battery and the Scots Fusiliers' Maxims under Captain De la Bere. The force attacked in two columns; one got through and set part of Thabi alight, but the other came under heavy attack "up a most awful gorge"[16]. Rather than risk a rearguard action in the dusk, Hill ordered the withdrawal. The Chamkannis were in force and so well concealed that De la Bere, covering the retirement, found that "all we could do was scour the woods and rocks with unaimed fire". Among the killed was Lieutenant Richmond Battye, 6th Bengal Cavalry, a member of a famous but ill-fated Army family of which a correspondent wrote: "It is now almost a tradition with the

The 15th and 36th Sikhs charging the houses west of Tseri Kandao on the night of 16 November. Drawing by W.B. Wollen from a sketch by Melton Prior. (Author's collection)

Battyes that all shall die on the battlefield"[17].

To dispel any triumphalism among the Chamkannis Hill attacked again next day, this time with the two Gurkha battalions - 2/4th and 1/5th - the Gurkha Scouts, 3rd Sikhs, and part of the 1st Queen's as rearguard. The Sikhs went for the village while the Gurkhas, preceded by the Scouts, scaled the heights from which the fiercest resistance had come the day before.

So steep were these in places that the Gurkhas had to haul each other up by hand. On reaching the top Lieutenant Lucas and his 80 Scouts were confronted by three strong sangars on successive ridges. As soon as the 5th Gurkhas were ready to support, Lucas attacked each in turn,

dividing his force in half and using the same fire-and-movement tactics that Engledue had employed with his Queen's. At the first the Chamkannis seemed ready to fight hand-to-hand, but fled at the last moment. Having cleared the third sangar Lucas reached the crest to shoot down the reverse slope at the fleeing enemy. So skilfully had these tactics been performed that not a single Scout was hit. With the Chamkannis on the run the destruction of Thabi went ahead, covered by the guns firing at any remaining hostile groups. When all was done the force retired unimpeded.

* * *

The peoples of this western region having satisfactorily

Officers of the redoubtable 36th Sikhs at Karappa. From left, standing: Lts. Craster, Browne, Van Someren; sitting, Lt. Munn, Capt. Custance, Lt. Col. Haughton and Maj. Des Voeux (enlarged), Capt. Searle; in front, Surgeon-Capt. Prall, Lt. Turing. Note the latitude allowed in the details of officers' field kit - single or double Sam Browne braces with or without cartridge loops, whistles on a button or pouched on a brace, pistol lanyards worn around the neck or the body. (R. G. Harris)

A certainly posed but still interesting photograph of two Gurkha Riflemen, possibly of the 1/3rd, helping a wounded lance-naik to the rear. (Author's collection)

been brought to heel, the Kurram Column returned to Sadda, while Lockhart with Gaselee's force marched south-east down the head of the Khanki Valley for 15 miles before turning north-east for the final ten miles back to Bagh, which was reached on 6 December. No opposition was encountered.

Meanwhile various punitive measures had been taken around Bagh. Some Afridi clans had made submission but others, notably the Zakka Khel, remained obdurate. The Orakzais had complied with the terms demanded of them and the Mastura Valley, still patrolled by the 1st Brigade, was peaceful. Winter was approaching fast, and the passes

would soon be blocked with snow. It was time to leave Tirah. All the heavy baggage, tents and surplus stores were already on the move south, and the whole force prepared to march in the lightest possible order consistent with enduring the worst of the cold.

Lockhart intended to move his base of operations from Kohat to Peshawar, in which direction the two divisions would converge but using separate routes: the 1st Division due east through the Mastura and Waran Valleys; the 2nd Division first north-east to Dwatoi, then east down the Bara Valley. Though moving, at most, only ten miles apart, they would be unable to support one another readily owing to an intervening range. While they marched, the Peshawar Column was to move out some 15 miles to Barkai on the Bara River to prepare a camping ground for both divisions.

Before departure Lockhart issued a further proclamation to those who had not submitted, to the effect that he was leaving to avoid the cold, but that he would remain within striking distance of their winter settlements. He warned them that "Afridis attacking the English is like flies assailing a lion; and, as an old friend of many of you, my advice is to submit, and so let your wives and families return from the cold mountains to their homes"[18]. It remained to be seen whether the Zakka Khel and their friends - their watchtowers destroyed, the autumn cultivation disrupted, their grain and fodder depleted - would heed his advice.

The Gurkha Scouts attacking the Chamkannis, 2 December, from a sketch by Lionel James. This emphasises the use of "fire and movement" to take the sangars manned by the tribesman. (The Graphic)

CHAPTER TEN

The Last Rearguards

The 2nd Derbys were not sorry to be leaving the Mastura Valley after five fairly uneventful months with the 1st Division. They had made themselves as comfortable as possible; supplemented their bully beef and biscuit with fresh local produce; and had even celebrated Inkerman Day, when their forbears of the 95th had so distinguished themselves 43 years before, with a battalion sing-song around a huge bonfire accompanied by their drums and fifes. Now it was daily getting colder, the first snow had fallen and, with the Orakzais quiet, it was time to go. To mark their departure another, larger sing-song was held, joined this time by the Devons and the Royal Artillery mountain gunners. Perhaps they sang a popular tune of the time, *Her bright smile haunts me still* - or even, in tribute to their foes, the Frontier parody *His bright knife haunts me still*[1].

The next day, 8 December, the 1st Division began its march in bitter cold, with alternating snow and rain falling somewhat incongruously upon the British soldiers' sun helmets. A week's marching lay ahead, following the Mastura River towards Bara Fort seven miles from Peshawar. The cold, the wet and the difficult terrain proved more taxing than the tribesmen who, no doubt thankful to see the backs of the intruders, made no effort to harass the march.

Only on the 9th was there any fighting, when the 1st Brigade made a successful foray northwards into the Waran Valley to complete the destruction begun by Kempster's 3rd Brigade between 13 and 16 November, and to punish the inhabitants for their attack on his rearguard. These were not deterred from attempting the same again, but Brigadier-General Hart handled the operations so skilfully that only one havildar was killed and four soldiers wounded, including two of the Derbys.

The hitherto unexplored Sapri Pass proved a formidable obstacle, particularly at night, only negotiated by the risky device of lighting bonfires along the track. The 1st Queen's picquets of the rearguard had a brisk fight, ambushing some Afridis at the exit from the pass, but all got clear without loss. By the 14th all the 1st Division was out of hostile territory and moving into the new camp around Bara Fort, prepared by Brigadier-General Hammond's Peshawar Column which had come out to meet them.

For Yeatman-Biggs' 2nd Division, with which Lockhart travelled, the 40-mile exodus from Tirah was to prove a far greater ordeal, one described by a correspondent as "a military achievement [that] will live in the military history of the century"[2]. It was conducted in vile, increasingly cold and wet weather, exacerbated by the constant crossing and re-crossing of icy waterways, carrying the lightest possible scale of equipment affording little shelter or dry clothing, and provisioned for only seven days. Even this required nearly 12,000 mules and ponies, forming an unwieldy

The energetic Brig.Gen.Westmacott (seated centre), commanding 4th Brigade, 2nd Division of the Tirah Field Force, with members of his staff. (Maj.T.C.S.Knox)

baggage train which, with its low-spirited, cold and frightened drivers, camp-followers and dhoolie-bearers, made for endless blockages and delays along the dreadful route, thereby stringing out the column with consequent loss of contact between advance- and rearguards.

On top of all this were the Afridis, operating on their own ground from commanding heights on either side of the route, well armed with Martinis and an increased number of Lee-Metfords. To them the long, straggling column seen daily below seemed not a force re-grouping to strike again, but a force in retreat and therefore in defeat, inspiring them to ever more determined efforts in revenge for wasted lands and destroyed villages. What the 1st Division had been spared during its withdrawal, the 2nd - already the harder-hit and more heavily engaged of the two - was to receive in full measure.

* * *

Westmacott's 4th Brigade led off on 7 December down the Dwatoi defile of less than happy memory, followed by the baggage train and hospitals, with Kempster's 3rd Brigade finding the rearguard. Though the route was as bad as in late November, and the weather colder, no opposition was met until Westmacott's advance-guard emerged from the defile, heading for the camping ground.

Westmacott immediately set about clearing the heights to establish picquets thereon to protect the slow progress of the baggage into camp. Instead of a night's rest, Captain Macfarlane's F Company of the 2nd KOSB - "a grand regiment", in the opinion of that perceptive judge Colonel

The camp at Dwatoi, photographed by Lt.Col.Haughton.
(Maj.A.C.Yate)

Haughton [3] – found that they were in for a nine-hour fight. At 3p.m. they attacked a hill "with pipers playing. The enemy retired to about 300 yards away. We had to lie close as bullets were coming in thick. We entrenched ourselves as well as we could, with loopholes in the walls. It was bitter cold and we were all wet through with wading during the day.

"When it got dark the Afridis began to fire at us. Suddenly one of the sentries called out, 'Stand to! They're on us!'. We opened fire immediately on a mob of men charging with loud shouts. Our fire checked them and they drew off. They established themselves all round us at short ranges, fired frequently, shouted abuse and threw stones. Privates Wait and Young were shot through the head when, as sentries, they tried to bayonet men trying to crawl up close. Up to 10p.m. we were much harassed and constantly threatened by rushes but after midnight they let us almost alone. It then came on to snow"[4].

That night marked the end of any fine weather and henceforth it was to be rain, sleet or snow all the way. Haughton, whose 36th Sikhs were, as usual, rearguard to Westmacott's brigade, spent most of the night trying to close up the baggage. He got only two hours' rest, lying down on "some soft stones" and, after "a good swig of rum and hot water" was up again at 6a.m., "making myself unpleasant to everyone with the baggage"[5]. Even so, the whole baggage train was not concentrated in the new camp until 1p.m. on the 8th.

When Haughton finally reported to Westmacott, he learned that one of his companies under the recently-joined Lieutenant Van Someren, with a company of 1/3rd Gurkhas under Lieutenant West, had been ordered to capture a hill which dominated the route ahead. Having had little sleep and only "a great hunk of tinned beef and bread" to eat, Haughton nevertheless decided to go out with another company to support Van Someren as he believed "the poor boy might have rather a nasty job". It was as well that he did so: although he found his "boy" had taken the hill against determined opposition, heavy losses might have ensued had it not been for his own flank move against enemy massing to counter-attack. As it was, the colonel's concern for his young officer kept him out all day, with

much steep climbing, and he did not get back to camp until dusk, "pretty well fagged out"[6].

The securing of this hill enabled Westmacott to make a punitive raid next day against the Kuki Khel who inhabited the Rajgul Valley west of Dwatoi, while Kempster's brigade took over the 4th's picquets. This was done most expeditiously and, though the withdrawal was harassed, without loss. The Kuki Khel were thereby deterred from attacking the rear of the 2nd Division when it began marching eastwards down the Bara Valley on the 10th.

The march was planned to take four days, each stage being only between eight and ten miles. However, the route along the meandering, rock-strewn and often torrential Bara River involved much icy knee-deep wading for men and animals or, when out of the water, clambering over the terraces of boggy rice-fields on either side. The men were permanently sodden below the waist from wading, and above from rain and sleet. A private in the Dorsets was heard to say: "Napoleon crossed the Alps. I've crossed this bloody Bara river forty times. I'm better than Napoleon!"[7]

When not marching in these atrocious conditions the infantrymen were climbing up and down, or shivering for long hours in picquet positions on top of, the flanking hills which rose beyond the rice-fields. On these the Afridis gathered to fire down, particularly at the massed target presented by the floundering baggage train, and ever more aggressively to attack the rearguards trying to withdraw once the baggage had passed.

The first day's march was one of the more trouble-free, but on the 11th the weather and the attacks worsened. The wounded and sick in the dhoolies had a fearful time; their bearers, weakened by the conditions, hardly had the strength to carry an empty dhoolie let alone one burdened with a wounded man. They had to be assisted by troops, which reduced the number of rifles available for picquet duty.

Such were the delays and so relentless the enemy pressure on this day that the last elements of the rearguard, commanded by Major Downman of the Gordons and consisting of 220 2nd Goorkhas, 70 Gordons, and 30 each of the Dorsets and 2nd Punjab Infantry, were overtaken by dusk, teeming rain and mist when still three miles from the main body's camp. They had with them 21 wounded, and the Afridis were closing in on all sides. Downman ordered all his men to fix bayonets and form a rough square around the wounded.

In the lead with some 15 Gordons was Captain Uniacke who, spotting a building ahead in the gloom, determined to occupy it. Running forward, they drew fire and took cover. Uniacke then ran on but soon realised that only four men had managed to keep up with him, and that a line of enemy lay between him and the building. Telling his men not to fire but "to shout like hell", he rushed forward. The enemy fired a few shots and ran. Uniacke and his handful raced into the building where he began shouting orders and blowing his whistle as though to a much larger force. His daring not only relieved the enemy pressure on Downman but gave the latter the direction in which to move. Soon the whole rearguard was within the building, whose loopholed stone walls afforded much better protection.

Here they remained throughout the night, relatively undisturbed; but with daylight the Afridis resumed a ceaseless

fire upon the post, causing more casualties and preventing any movement outside. Eventually reinforcements fought their way back from the main body - which had been fired on throughout the night - and Downman's men finally reached camp at 1p.m. after "36 hours wet through, with little food or sleep and plenty of fighting"[8]. Some 50 casualties had been sustained on the 11th, and double that number of followers and baggage animals.

Lockhart ordered a rest on the 12th and the march was resumed on the 13th, with Westmacott now finding the rearguard. With his proven reliability he was undoubtedly the man for the job for, as the Scots Fusilier De la Bere observed, "the enemy seemed to realise that it was their last chance at us, and they gave the rearguard an awful time of it, pressing on and exposing themselves far more than usual"[9].

The Afridis began attacking before the tail end of the baggage had left camp and while the rearward picquets were still in position. The brunt of the fighting was first borne by the 3rd Gurkhas and four companies of the Borderers. Once the baggage was away the picquets fell back, covering each other and supported by the guns of No.5 (Bombay) and No.8 (RA) Batteries. By now the troops were thoroughly experienced in such withdrawals and the last companies got clear without loss. One Borderer, Private Forsyth, had a narrow escape from capture. He had fallen, wounded in the face and overlooked by his comrades, but managed to run after his company just before tribesmen reached him, though being hit again in wrist and thigh before he caught up. The fighting had been so intense and the enemy so numerous that the rearguard did not clear the camp until four hours after the advance guard had left, and the 3rd Gurkhas and some of the Borderers had expended all the ammunition in their pouches.

Such were the difficulties of the route - particularly when the valley narrowed into two defiles - and so determined the Afridis' pursuit that the baggage train became ever more chaotic, with unled mules, abandoned

Officers of the 2nd King's Own Scottish Borderers and attached staff, including Lt.Col.Dixon, commanding (seated centre), Capt. Macfarlane, F Coy. (seated second left); the officer seated at far right wearing a round hat is the chaplain. (Maj.T.C.S.Knox)

kit and drenched, panic-stricken drivers and followers. More and more soldiers had to help with the casualties, reducing the fighting strength, as the bearers were too busy frantically trying to save themselves.

Fortunately, in complete contrast to this shambles separating the two brigades was the unfailing steadiness of the rearguard. The admirable Westmacott was everywhere in evidence, directing and encouraging. With the enemy in such strength along the flanking heights and forever trying to envelop the column, the fighting was continuous; all his battalions - Borderers, 3rd Gurkhas, 36th Sikhs, Northamptons and half the Scots Fusiliers - became engaged, supporting and covering each other as they gradually fell back. Had it not been for this masterly rearguard action the chaos among the baggage might have ended in massacre, particularly at the second defile where a serious blockage occurred. So fast did the Afridis move that there was a danger they might get ahead and confine the rearguard to this death-trap. Westmacott was equal to the threat and so deployed his men that it was averted, the

Westmacott's rearguard confronting the last Afridi rush just before nightfall on 13 November. Drawing by J.Nash from a sketch by the correspondent Lionel James. (Northamptonshire Regiment Museum)

The camp below Fort Ali Masjid at Christmas 1897, from where the 1st Division marched into the Bazar Valley to destroy the centres of the Zakka Khel Afridis. (Lt.Col.P.J.Mercer)

baggage passing safely through.

Even then their ordeals were not over, for the route then left the river and passed over a plateau thickly covered in dense scrub and intersected by nullahs, affording excellent cover for attackers who pressed in ever more closely. By now it was getting dark and Westmacott, realising that it was unsafe to try to reach the 3rd Brigade in such terrain, decided to halt on a ridge for the night.

His five battalions were so reduced by casualties and men detached to carry the wounded that they only averaged between 100 and 200 effectives each. They had done their work, held their ground and were nearly out of hostile territory. They had neither water, food nor blankets, and had been engaged all day; but perhaps they might now get a well-deserved rest before completing the march on the morrow. It was as the correspondent, Lionel James, experienced, "a vain hope".

"Suddenly there was a cry, and the officers had only just time to extend their men before the enemy were upon them. The Afridis made a terrific rush, so that even among the brushwood more Afridis were seen than had ever been seen collected at close quarters before. It was a trying time, for they came under cover of a sweeping fire. For a moment it seemed that the men who had been fighting all day would be enveloped, over-run and swept away. It was but momentary. The officers threw themselves into the line, magazines worked freely, and the very bushes seemed to fade away before the hail of lead; from the very bayonet-point the tribesmen were swept back – back into the closing darkness – and they never tried a second time"[10].

Among the 25 fatalities was Lieutenant West of the 3rd Gurkhas, "foremost in every fight"[11]. A further three officers and 80 men had been wounded, for whom little could be done, and all spent a wretchedly cold, uncomfortable night after such an arduous day, with the ever-present threat of a renewed assault.

None came until daylight on the 14th, when the Afridis recommenced their harassing fire as the rearguard again withdrew – but now, having learned the mettle of Westmacott's men, with far less ardour than before. By midday the brigade reached the picquets of Hammond's Peshawar Column. Under its protection the 3rd Brigade and baggage had arrived earlier, having spent an undisturbed night thanks to the previous day's resistance by Westmacott and his men. For their efforts the 4th Brigade received a special congratulory order from Lockhart.

The 2nd Division's march out of Tirah was now accomplished. It had been costly, not only in casualties, which between 7 and 14 December totalled 164 killed and wounded, but also in the strain imposed by the weather, the marching conditions, and the ubiquitous enemy, masters of their weapons and their terrain. To Hammond's fresh troops all ranks of this tough-campaigning 2nd Division, though "fit and hard", appeared "drawn, pinched, dishevelled and thoroughly worn"[12]. Especially so were the long-suffering wounded, carried in on stretchers, on beds seized from villages or supported in jolting agony upon mules. Nevertheless their three months' toil in Tirah was over; and the Afridis, their lands ravaged and many of their men killed, were left with much food for thought.

* * *

The 2nd Division was in need of a rest, as was Lockhart himself, the rigours of the retreat having taken further toll of his strength; this luxury he was not yet ready to allow himself, however. He next intended to complete his action against the Zakka Khel – as he had warned in his final proclamation – by attacking their other settlements. These lay in the hitherto unvisited Bazar Valley, running parallel to and north of the Bara Valley. Simultaneously the Khyber Pass, abandoned to the Afridis since their August attacks, was to be re-occupied.

The latter task Lockhart delegated to Hammond, while he accompanied the 1st Division into the Bazar Valley. By Christmas Eve both forces were concentrated near Fort Ali Masjid, ready to advance the next day; there was to be no seasonal cheer for these troops in 1897.

Lionel James described the Bazar Valley as "a huge rolling plain, one arid, bare, rocky wilderness" in which, from its entrance, "not a vestige of human habitation or existence could be seen, save for the weary track which faltered its way among the rocks"[13]. In the centre of the valley, screened by a ridge, lay the 1st Division's objective: the main Zakka Khel centre of Chena, a collection of walled, impoverished-looking dwellings with strong watchtowers and some six acres of cultivation. To James its desolation typified and explained the Zakka Khel's grim stubbornness.

It took the 1st Division a week, beset by cold, piercing

Men of the 2nd King's Own Yorkshire Light Infantry - the battalion which fought at Shinkamar on 29 January - with a mule-mounted Maxim gun. Note the 1894 ammunition pouches, with the flap and fastening strap on the inside surface; and the low position of the slung Lee-Metford Mk I, whose lower sling swivel was in front of the magazine rather than on the butt. (R.J.Marrion)

winds and icy rain, to enter the valley, with each brigade using a different route, one considerably more difficult than the other's; to scour it, destroying the deserted dwellings and searching for the food stocks, all removed or burned; and to withdraw, both brigades using the same route. Some skirmishing occurred and casualties were sustained, particularly among the rearguards; but by the turn of the year the 1st Division was safely encamped around Jamrud Fort west of Peshawar.

Meanwhile Hammond's column, which included the 2nd Oxfordshire Light Infantry ("the 52nd") and the 45th Sikhs - last met in these pages fighting respectively against the Mohmands and at Malakand - had traversed the Khyber Pass from Ali Masjid up to Landi Kotal, past the burned-out, looted forts. The pass was deserted. The advance and repair work to the forts, immediately put in hand, were largely unopposed, save for the occasional sniping at the picquets installed along the route to protect the forward movement of stores and supplies.

Only on 30 December were any serious attacks made: upon picquets at Ali Masjid, and upon the 52nd after destroying a village near Landi Kotal. In the late afternoon two 52nd picquets were withdrawing covered by a third, when they were fired on by hitherto concealed tribesmen who began to close in. Three men were quickly wounded and the picquets took cover in a shallow nullah. Two of the wounded could still walk, but the third's wound required immediate dressing, which was done by the commanding officer, Colonel Plowden. Once the wounded had been sent ahead the retirement continued.

Then Corporal Bell was killed. Plowden and two subalterns, Owen and Fielden, dragged the body away. Although the 52nd were firing back the enemy shooting intensified, especially when an open space had to be crossed; here Private Butler was shot in the leg. Lieutenant Carter pulled him up on to his back but Butler was hit again and killed, which threw Carter to the ground. Fielden ran to their aid and together he and Carter got Butler's body to cover. Then Plowden and Owen, still carrying Bell's corpse, were both wounded, as were seven other men. With 17 dead and wounded, with the enemy growing in numbers and closing in on three sides, the party could not move and

would have to fight it out. Scribbling a note asking for help, Plowden told his orderly Bugler Crowhurst to take his charger and gallop off to Landi Kotal for reinforcements.

Meanwhile Captain Davies, who had earlier retired with his picquet, had heard the firing and doubled his men back to the rescue. Nearing the beleaguered party he saw the enemy apparently massing to rush in with swords. Ordering his men to fix bayonets he led a charge at the swordsmen, who broke and ran. This gave a breathing space, but the enemy riflemen were still in position; Davies had no choice but to add his rifles to the first party to try to hold their ground in the hope that the bugler would get through.

This Crowhurst succeeded in doing - most

Some of the officers killed in Tirah. From top left: Capt.De Butts, RA (29 October); 2/Lt.Macintire, 1st Northamptons (9 November); Lt.Wylie, 2nd GR (16 November); Capt.Lewarne, 15th Sikhs (16 November); Lt.Col.Haughton, 36th Sikhs (29 January 1898); Lt.West, 3 GR (13 December). (Author's collection)

commendably, considering he was an ordinary private soldier not normally mounted, and had to cross unfamiliar and hostile country. Eventually, after dusk had fallen, reinforcements reached the still-fighting 52nd and extricated them safely with all their dead and wounded. Among those recommended for gallantry awards in this action was Sergeant-Major Dempsey, who had reached the highest non-commissioned rank after only 11 years' service. Sadly he never lived to receive his Distinguished Conduct Medal, for he died in hospital from the wound he had suffered.

Another NCO of whom news was received at the end of the year was the astonishingly lucky Colour-Sergeant Walker of the Royal Scots Fusiliers. Wounded above the elbow, he had been captured by Afridis during the 2nd Division's retreat down the Bara Valley. Long given up for lost, he had been perceived as a useful hostage by his captors, who allowed him to send in a letter to Peshawar to assure the authorities that, though pained by his wound, he was alive and well. It would be several weeks before he was released, but when he was he reported that, surprisingly, he had been well treated.

* * *

As 1898 dawned, Lockhart had three brigades holding the Khyber, with two of the now rested 2nd Division continuing the blockade line along the north-east boundary of Afridi territory. A hundred miles to the north-east Sir Bindon Blood was about to chastise the Bunerwals, as described in Chapter Five. All other tribes who had been in arms had made submission.

The new year brought the end of the Afridi campaign in sight, but with it a tragedy. To continue the economic pressure on the Afridis four columns, from Ali Masjid in the north, round through Jamrud and Bara to Mamanai in the south, were to converge in an arc to capture a herd of cattle with its guards which was believed to graze daily in the Kajauri Plain west of Bara Fort. Either the information was wrong or the Afridis were alerted, for the first three columns returned to their bases having seen nothing. The Mamanai Column, consisting of the 2nd King's Own Yorkshire Light Infantry – new to the Frontier, having just relieved the Northamptons – and four companies of Haughton's 36th Sikhs, with two guns, saw a few cattle but many more Afridis.

At the Shinkamar Pass Haughton and his men advanced unopposed beyond it to search some caves, while the KOYLI took up positions to cover his withdrawal. When that moment came a mass of Afridis crowned a height above the pass which had been left unpicquetted through a misunderstanding. Haughton's retreat was cut off.

Colonel Seppings of the KOYLI sent up two companies under Lieutenants Dowdall and Walker to drive the enemy off. This they did, but then came under intense fire from 250 yards away. Both officers and another – Hughes – were killed, as were several men, and others wounded [14].

Their action had enabled Haughton to send his Sikhs back down the pass covered by the KOYLI's main body, but he, seeing the plight of the Yorkshiremen on the height, hurried up to them with his Adjutant, Lieutenant Turing, and a few Sikhs. When he got there the Afridis were closing in on two sides. He ordered the wounded to be carried off at best speed. He and Turing picked up Lee-Metfords and, with two Sikhs and two Yorkshiremen, opened rapid fire to cover them. Turing and the Sikhs were soon killed. Haughton told the two KOYLI to fix bayonets, saying,

The end of hostilities: members of the Afridi jirga at Peshawar. (Maj.A.C.Yate)

"We'll shoot away the ammunition we've got, and then show them how British soldiers die". He fired a few more rounds, then was shot in the head. "He fell, like the grand soldier and gentleman he was, in endeavouring to save others"[15]. One Yorkshireman was killed; the other got away, to tell the tale of how one of the most outstanding and admired figures of the whole campaign had died – in the very last action of the Pathan Revolt.

Despite this being the KOYLI's first action, and despite the loss to the 36th of their revered colonel, both battalions fell back steadily in the face of the Afridi pursuit. Some dead had to be abandoned, but not one casualty nor one rifle was left behind. Seppings had earlier heliographed to Mamanai for help, and at 4p.m. Westmacott arrived with 300 Scottish Borderers and 3rd Gurkhas to cover the move back to Mamanai.

In this action of Shinkamar, apart from the loss of John Haughton and his party, the 36th Sikhs had few casualties, but the KOYLI had lost three officers and 26 killed, another three officers and 32 wounded – a heavy bill for a first action at the end of a campaign. As a result of a special plea by Westmacott, and his despatch of an Afridi corpse to its village, the Afridis returned Haughton's unmutilated body to Mamanai, from where it was taken and buried with full honours in Peshawar military cemetery.

Haughton was not the only major figure whose death coincided with the end of operations. Major-General Yeatman-Biggs had seen the campaign through despite being dogged by ill-health since assuming command of 2nd Division, but on 4 January he died at Peshawar. Lockhart himself, unwell at the start and never fully regaining his fitness, had shared all his men's privations and dangers; these certainly took their toll, for he was to die two years later, aged only 58.

The total battle casualties of the Tirah campaign had been 287 killed, 853 wounded and ten missing. These included 23 British and four Indian officers killed, 56 and 16 wounded. This high proportion of one officer casualty to every 11 other ranks – twice the proportion of officers to men in the force – must be an indication both of the enemy's marksmanship and of officers' readiness to lead from the front.

These pages have seen the price of leadership and loyalty to their soldiers – what Kipling called "the dark art and mystery of managing men"[16] – being paid by officers of all ages: the youthful, like the Northamptons' 2nd Lieutenant Macintire with less than two years' service, the more experienced, like the ever-foremost Lieutenant West of the 3rd Gurkhas aged 29, or the Gunner, Captain De Butts, with 15 years' service, and of course the inspiring Haughton who, after 26 years with his faithful Sikhs, gave his life for men of a British regiment. For such officers soldiers, be they British, Indian or Gurkha, would give their utmost – as we have also seen in this account.

* * *

Although Shinkamar was the last action of any consequence, another two months elapsed before the last Afridis submitted and paid their dues. Then was seen a remarkable aspect of the Pathan character. On 5 April Lockhart started from Peshawar on his long journey home for a much-needed rest. At the station to see him off were hundreds of Afridis, Zakka Khel among them, cheering him to the echo and swearing that, in future, they would fight not against him but on his side. Thus they showed their respect for a man they felt knew and understood them, who had not wavered from his task, and had always dealt and fought with them fairly.

To the men who had fought for him in the formerly unpenetrated but now subjugated Tirah, Lockhart offered his praise and thanks for their "bravery and devotion" when "subjected to great hardship and exposure, harassed at night by assaults at close quarters or by distant rifle fire, and engaged in long and trying rearguard actions against enemies unrivalled as skirmishers and marksmen".

Although armchair pundits at home and in India were quick to criticise his command he, with his long experience of such operations, felt able to conclude: "In no previous campaign on the North-West Frontier have the difficulties to be overcome been more formidable; in none has the punishment inflicted been more exemplary, or the submission been more complete"[17]. More campaigns would be fought by the British and Indian Armies on the Frontier for another fifty years; but never again would so many tribes take up arms within the space of one year, nor so large a force be deployed against them.

Armchair generalship from Punch, 12 February 1898, before the Afridis finally submitted. "All right, my lads. You're not to blame. But we've got to find out who is!" (Lt.Col.P.J.Mercer)

"SOME ONE HAS BLUNDERED."

BIBLIOGRAPHY

The published works consulted are as follows. Other sources are given in NOTES & SOURCES.

Aggett, Maj.W.G.P., "History of The Devonshire Regiment - Vol.II"(1995).

Anglesey, Marquess of, "History of the British Cavalry -Vol.3, 1872-98"(1982).

Atkinson,C.T., "The Dorsetshire Regiment - Vol.II"(1947).

Barthorp, Michael, "The North-West Frontier: British India and Afghanistan, 1839-1947"(1982).

Callwell, Col.C.E., "Small Wars"(1906 edn., reprinted 1990).

Caroe, Sir Olaf, "The Pathans, 550BC-AD 1957"(1958).

Cavendish, Brig-Gen.A.E.J., "*An Reisimeid Chataich:* The 93rd Sutherland Highlanders"(1928).

Churchill, Winston S., "The Story of the Malakand Field Force"(1898, reprinted 1989).

Churchill, Winston S., "My Early Life"(1930, 1959 paperback).

Davies, Capt. H.R., "With the Mohmand Expedition", Oxfordshire Light Infantry Chronicle (1897).

Davis, Col.John, "History of the 2nd Queen's Royal Regiment - Vol.V"(1906).

De la Bere, Capt.H.P., "With Machine-Guns in Tirah", United Services Magazine, Vol.XX (1899-1900).

Farwell, Byron, "For Queen and Country"(1981).

Fincastle, VC, Viscount, and Eliot-Lockhart, Lieut.P.C., "A Frontier Campaign: The Malakand and Buner Field Forces"(1898, reprinted 1990).

Gathorne-Hardy, Jonathan, "The Public School Phenomenon"(1977).

Greenhill Gardyne, Lt-Col.C., "The Life of a Regiment: History of the Gordon Highlanders - Vol.II"(1903).

Grierson, Lt-Col.J.M., "Scarlet into Khaki"(1988 reprint of "The British Army by a Lieutenant-Colonel", 1899).

Gross, John (Ed.), "Rudyard Kipling"(1972).

Gurney, Lt-Col.Russell, "History of The Northamptonshire Regiment, 1742-1934"(1935).

Hamilton, Gen.Sir Ian, "Listening for the Drums"(1944).

Harfield, Alan, "The Indian Army of the Empress, 1861-1903"(1990).

Harris, John, "Much Sounding of Bugles"(1975).

Heathcote, T.A., "The Indian Army: The Garrison of British Imperial India, 1822-1922"(1974).

"Highland Light Infantry (HLI) Chronicle"(1897, 1898).

Hobday, Maj.E.A.P., "Sketches on Service in the Indian Frontier Campaign, 1897"(1898).

Hutchinson, Col.H.D., "The Campaign in Tirah, 1897-98"(1898).

"Illustrated London News"(1897).

James, Lionel, "The Indian Frontier War"(1898).

Kipling, Rudyard, various works, 1886-1937; see Notes & Sources.

Longford, Elisabeth, "Wellington - The Years of the Sword"(1969).

Macmunn, Sir George, "Romance of the Indian Frontiers"(1931).

Mason, Philip, "A Matter of Honour: the Indian Army, its Officers and Men"(1974).

Masters, John, "Bugles and a Tiger"(1956).

Myatt, Frederick, "The British Infantry, 1660-1945"(1983).

"Navy and Army Illustrated"(1896-98).

Nevill, Capt. H.R., "North-West Frontier, 1849-1908" (1912, reprinted 1992).

Newbolt, Sir Henry, "Poems Old and New"(1912).

Oatts, Lt-Col.L.B., "Proud Heritage: the Story of the Highland Light Infantry - Vol.3."(1961).

Richards, Frank, "Old Soldier Sahib"(1936).

Roberts of Kandahar VC, FM Lord, "Forty-One Years in India"(1900).

"Rifle Brigade Chronicle"(1897).

Shadwell, Capt. L.J., "Lockhart's Advance through Tirah" (1898).

Singer, Andre, "Lords of the Khyber"(1984).

Slessor, Capt.A.K., "The 2nd Battalion Derbyshire Regiment in Tirah"(1900).

Spiers, Edward, "The Army and Society, 1815-1914"(1980).

Spiers, Edward, "The Late Victorian Army, 1868-1902"(1992).

Victorian Military Society(VMS) Journal, "Soldiers of the Queen"(1985,1991).

"Wellington College Register, 1859-1962"(1963).

"Wellington College Year Book"(1897, 1898).

Wolseley, Gen.Viscount, "The Soldier's Pocket-Book"(1886).

Woods, Frederick (Ed.), "Young Winston's Wars: Despatches of Winston S.Churchill, 1897-1900"(1972).

Woollcombe, Robert, "All the Blue Bonnets: History of the King's Own Scottish Borderers"(1980)

Wyndham, Horace, "The Queen's Service"(1899).

Yate, Maj.A.C., "Lieutenant-Colonel John Haughton: A Memoir"(1900).

Younghusband, Capt.G.J., "Indian Frontier Warfare"(1898).

NOTES AND SOURCES

For full details of published works, see Bibliography under author.

Chapter One: The Frontier and its People
(1) Masters, p.218.
(2) Quoted Barthorp, p.12.
(3) Kipling, "The Young British Soldier", from "Barrack-Room Ballads"(1892).
(4) Quoted Mason, p.338.
(5) Roberts, p.286.
(6) Gen Sir Andrew Skeen, quoted Singer, p.110.
(7) Ibid., p.111.
(8) India's seat of government until 1912, thereafter Delhi.
(9) Remark made to Hon. Mountstewart Elphinstone, first official to encounter Pathans in 1809, quoted Singer, p.47.

Chapter Two: The Soldiers
(1) In 1903 the five junior regiments became respectively the 9th, 6th, 7th, 8th and 10th Gurkha Rifles.
(2) Wolseley, p.419.
(3) Newbolt, p.65 ("The Guides at Cabul, 1879").
(4) Heathcote, pp.140-142.
(5) Kipling, "Something of Myself"(1937) p.22.
(6) Kipling, "Stalky & Co."(1908 edn.) p.271.
(7) Newbolt, p.232 (Note to "Clifton Chapel".) "Wellington College Register, 1859-1984", p.22, Wellington Year Book, 1897, 1898.
(8) Gathorne-Hardy, p.442.
(9) Kipling, "Arithmetic on the Frontier", from "Departmental Ditties" (1886).
(10) Newbolt, p.76 ("Clifton Chapel") and p.78 ("Vitai Lampada").
(11) Spiers ("Late Victorian Army") p.103.
(12) From "Wee Willie Winkie and Other Stories"(1907 edn.) p.101.
(13) Hamilton, p.120.
(14) Spiers ("Army and Society") p.50.
(15) Ibid.,p.46.
(16) Quoted Longford, p.322.
(17) "The Incarnation of Krishna Mulvaney" from "Life's Handicap" (1907 edn.) p.23.
(18) Sir George Younghusband, quoted in Michael Edwardes, "Oh to Meet an Army Man" from Gross, p.44.
(19) As in fn.17, "The Mutiny of the Mavericks" and "Drums of the Fore and Aft".
(20) Quoted Oatts, pp.13,14.
(21) As in fn.17.
(22) "Navy and Army Illustrated", 6 Mar 1896, pp.127-128.
(23) Wyndham, p.118.
(24) Richards, pp. 75, 76, 109, 199.
(25) "The Courting of Dinah Shadd" from "Life's Handicap"(1907 edn.) p.43 and "Barrack-Room Ballads".
(26) Richards, p.155.
(27) "The 'Eathen", from "Barrack-Room Ballads".
(28) Harris, p.166.
(29) "Screw Guns", from "Barrack-Room Ballads".
(30) Not including Foot Guards. Seventeen more battalions were added in 1897-1899.
(31) "The Young British Soldier" from "Barrack-Room Ballads".
(32) The Rifle Brigade and King's Royal Rifle Corps were not territorially based and each had four regular battalions.
(33) Rifle Brigade Chronicle, 1897, p.113.

Chapter Three: Treachery in Tochi
(1) Macmunn, p.190.
(2) C-in-C India's report, quoted in VMS Journal ("Soldiers of the Queen") No.42(1985), p.21.
(3) 6th Jats, 14th Sikhs, 25th and 33rd Punjabis.

(4) Rifle Brigade Chronicle, 1897, p.117.
(5) Ibid., pp.117-118.
(6) Ibid., p.120.
(7) Ibid., p.121.
(8) Ibid., p.122.
(9) When, as 95th Rifles, their proud boast had been that they were always "first in the field and last out of it".
(10) Rifle Brigade Chronicle, 1897, p.135.
(11) Cavendish, p.225.
(12) Quoted Hutchinson, p.156.
(13) Peter Hopkirk's "The Great Game"(1990) about Anglo-Russian rivalry in the region does not even mention the Pathan Revolt.
(14) From "Oonts" ("Barrack-Room Ballads").

Chapter Four: War-Drums in Malakand
(1) Churchill, ("Malakand Field Force") p.63.
(2) Ibid., p.70.
(3) Despatch of Maj-Gen.Sir Bindon Blood, KCB, dated 20 Aug 1897, quoted Ibid., p.225. Rattray lived to become a lieutenant-colonel and was killed at the Battle of the Hai in the Mesopotamian Campaign in 1917. Wheatley later became a brigadier-general, a CMG and died in 1954. Also consulted: Lieut.Rattray's own account of Chakdara, quoted in a MSS letter by his brother, dated 30 Oct 1897 (Mr.Rulzion Rattray).
(4) Fincastle and Eliot-Lockhart, p.74.

Chapter Five: Blood on the Warpath
(1) Churchill, ("My Early Life") p.136.
(2) "S.T.A.R." (a sergeant), HLI Chronicle, Oct 1897, p.134.
(3) In 1897 there were no posthumous VC awards so Maclean's citation stated he would have received it "had he survived". It was confirmed in London Gazette, 16 Jan 1907.
(4) Churchill, ("Malakand Field Force") p.86.
(5) Despatches of 9 and 12 Sep, 1897, quoted Woods, pp.13,16.
(6) Churchill, as fn.1., p.143.
(7) Churchill, as fn.1., p.144, as fn.4., p.125.
(8) Churchill as fn.1., p.145.
(9) Ibid., p.146.
(10) Ibid., p.151.
(11) Churchill, as fn.4., p.133.
(12) Ibid., p.135.
(13) Ibid., p.156.
(14) James, p.51. The Dum-Dum bullet was outlawed in 1899.
(15) Ibid., p.200. White stones were tribesmen's ranging marks.
(16) Ibid., p.162.
(17) Fincastle & Eliot-Lockhart, p.170.
(18) Ibid., p.171.
(19) Churchill, as fn.4., p.168.
(20) Their nickname deriving from their former regiment, 50th Foot, which had black facings.
(21) Churchill, as fn.4., p.170.
(22) Ibid., p.171.
(23) Sergeant Baird, HLI Chronicle, Jan 1898, pp.173-5.
(24) Ibid., p.176.
(25) HLI Chronicle, Jul 1898, pp.249-250.
(26) Quoted Oatts, p.29.
(27) As fn.25., p.252.

Chapter Six: The Mohmand Dog
(1) Churchill, ("Malakand Field Force") p.88.
(2) MSS letter from No.3345 "Fred"(rank and surname unknown) of F Company, 1st Somerset Light Infantry dated "Peshawar 31/10/97" to his mother. (National Army Museum).
(3) Ibid.
(4) Report in "The Pioneer" (1898), quoted in VMS Journal "Soldiers

of the Queen" No.67(1991), p.22.
(5) James, pp.17-18.
(6) Davies, p.80.
(7) Churchill as in fn.1., p.158. Imperial Service troops were provided by the Indian princely states.
(8) James, p.26.
(9) Ibid., p.65.
(10) As fn.2; Hobday, p.148.
(11) As fn.2.
(12) Davies, p.82.
(13) Ibid., pp.84-85.
(14) James, p.70.
(15) Davies, p.86.
(16) As for fn.2.
(17) James, p.82.
(18) The next Mohmand uprising of 1908.

Chapter Seven: Khyber, Kohat and Kurram
(1) Macmunn, p.138, and I.Samuel, 9.2.
(2) Churchill, ("Malakand Field Force") p.194.
(3) Macmunn, p.217.
(4) Churchill, ("My Early Life") p.137.
(5) Macmunn, p.218.
(6) De la Bere, p.165.
(7) Uppingham School Magazine, June 1898, quoted Yate, p.65.
(8) Letter dated "Fort Lockhart, September 13 1897", quoted Yate, p.136.
(9) "The Pioneer", quoted Nevill, p.268.
(10) Unnamed member of relief force, quoted Yate, p.134.
(11) Letter dated "Fort Lockhart, September 16 1897", quoted Yate, p.140.
(12) Illustrated London News, 25 September 1897, p.410.

Chapter Eight: The Heights of Dargai
(1) Hamilton, p.231.
(2) The Scouts were later increased to 6 officers, 500 men.
(3) Atkinson, p.35.
(4) Slessor, p.44.
(5) Ibid., p.28.
(6) Letter to Sir Charles Gough dated 16 Jan 1898, quoted Yate, p.226.
(7) Slessor, p.25.
(8) Hamilton, p.232.
(9) Quoted Shadwell, p.50.
(10) Macmunn, p.233.
(11) Ibid., p.231.
(12) Slessor, pp.56-57.
(13) Macmunn, p.227. "Zakhmi dil" = Bleeding Heart; dole, sarnai = Pathan drum, pipe.
(14) Not to be confused with Dargai near Malakand (Chapter Four).
(15) Ever since its 2nd Battalion's experience, as 58th, in the First Boer War, the Northamptonshire Regiment had paid particular attention to shooting, winning many competitions.
(16) Letter quoted, Woollcombe, p.75.
(17) Capt.V.R.Ormsby, 1/3GR. MSS account. (Gurkha Museum).
(18) Shadwell, p.122.
(19) Hutchinson, p.61.
(20) Greenhill Gardyne, p.348.
(21) This regiment always spelt its title thus.
(22) Lt-Col.E.A.Travers, 1/2GR. Letter dated 22.10.1897. (Gurkha Museum).
(23) Slessor, p.71.
(24) Granted to the old 39th as being the first King's battalion to serve in India in 1754.
(25) As fn.22.

(26) Slessor, p.72.
(27) Lieut.Tillard, 3 GR, quoted Ormsby, as in fn.17.
(28) Slessor, p.73.
(29) Atkinson, p.35, fn.
(30) Slessor, p.74.
(31) Ibid., p.74; Hutchinson, p.71.
(32) As fn.27.
(33) Greenhill Gardyne, p.351.
(34) Ibid., p.341.
(35) Yate, p.6. The artists were R.Caton Woodville and Vereker Hamilton.
(36) Lt-Col.M.J.Evetts, MC, late Royal Scots Fusiliers, letter to the author.
(37) Newbolt, p.68, ("The Gay Gordons: Dargai, October 20th 1897")

Chapter Nine: The Scouring of Tirah
(1) Lockhart's Dargai despatches, quoted Slessor, p.88.
(2) Slessor, p.102.
(3) Illustrated London News, 27 Nov 1897, p.763.
(4) Slessor, p.102-103.
(5) Princess of Wales's Own; from 1920, Green Howards.
(6) Shadwell, p.164.
(7) Ibid., p.165.
(8) 1st Bn. Northamptonshire Regiment MSS Record of Service, 1 Nov 1897.(Regimental Museum)
(9) Shadwell, p.120.
(10) Letter to Capt.A.H.Barthorp dated "Tirah Maidan, Nov 3".(Northamptonshire Regimental Museum)
(11) Ibid.
(12) As fn.8, 9 Nov 1897.
(13) Diary 1898 of Capt.A.H.Barthorp.(Author)
(14) Hutchinson, p.125.
(15) Quoted Atkinson, p.47.
(16) De la Bere, pp.169-170.
(17) "The Pioneer", quoted Hutchinson, p.181. His father and three uncles were all killed in action with the Indian Army.
(18) Quoted Hutchinson, p.185.

Chapter Ten: The Last Rearguards
(1) Attributed to Lieut.R.S.Baden-Powell, 13th Hussars; letter to the author by Lt-Col.David Murray, late Queen's Own Cameron Highlanders.
(2) James, p.264.
(3) Quoted Yate, p.182.
(4) KOSB officer's letter, quoted Hutchinson, pp.189-90.
(5) Letter dated "Dwatoi, 9 Dec", quoted Yate, p.181.
(6) Ibid., p.182.
(7) Quoted Atkinson, p.48.
(8) Greenhill Gardyne, p.364.
(9) De la Bere, p.171.
(10) James, pp.262-3
(11) Shadwell, p.284.
(12) James, p.267.
(13) Ibid., p.278.
(14) A poignant memento of Lt.Thomas Dowdall's death survives - his Sam Browne belt, the cross strap torn by the bullet which killed him. An unusually full collection of personal and service documentation relating to Lt.Dowdall is on loan to the India Office library.
(15) Officer's letter, quoted Yate, p.202.
(16) Kipling, "Only a Subaltern".
(17) Lockhart's final despatch and Special Order of 4 Apr 1898, quoted Hutchinson, pp.222-3.